Greenhill Books

Greek and Roman Warfare

Greek and Roman Warfare

Battles, Tactics and Trickery

John Drogo Montagu

Greenhill Books, London
MBI Publishing, St Paul

Greenhill Books

Greek and Roman Warfare
Battles, Tactics and Trickery

First published in 2006 by Greenhill Books/Lionel Leventhal Ltd, Park House,
1 Russell Gardens, London NW11 9NN
and
MBI Publishing Co., Galtier Plaza, Suite 200, 380 Jackson Street,
St Paul, MN 55101-3885, USA

ISBN-13 978-1-85367-685-7
ISBN-10 1-85367-685-3

Edited and typeset by Palindrome
Printed in the United States of America
Book Club Edition

To the memory of Tony (E. A.) Beaulah

Contents

Part Two
Tactics in Battle

List of Battle Plans

Preface

I t was not my idea to write this book. The suggestion and the stimulus came from my publisher, Lionel Leventhal, who deserves the credit for the unusual approach to the subject. A chronological exposition has a straightforward plan; a hotch-potch mass of assorted observations is a very different matter. I have to admit that it took me a long time to alter my frame of mind, and my early attempts were nothing short of disaster. I would have abandoned the project altogether if the idea had left me in peace, but it refused to go away. Then suddenly it seemed to gel. From that time on I enjoyed the challenge immensely.

I wish also to acknowledge my profound debt to the late Tony Beaulah, to whom this book is dedicated and whose recent demise saddened me greatly. A retired teacher of the Classics and English, he was my only personal contact with the Classics and the only friend I could ask to read the script. I feared that he might regard it as elementary and naive, but in putting my mind at rest he did more than anything else to boost my morale when I was beset with doubts. His detailed comments were meticulous and invaluable.

General Introduction

Then are many books on the art of warfare in the ancient world, so why another? To this oft-used opening gambit there is a ready reply. Of the existing works many put heavy emphasis on arms and armour, formations and their detailed organisation and intrinsic manoeuvres, and on the functioning of armies under all the circumstances away from the field of battle. These aspects can be regarded as the 'hardware' of warfare, the basic necessities. Less attention has been paid to the 'software.' This covers nearly everything else from generalship and human behaviour to strategy, planning, secrecy, surprise, and deception, and indeed the whole gamut of tactics, trickery and guile. These are functions which are less visible than the hardware but which are probably more active in determining the course of confrontations. It is well known that total military numbers alone do not necessarily determine a victory. A well-planned ambush or turning movement can overcome numerical odds. To the knowledge of the writer there has been no work which examines the military history of the ancient world from this thematic angle.

'God of battles, was ever a battle like this in the world before?' Tennyson's meaning is abundantly clear, but no two battles could ever be the same, even assuming that the same armies were involved on the same site. The number of imponderables involved is too vast to allow of anything more than resemblances. Personalities and peccadillos, geographical factors and climatic conditions are but a few of the many determinants of an outcome, to say nothing of trickery of various kinds or that extra dash of ingenuity and initiative. When accounts of battles are reduced to bedrock, the basic formula tells us, quite simply, that A engaged B in battle and that A or B won (if the result was not indecisive). This formula is encountered quite commonly, particularly in the ancient literature, but it almost invariably refers to those confrontations about which nothing else is stated or even known. The more one knows, the more the special factors become apparent and, with them, the possible reasons for the outcome. It is no longer a standard question of who won the battle but why? What were the factors, adverse or otherwise, which resulted in a victory on one side or a defeat for the other? This statement is no tautology when all the factors are taken into account. Good tactics may win a battle; a blunder may lose one. It is only when battles are analysed on this sort of thematic basis that similarities, differences and trends begin to appear, and each battle is then seen to be a unique occurrence.

The overall source for this work was a survey of nearly 700 battles (excluding sieges) in the Greek and Roman worlds down to 31 BC which had been recorded by the ancient chroniclers.[1] This yielded a large number of observations on most aspects of the warfare of the era, the 'software' in particular. It ranged through the whole gamut of tactics and human pro-clivities to personal snippets like the affair of the consul who, out of jealousy of his consular colleague, outraged the Senate by abandoning his campaign and demanding a triumphal procession for himself![2] (The débâcle resulted in the postponement of the Senate's plans until the following year.)

The object of the present work is to bring all the 'software' together and to attempt to assemble it in some sort of definitive order. It was evident at the outset that there were problems which would need to be addressed. First, there is a huge overlap between the elements of surprise and deception. Of the tactical (as opposed to the human) elements surprise was undoubtedly the most common single factor in the whole history of classical warfare. It often occurred by itself without any intentional deception, as in nocturnal attacks on sleeping camps. Alternatively, surprise was frequently combined with a deception which itself may have taken varied forms as, for example, in feints and ambushes. These form two large distinct groups which will be considered separately under the headings of 'Surprise' and 'Surprise with Deception.' (Deception alone in the absence of any intended surprise forms a third category). The second problem concerns the individual observations and events which provide the raw data. Many of these highlight more than one theme so that there is also an overlap in a different dimension. To prevent the need for much page-turning by the reader, the events which are relevant to more than one theme are recounted under each heading. Cross-references are kept to a minimum and are generally inserted when an event is described under another heading in more detail.

In Part Two of this work a number of the larger battles have been described in their entirety. They have been selected to include those with a high content of thematic features, either in the battle itself or in the preliminary run-up, with the object of presenting the total picture. When any entry in the first part of this work relates to one of these battles, the reader is referred to the relevant account in Part Two. In these accounts the battles themselves are not referenced exhaustively; the emphasis is placed on the various factors which are the subject of this work. The references in Part One are given at the end of each chapter (avoiding the aggravations that arise when they are collected at the end of a work).

The battle descriptions in Part Two have provided an opportunity for reviewing some of the plans which were included in my earlier work. In general, only minor changes have been made in an attempt to add clarification or to give a more faithful portrayal of a detail in the text. The plan of the battle off Ecnomus did, however, warrant larger amendments, and the battle of Chaeronea required a complete overhaul. To the author's knowledge some of the battles included here have not been previously illustrated schematically, e.g. Gabiene, Magnesia, Pydna and the Trebia. A few others were not considered amenable to such treatment or would derive no gain from it.

Note

1   J. D. Montagu, *Battles of the Greek and Roman Worlds*, London, Greenhill, 2000.
2   Livy, 8.12.8–10.

Part One

Human and Tactical Elements

1

The Element of Doubt

'Although God cannot alter the past, historians can' (Samuel Butler, *Erewhon*). Herein lies the healthy element of doubt that besets considerations of historical writings. God may ordain the order of events, but our knowledge and perception of them depend upon the accounts of them which are handed down to posterity, in other words our sources. However, they in turn were frequently reliant upon *their* sources, quite probably from an earlier age. Modern experiences show clearly that two men fighting in the same battle may see it and describe it in a very different light, and yet these are contemporary accounts from people who were actually there. The concern here is with the various mechanisms that can be involved in the unwitting or sometimes deliberate distortion of such accounts and the deviation of 'history' from the true facts.

In common parlance the word 'history' is used loosely to mean a succession of events. In a more specific sense it may be defined as a *record* of events, in which the recording is the operative factor rather than the actual events themselves. The word 'history' is derived from the Greek word *historia* meaning enquiry, and the function of the historian is not only to record the events as faithfully as he can but to analyse and interpret them in their context and to report the circumstances which brought them about, influenced them, and led to the consequences. But as motives, actions and events can be viewed in different ways by different people, historians not uncommonly disagree among themselves in their interpretations of events. Yet, all are concerned with the same basic data. Even in this century with its advanced communications technology new slants are periodically published on aspects of the two World Wars. The more remote the events in time, the more numerous are the causes for uncertainty and disagreement.

In the history of any long-standing civilisation an account of an early conflict may well be folk lore which has become incorporated in the nation's legendary past. Even so, it may have some factual foundation. The Trojan War (*c*.1200 BC) is a case in point. It is a magnificent legend, and the heroic deeds of derring-do recounted in Homer's *Iliad* are splendid myths. Nevertheless, it is unsafe to assume that all of this is entirely devoid of any element of truth. There may have been no wooden horse, but it is now generally held that there was an expedition around 1200 BC, which was almost certainly concerned with trade, especially in corn. Troy has been identified with the modern Hisarlik in Asia Minor, situated not far from the Hellespont (Dardanelles). It was in an excellent position to control all the sea traffic through the Hellespont and Bosphorus to the Black Sea, which the ancients euphemistically called the Euxine or 'well-behaved' sea in the hope that it would respond in kind. A trade war was by no means an unlikely event.

The history of at least the first two centuries of the Roman Republic is particularly prone to doubts owing to the absence of any official records apart from the *Fasti*, the calendars of days allowed for business, which listed only the magistrates and functions such as triumphs. There was no Herodotus, let alone a Thucydides, who lived in or near these times. It is self-evident that a historian must have his own sources of information, and Livy (59 BC–17 AD) had to rely on earlier sources such as Fabius Pictor, the first Roman historian, who flourished in the late third and early second century. This leaves a sizeable gap after the traditional date of the foundation of the Republic, 509 BC. When the sources are incomplete, there will be a tendency on the part of the historian to fill the gap from local legend and hearsay, helped by a fertile imagination. When all else failed, Livy's aim was to write good stories.

In a bygone era in which communication was almost exclusively by word of mouth, a potent factor which might affect the accuracy of a story was the fallibility of human memory. In the first historical narrative known to us Herodotus chronicled the Persian Wars. He obtained his information principally from verbal accounts which he obtained from people who had taken part in the events that he related or from their families and descendants. As he was probably born around the time of the Persian Wars, the period between the events he describes and his researches could have blunted the memory of anybody who had been a witness or impaired the recollection of any kinsfolk to whom the tale had been related. There are gaping holes in Herodotus' account of the battle of Marathon. He left it to later historians to attempt to complete the picture by deduction and speculation, in which there can be no certainty of truth.

Another likely source of error on the part of the ancient historians lies in the size of armies and the number of casualties. By and large, the historians of the Greek battles have recorded credible figures for the Greek armies, but the numbers quoted for foreign armies are a very different figure of speech. They are frequently astronomical, for example Herodotus' estimate of 1,700,000 for Xerxes' infantry alone.[1] Such figures may be just inspired guesswork with more guessing than inspiration. But there are other mechanisms which might have been at work. The historian could have inflated the enemy's numbers and casualties for patriotic reasons, thereby exaggerating a victory or lessening a defeat. Conversely, there could have been a tendency to minimise the figures for the 'home team' if hard facts and figures were not available.

Perhaps the most widespread source of distortion in recorded history is bias on the part of the writer. Livy, as an example, was a great patriot and it showed up in his writings (although even he could not minimise the Roman shame after the disgraceful ambush of two consuls at the Caudine Forks, see p. 68). In particular, military figures like Caesar who recorded their own deeds are likely to have been prejudiced and at risk of enhancing them in a favourable light. As a purely subjective phenomenon, prejudice is not easily detected in oneself and is much more difficult to counteract. An example will illustrate the point. Xenophon entertained many prejudices, among them a loathing of Thebes. This is evident when he totally ignores the great Theban general Epaminondas and makes no mention of him, even in his description of the general's most famous victory at Leuctra (pp. 136 f). Epaminondas' military prowess passes without notice until the final battle at which he was killed.

Corruption is a potent and pernicious source of error in historical documents. It is in a different category from the errors and distortions described above in that it cannot be laid at the historian's door. The term refers to an inadvertent alteration of the text when a document is copied, as many have been, down through the ages. 'Mistyping' would be the modern equivalent. Place names may be changed to similar ones, and words or phrases may suffer distortion. But the symbol which is most at risk from corruption is the numeral. It is also the most damaging because there is no inherent indication that it has occurred. A single corrupted numeral merely becomes another numeral. To quote an extreme example, a figure of 10,000 is not in the same league as 1,000 or 100,000. How much havoc can be created by the addition or deletion of a single '0'!

On another tack, doubt can be cast upon the interpretation of a phrase or, more usually, a single word, particularly a Greek one. In the course of this work, the author happened on two instances of substantially different interpretations of the same phrase. One concerned the battle of Chaeronea (338, pp. 142 f); the other the battle of Corinth known as 'the Nemea' (394, pp. 131 ff). In neither instance did the interpretation of the dubious word or phrase seriously affect the perceived outcome of the battle, but in both cases the account of a tactic was rendered ambiguous. These are matters concerned with historical veracity. They are discussed in some detail in the accounts of the battles concerned.

Finally, doubts can be entertained about the fundamental historicity of some reported events. Did they happen at all? As an example, doubts have been voiced about the historical nature of the reported diversion at Camarina in 258,[2] which is said to have involved a heroic military tribune and his 300 men.[3] The name of the tribune involved is given variously in the different accounts, which has evoked the doubts, although it must be added that several sources including Livy, Pliny, Florus and others are in agreement while only the two earlier ones dissent. Nevertheless, the case remains open.

On a more positive note, doubting in the realm of history is a healthy pastime. Without doubts and divergences of opinion there would be no progress in the consolidation of reported events. Words like 'presumably', 'probably', and 'possibly', will inevitably continue to loom in the historian's vocabulary, but there is always the hope that future discoveries may from time to time replace them with certainty – perhaps!

Notes

1   Herodotus, 7.60.
2   J.F. Lazenby, *The First Punic War*, UCL Press, 1996, pp. 75–6.
3   Frontinus, I.5.15; Livy, *Epitome* 17 and later writers.

2

The Element of Planning

Good planning is the cornerstone of successful warfare, embracing every aspect of it in the realms of both strategy and tactics. It confers a huge advantage over the unplanned, haphazard and makeshift performances which so often predominated in the world of classical military events. Whereas strategy is more concerned with wars, tactics lie in the province of battles. The two elements have often been regarded as distinct entities but that is far from the truth. Strategy produces the master plan, which determines the tactics and formulates their objective. But as tactics develop, they influence future strategies. The two are heavily interlinked with a nebulous division occasioned by considerable overlapping.

Strategy covers the broad picture of warfare. It is made in advance and is long-term in its planning. It requires knowledge of the enemy's size, methods, aptitudes and capabilities, embracing any information obtained from reconnaissance or from outside sources. Apart from purely military considerations it has to be subservient to politics and economics and, in particular the national interest. There is no universally agreed definition of strategy. Such a thing could scarcely be expected in view of its development throughout the ages, its dependence on advances in weapons and technology, and its geographical variations around the world. As a result, the stated principles involved vary from one exponent to another. Tactical planning is more immediate, often taking place after a confrontation of forces but before the onset of hostilities. Under these circumstances it is probably determined largely, sometimes entirely, by the enemy's actions, his deployment and apparent intentions. After the parties close and hostilities commence any further tactics or movements on either side can usually be regarded as either defensive or opportunistic and dictated by the exigencies of the moment. The battle of Pydna (p. 220), which terminated the Third Macedonian War in 168, offers a clear example of such an unplanned manoeuvre. When King Perseus's Macedonian phalanx advanced inexorably over the plain, bristling with *sarissae* (long pikes) to the fore, the Romans were unable to hold it. Disaster loomed until a distraught consul, Aemilius Paulus, noticed that the phalanx had advanced on to uneven ground at the foothills of the mountains. This caused the phalanx to lose its cohesion and gaps began to appear between its ranks. Aemilius immediately divided his men into small groups and told them to infiltrate the gaps and attack the phalangites on their flanks. Armed with their long pikes, the latter were unable to turn to defend themselves. They had no alternative but to discard them and resort to their short swords, which were no match for the Roman swords. Impending disaster was turned into a resounding victory. Aemilius's order was a sudden decision based on acute observation of a changing situation. As such there was no plan.

In the early days of classical warfare strategy in the modern sense was virtually non-existent. The term originally meant the art of generalship, and it was the general (Greek: *strategos*) who deployed his troops and devised the tactics, such as outflanking movements, surprise attacks, ambushes and other forms of deception. In short, he was the planner. In the history of ancient Greece there are many accounts of battles which show little evidence even of tactical planning; there is still less evidence of any long-term plan. This is particularly true of the many encounters between the city states. The usual impression given by the chroniclers is of two military forces which confronted each other and then battled out their grievances without more ado. This impression might emanate in part from the brevity of many of the accounts but the general picture of a lack of planning remains unchanged. One obvious exception was the battle of Salamis (480) and the victory for the Greeks, thanks to Themistocles. It was he who turned Athens into a naval power and whose convictions and strategy were responsible for the victory. This is detailed further below.

Much the same may be said of early Roman warfare, particularly during the first two centuries of the Republic. During this period Rome was entirely involved in the struggle for the control of Italy. It was an almost endless succession of battles on Italian soil with only one plan, the conquest of the country. Rome was not involved in any conflicts outside Italy until the First Punic War erupted in 264. In these early days warfare consisted largely of battles with little or no advance planning. More often than not hostilities were prompted by uprisings of the neighbours or incursions from further afield so that warfare was waged on an almost ad hoc basis. They were also the days of personalised conflicts, in which there was no place for any plan other than to kill the opposing commander. As the general decided the course of events on his side, so he became the chief target. If he was put out of action, the action itself usually ground to a halt and the leaderless army withdrew and lost the fight. In the absence of any other plan these conflicts cease to be of concern here. They are elaborated later (pp. 109 ff).

Although there was little evidence of planning in the early days, there were nevertheless a few exceptional examples of forethought which amount to simple plans. We know from Herodotus that in one of the earliest recorded attacks – on Mount Parnassus[1] around 500 – the Phocian leader

Tellias undoubtedly planned his attack on the Thessalians up to a point because he had to wait until the moon was full. He then took 600 men and painted their bodies and weapons with whitewash and sent them out to attack the enemy and to kill everyone who was not white like themselves. This method of identification provides further evidence of elementary planning. Needless to say, these ghostly apparitions created utter panic in the enemy camp, but this was not the intended object of the whitening. Tellias also had other similar ruses up his sleeve. For example, he would dig a trench in a pass that the enemy cavalry used and would bury in it large empty pots lightly covered to disguise them. This again shows some primitive planning in advance. These instances remind us of the many other tactics which required a small element of forethought. In the case of ambushes, for instance, someone had to originate it, to decide on the site and perhaps arrange a signal to indicate when the concealed party should break cover.

Not long after the tricks of Tellias there occurred a major battle the name of which has resounded through the ages – Marathon (490). But although the name is among the best-known in the whole history of warfare, Herodotus' account of the battle has raised a number of debatable issues, one of them being the question of planning. In brief, the Greeks found it necessary to extend their line to cover the longer Persian line. They achieved this by thinning their centre, probably to a depth of only four men, while leaving the wings at full strength, usually eight deep. In the action the Persians broke through the thin Greek centre and put it to flight, but the Greek wings worsted the enemy's wings. Instead of pursuing the fleeing Persians, the Greek wings rallied and may even have joined together in the rear of the Persian centre (Herodotus' precise meaning is debatable). Noting that their colleagues were attacking the enemy in the flank or rear, the fugitive Greeks turned and attacked their pursuers from the front. Caught between two fires, the Persians fled back to their ships. Many modern historians, such as N. G. L. Hammond, regard the Greek tactics (thinning their centre and thus allowing the Persians to advance and be taken in the rear) as a superb stroke of tactical planning.[2] Others, for example L. Montross[3] and J. F. Lazenby[4], doubt whether Greek generalship at that time had advanced sufficiently to plan such refined manoeuvres. They incline to the perhaps more likely view that the tactics at Marathon were fortuitous. The wings just happened to be in the right place at the right time to support their beleaguered centre as they would naturally have wished to do. This highlights the risk of diagnosing planning when little or none may have taken place. In discussing these affairs from the Greek angle it is easy to forget the other side of the coin. It was the Persians who had developed a definite strategy. Their invading force was far too small for a military conquest, but they had with them Hippias, a supporter of Persia and former tyrant of Athens who had been expelled from the city. The principal object of the expedition was probably to reinstall him, thereby gaining an indirect influence and control over affairs in the state. Moreover, they may have planned to achieve this by luring the Greeks out of Athens to Marathon and then sailing round to capture the undefended city.

At the time of the battle of Marathon there was an Athenian among the Greeks who showed all the foresight necessary for advanced strategical planning. This was Themistocles. He was totally convinced on two points: first that the Persians would invade again with much larger forces, and second, that success in defeating them could only occur at sea. He put all his energies into forcing a motion that Athens should institute an urgent and vigorous ship-building programme. When the second Persian invasion took place only ten years after Marathon, the first major – and naval – battle took place in the vicinity of the island of Salamis (480). Themistocles was again convinced that the Greeks' only hope of defeating the large Persian fleet was to fight in the narrow waters of the bay. Against considerable opposition, notably from the Spartan commander-in-chief Eurybiades and by means of a ruse (see pp. 84–5), Themistocles got his way, with the result that is known worldwide. Had it not been for his foresight and strategical planning, the whole course of western civilisation might have taken a different turn.

When the warriors of old fought as a disorderly horde, each man for himself, there was no real scope for planning. It was not until the leaders decided to amass their troops into an organised body, a phalanx, that any sort of planned refinement became thinkable. The decision was of far-reaching importance, but the earlier phalanxes were handicapped by being inflexible. In a further major advance, the element of flexibility became the great issue, and the more flexible and manoeuvrable Macedonian phalanx rose to pre-eminence. Still further improvements resulted in the Roman legion, which was subdivided into smaller units and which exceeded all before it. Flexibility was the essential ingredient, and it was not until this was achieved that deployments and tactics became malleable elements which could be planned to fit the needs. Examples are provided by the clear lanes through the legions which were planned by Scipio to allow the harmless passage of the enemy's elephants at Zama in 202 (p. 202), and Caesar's withdrawal of one cohort from the third line of each legion to form a fourth line with a specific purpose at Pharsalus (Farsala) in 48 (p. 232).

The phalanxes and then legions were tactical entities concerned with the immediate battle; their formation, deployment and subsequent movements were tactical issues. The phalanx was a tightly knit body of men, each of whom was dependent on his neighbour. His shield, held on the left arm, protected not only himself but also the right side of the man on his left. As Thucydides has pointed out, this explains why on the march each man tended to drift to the right in search of the added protection afforded by his neighbour's shield. Hence, the whole phalanx tended to incline to the right, which led to battle lines in which each right wing became extended and threatened the opposing enemy wing.[5] It is evident that planning played no part in this effect and that the various defensive measures which it evoked were dictated by the exigencies of the moment. The root cause of all these events was the hoplite's unprotected right side. From this it also follows that flank attacks against hoplites were more effective when launched against the right side. In the classical era the Greek phalanx was usually formed eight men deep. When a man fell, the man behind him took his place. Fighting in battle was usually a matter of shoving and shouting, and sheer weight was one important determining factor. This would seem to be the rationale for an increase in depth of the Theban phalanx to as many as twenty-five men at the battle of Delium (424), in contrast to the Athenians' eight per file. As a result, in the words of Thucydides, the Thebans on the Boeotian right 'got the better of the Athenians, pushing them back step by step and keeping up their pressure'.[6] The increased depth of the Theban phalanx at Delium seems to have been the start of a Theban trend toward greater mass. This culminated at the battle of Leuctra (p. 136) in which the great Theban general Epaminondas further increased the depth of the phalanx to forty-eight shields (371).

Epaminondas was the first great Greek tactician, and he brought tactics into full play in Greek warfare. There was nothing very new in his overall strategy at Leuctra. It was quite simply to defeat the Spartans and to dislodge them from their position of leadership (hegemony) among the Greek states. However, his tactics to this end were well-planned and unique at that time. They are described in connection with the battle, but it is worth mentioning here that he put the emphasis first on concentration of attack and second in directing the whole weight of his phalanx at the enemy command post. It is unfortunate that he was killed in his second great battle, at Mantinea (362),[7] and that Plutarch's biography of him has not survived, so that little is known about the man himself.

After Mantinea the short period of Theban hegemony came to an end. Greece descended into chaos with the Social War followed by the Third Sacred War. At this point, following his accession after the battle of Methone (359), Philip II of Macedon stepped onto the stage. He was not only a great tactician but also an expert strategist and diplomat. His primary claim to fame lay in his brilliant reorganisation of the Macedonian army into the best-trained and most efficient fighting force of the time. The reader is referred to works on the subject for details of its organisation, for example, by Peter Connolly.[8] It is sufficient here to mention only the pikes up to 6.3 metres (nearly twenty-one feet) long with which the phalangites were armed and the large emphasis on cavalry. This model army was the first part of his overall strategy. His further aims were twofold: first, to obtain control of Greece and, second, to conquer Persia on the pretext of avenging the damage caused to Greece by Xerxes' invasion. With Greece in a mess, Philip's diplomatic talents came to the fore as he started to interfere in their affairs, on occasions ensuring that he was actually invited by some party or other to do so to the benefit of his own ends. This led, twenty-one years after has accession, to the battle of Chaeronea in 338 (p. 142) in which he defeated the combined Athenian and Theban force totally and gained control over Greece. The first part of his great plan had succeeded brilliantly; strategical diplomacy was to follow. In victory, he was harsh toward the Thebans but he treated the Athenians with unexpected leniency. He knew that he would need help from them, from their navy in particular, in the second phase of his plan – the invasion of Persia. His assassination prevented him from executing the plan, which was left to his son Alexander to undertake.

Alexander willingly adopted his father's plan against Persia, but it could not be put into action forthwith. Like his father he was a great strategist and he realised that he could not campaign in Asia while leaving hostile tribes in his rear. They would immediately avail themselves of a heaven-sent opportunity to invade Macedonia. This was the strategic rationale behind the whole of his first campaign, which was designed to subdue the unruly Thracian and Illyrian tribes. Later, during his great anabasis (march up-country), a good example of Alexander's capacity for detailed planning was forthcoming on the eve of the battle of Gaugamela (331), when he was confronted with an army believed to outnumber his force by a factor of around five. Alexander is said to have shut himself away in deep thought for several hours, working out his plan of battle. As soon as he was satisfied, he fell into a deep slumber and had to be awoken next morning.[9] It is well known that his victory that day was one of the greatest decisive achievements in military history.

Further proof of Alexander's skill as a strategist is shown by his relations with the defeated Persians. In the western 'liberated' provinces he put the emphasis on cooperation; in the east, where loyalties were different and liberation meant nothing, he upgraded it to partnership. Any satrap who submitted without a fight was re-installed in office, and the Persian administration was left intact where possible. The many new towns that he founded served initially as police stations and then became trading posts and eventually centres of Hellenistic culture. He himself adopted Persian garb and customs, to the disgust of his men, who simply did not understand his thinking. But there was method in his plans. He knew full well that with his numbers he would be totally incapable of policing the vast empire that he was conquering. The only possible solution was a joint partnership with the Persians. All of these acts are evidence of a well-developed strategical plan designed to leave Alexander himself and his men free for other activities. These included further plans for other expeditions and conquests which he was hatching at the time of his death.

In the Hellenistic period (after Alexander) warfare failed to retain his subtlety and gloss. Among the Diadochi (Successors of Alexander) the keywords were power and the lust for it. They were continually at each other's throats in battles which were 'hammer and tongs' affairs with no hint of a strategical plan other than to enlarge their particular empire at the expense of the other. Such were the conflicts at Paraetacene (317, p. 155) and Gabiene (316, p. 161), Ipsus (301, p. 165) and many others. The battle of Corupedium in 281 saw the two surviving generals of Alexander, Lysimachus and Seleucus, fighting it out for mastery of the whole empire at the ages of seventy-four and seventy-seven respectively, as quoted by Justin.[10] The death of the rival was their only aim. Lysimachus was killed but Seleucus savoured his victory for only one year before he was assassinated. So ended the era of the Diadochi, but their successors carried on in similar vein. During the post-Alexandrian period there were numerous further wars, notably the Syrian and Macedonian Wars, the war against Antiochus and the wars of the Achaean League. These provided evidence of tactical innovations but little in the way of underlying strategy. One exception, at least, was the war against Antiochus, which was triggered by an invitation to him by the disgruntled Aetolians to 'liberate Greece'. It was unlikely that they intended anything more than a gesture of displeasure to the Romans, but Rome saw it in a different light. Only three years had elapsed since Hannibal had escaped from Carthage and joined Antiochus at Ephesus, asking him for the military means to stir a revolt at Carthage or even to invade southern Italy. The suspicions in the air provided sufficient strategical grounds for the Romans to put a stop to the plans of Antiochus. Under the terms of the peace Hannibal had to surrender, but when the net closed he escaped and committed suicide.

There was also the Chremonidean War, in which Ptolemy brokered a settlement between Athens and Sparta (the first for two centuries) as the joint champions of Greek liberty against Macedonian rule. But Ptolemy did not play his part in providing the necessary active military support, and the one battle at the Isthmus in 265 was a fiasco.[11] These examples take us back to the initial premise that strategy in the Hellenistic world tended to be on an obvious superficial plane with little subtlety.

What has been said above about the paucity of strategy and planning in Greek warfare applies just as much to Rome but again there were exceptions. Among the strategists were Hannibal and perhaps Caesar, but the greatest of the Romans was the enigmatic Scipio Africanus. Starting with Hannibal is to start with the origins of the Second Punic War. Hannibal had been brought up by his father, Hamilcar Barca, to harbour an abiding hatred for all things Roman. It had become increasingly clear after the First Punic War that another conflagration between Rome and Carthage would not be long delayed. An affair at Saguntum provided the trigger. Saguntum was the only city south of the Ebro river which was not in Carthaginian hands. The Romans had undertaken to protect it, turning it into a sore in the Carthaginian side. When Hannibal decided to defy the alliance and make ominous preparations to attack the place, the Romans protested to Carthage and demanded that Hannibal be handed over to them. The Carthaginian senate's refusal and their support of Hannibal ignited the Second Punic War (218) and it seems clear that Hannibal engineered the whole affair for that specific purpose.[12] It was certainly good Carthaginian strategy. The Romans assumed that the forthcoming war would be fought largely in Spain and on the seas, which they commanded, but Hannibal had other ideas. As everyone knows, he put in motion one of the greatest plans in the history of classical warfare, carrying the war into Italy by crossing the Alps. He was aware that he would have to rely on recruiting Gauls, but this was already being dealt with as another part of his strategical plan. His emissaries had made contact with them and were able to tell him which tribes were friendly and which were not. At the Trebia (218, p.175), Trasimene (217) and Cannae (216, p.180) everything went according to plan, but then it faltered. Quintus Fabius Maximus was appointed dictator and he had a strategy of his own – to dog, delay and harass Hannibal, wearing him down while refraining utterly from any confrontation. As before Hannibal had relied on some of the southern states rallying to his banner, but they failed to do so. Then again he had no siege train or equipment without which any attack on Rome would be unthinkable. His only hope lay in his brother Hasdrubal's attempt to join him via the Alps. The Roman army in the north of Italy should have been able to stop Hasdrubal, but one man, the consul Gaius Claudius Nero, was not happy about the prospects and wanted to increase the odds. He had a strategy which, with supreme initiative, he put into effect. It involved marching a part of his force in secret for about 250 miles to reinforce his consular colleague in the north. It was a resounding success, which ended in a total victory for the Romans on the Metaurus river (207, p.191) and the death of Hasdrubal. Although Hannibal continued to hang on in the south for a further four years, he achieved nothing of significance and had no further hope of rescue.

Publius Cornelius Scipio, a strong contender for the title of Rome's greatest strategic and tactical genius, was a pious man who believed that he obtained his inspiration from the gods. In his turn, he inspired his men. In addition to being a great military planner, he was also a good diplomat. When, at the age of twenty-five, Scipio landed in Spain in command of a new army and set up his headquarters at Tarraco (Tarragona), he found himself opposed by no less than three Carthaginian armies. They were all in the interior and were separated from each other, but he could not afford to attack any one of them for fear that they would unite and outnumber him. Instead he adopted an ingenious strategy, leaving the enemy alone and making his attack against their largest base and most important port and arsenal, Cartagena (New Carthage, 209). This stroke was planned to a nicety. During the preceding winter Scipio had carefully questioned every arrival from New Carthage concerning every aspect of the place. As none of the enemy forces was within ten days' march of his objective, he besieged it by land and sea and captured it after one day of fighting (p. 91). Although he had an axe to grind against the Spaniards as a result of the deaths in action in Spain of his father and uncle, he never allowed his feelings to interfere in his dealings with the natives. Towards them he was lenient and, at times, performed acts of great kindness. After the siege of New Carthage, for instance, he set free all the citizens and restored their property to them, and he released the Spanish hostages and sent them to their homes. This was excellent diplomacy, which reaped dividends in the form of new allies and recruitment. After the capture of New Carthage three of the most powerful Spanish chieftains went over to him and many tribes followed in their wake. Every Spanish recruit meant another deserter from the Punic cause, and the Carthaginian generals were bitterly aware of the shift and felt the pinch. Everything that Scipio did seemed to be planned to the last detail. He was at his best in the battle of Ilipa in Spain in 206, to some minds the most fascinating battle in the history of classical warfare (p. 197).

Scipio's final masterpiece of strategy against Hannibal was the battle of Zama (p. 202), which was fought on Scipio's terms. He chose the battlefield and ensured that Hannibal was camped on a hill with a deficient water supply, whereas he himself was well supplied. After the final defeat of Hannibal, Scipio's foresight and diplomacy again came to the fore. In the formulation of the peace treaty his terms were magnanimous. Carthage was allowed to retain ten ships for self-defence and she was encouraged to resume her former place as a centre of trade. At this she again became successful and prosperous, which was not to the liking of some Romans. 'Rome must be destroyed' was Cato's clarion call at the end of every speech in the Senate. Tragically it led to the Third Punic War, the only aim of which was the total destruction of a peaceful but too prosperous rival.

Caesar was more tactician than strategist. If he had an overriding strategy, it was simply to secure his own dominance in the eyes of his fellow countrymen. His writings bear witness to his frequent lack of foresight. As General Fuller has put it: 'not one of his campaigns was adequately prepared, and some not prepared at all'.[13] As examples, both of his invasions of Britain are summed up as 'amateurish in the extreme.' On his own admission, Caesar set out on his first invasion too late because 'the winter sets in early in those parts.' With what was either an incredible lack of foresight or a blind trust in providence, he took no extra ships or equipment. When a violent storm arose, a number of his ships were shattered and many others lost their anchors or tackle. Every available man was put to repairing them, using parts from those that were totally unserviceable, while some equipment had to be ordered for despatch from the Continent. In the end all but twelve of the ships were saved.[14] From the climatic angle the second invasion was a copy of the first but the storm was greater, involving the total loss of 40 ships. Lessons had not been learnt. On this occasion it was necessary to send to the Continent for expert craftsmen.[15] As a tactician, his keywords were speed and audacity, but his remarkable fleetness was often compounded with a haste which landed him in difficult situations. Almost invariably he managed to extricate himself from his self-imposed dilemmas but only by means of impromptu performances. At the river Sambre (Sabis, 57), for instance, he failed to spot the ambush set by the enemy and was only saved from chaos and impending disaster by the courage of the famous Tenth legion.[16]

Like Caesar, Pompey also aimed for the dominant position, but the world was too small for the two of them. While lacking the genius of Caesar, Pompey had superb organising abilities. In 67 he was given a free hand in eradicating the Mediterranean pirates who had cast a blight on sea trade and commerce, severely affecting Rome. He was given the command for a period of three years and began by dividing his ships into thirteen sections, each with its own area of operation. His methods were so successful that he accomplished the feat in three months.[17] He solved the problem of the disposal of the thousands of captured pirates not by killing them but by resettling them well inland as colonists in undermanned areas. It was a sage piece of strategy.

Notes

1   Herodotus, 8.27.
2   N. G. L. Hammond, *A History of Greece to 322* BC, 2nd edn, 1967.
3   L. Montross, *Encyclopaedia Britannica*, s.v. *Tactics*, 1962.
4   J. F. Lazenby, *The First Punic War*, UCL Press, 1996, pp. 69–70.
5   Thucydides, 5.71.
6   Thucydides, 4.96.
7   Xenophon, 7.5.21–27; Diodorus, 15.84–87.
8   P. Connolly, *Greece and Rome at War*, Greenhill, 1998, pp. 66 ff.
9   Diodorus, 17.56; Plutarch, *Alexander*, 32.1.
10   Justin, 17: 1.7–2.1; Orosius, 3: 23.58–62.
11   Plutarch, *Agis*, 3.4.
12   Livy, 21.6–18.
13   J. F. C. Fuller, *Julius Caesar: Man, Soldier & Tyrant*, Wordsworth, 1965, p. 316.
14   Caesar, *Gallic War*, 4.28–31.
15   Caesar, *Gallic War*, 5.10–11.
16   Caesar, *Gallic War*, 2.16–28.
17   Plutarch, *Pompey*, 28; Appian, *Mithridatic Wars*, 96.

3

The Human Element

The human element with all its manifestations was undoubtedly the dominant factor in warfare in the ancient world. Little went on in an army in battle that was not ultimately attributable either directly or indirectly to the commander himself and, through him, to his junior officers. The strategy (if any), tactics and general conduct of his army stemmed from him, while his attitudes, such as his optimism, enthusiasm or encouraging nature, may have filtered down from the top to the rank and file. In view of all these factors the importance of human behaviour in determining the outcome of a battle cannot be overstressed. It is central to the whole issue. It does, however, differ in one important respect from the other elements considered in this work, namely surprise, deception, and planning, in that these are devised with the sole object of winning, in which they may or may not succeed. In contrast, such is human frailty that the human element also has a greater potential for losing the battle. It has to be remembered, however, that these remarks apply to both sides of a conflict.

The welter of diverse factors that make up the human element include innate, intellectual, emotional, behavioural and somatic components. For purposes of discussion these various factors can be divided into four main groups. The first covers only the unique quality called military genius. The second group comprises universal characteristics which are inherent in everybody and which range on a bipolar scale between high and low extremes, for example, morale and physical fitness. The third and fourth groups between them deal with the wide range of temperamental and behavioural features which play such a large part in the outcome of military actions. The favourable or winning characteristics form the third group; the fourth and perhaps not surprisingly larger group covers the unfavourable attributes which are conducive to losing an action.

Military Genius

Any consideration of the human element must start at the top with the commander-in-chief. A few commanders possess that indefinable quality called military genius, which seems to be innate. No one without it can hope to achieve that peak. It covers not only excellence in planning, in action and in man management but also in example, to such an extent that the troops come to worship their leader and would follow him to the end of the world. Another important asset, notably found in such people, is the ability to put oneself in the enemy's shoes and to divine his thoughts and reactions to situations. Any commander blessed with military genius illustrates the peak toward which all other commanders should aspire. Alexander the Great is the quintessential example of a genius that leaps into the mind. Admittedly, his ultimate test came in the depths of what is now Pakistan, when his men adamantly refused to go another step, wading through mud and crossing swollen rivers, inadequately clothed and in the height of the monsoon weather. To add to their misery they had not seen their families for about eight years. Even then their love for him ensured that there was no bitterness once he realised that he had to give in – for the first time in his life. Up to that point he had been invincible. Cyrus the Great must have been another military genius. Although we know much less about him, the fact that he was Alexander's idol indicates as much. Hannibal, unbeaten until Zama, perhaps shared the laurels with Alexander. Julius Caesar, also, had military genius, but he was at times too hasty and made too many mistakes to be in the top flight. Undoubtedly the greatest among the Romans was Scipio Africanus. Plutarch more than once refers to him as Scipio the Great.[1] Epaminondas, probably the first among the great tacticians, also ranked among those with genius during his short life.

Universal Characteristics

In warfare in the classical era, the commander was responsible for the welfare of his men, their morale, discipline, physical fitness, and training. which had to be seen to start at the top. These characteristics are possessed by everybody in varying degree, ranging between high and low extremes. To them can be added piety and superstition as customs and attitudes which in that era were also to all intents and purposes universal.

Morale

Of all the various components in the human element none can surpass morale in importance, largely because it is infectious and is usually trans-mitted to a whole body of men from top to bottom. Less is said in the ancient chronicles about the morale of the men at times when it was presumably good in contrast to the bad times. There appears to be a general assumption that it was high unless stated to the contrary. In one, a perhaps exceptional report by Livy relating to the capture of Pedum in the Great Latin War (338), he says that this raised the morale of the consuls – and their armies as a whole – to such a peak that they toured round the Latin cities capturing each one in turn and subduing the whole of Latium.[2] But this only highlights the well-known fact that success breeds a high morale. Conversely, there are a number of references to the depressing effect of defeat in both the Greek and Latin worlds but they too add up to nothing more than the obvious. The most informative account on this topic relates to the Carthaginian morale at the Bagradas river (Medjerda) in 255 during the First Punic War. Though still defiant, the Carthaginians were utterly dispirited by defeats and afraid to descend from the heights into the plains where the Romans were encamped. To rectify this situation the Carthaginians recruited reinforcements from Greece. These included a veteran Spartan officer called Xanthippus, who rapidly assumed command of the army and trained the men in the best Spartan traditions. Morale soared to such a high level that Xanthippus overcame their fears and persuaded them to descend into the plain and confront the Romans. His success was such that they won a devastating victory, virtually annihilating the enemy.[3]

In the Greek world, the most common demoralising factor among the men was the death of their commander or leader. At Plataea in 479 the death of Masistius, the Persian cavalry commander, had a pronounced two-way effect. The Persians mourned in their usual way, cutting off their hair and the horses' manes amid much lamentation. The Athenians, on the other hand, made capital out of the corpse. They put it in a cart and wheeled it through their lines. The very sight of it elicited a tremendous boost to their morale.[4] That the death of a leader should have opposite effects on the adversaries is understandable, but that it did on one occasion arouse conflicting sentiments within one force requires a little explanation. When Callicratidas, the Lacedaemonian admiral, was killed in the naval battle of Arginusae (406), the Peloponnesian right wing gave up and turned to flight. The left wing, however, maintained its fighting spirit and continued to battle stoutly as long as it could.[5] This unexpected response is explained by the composition of the wing. It consisted of Boeotians and Euboeans who had revolted from Athens and who were therefore afraid of the consequences if they were captured. They were in effect fighting for their lives.

Although the death of a leader was often a potent cause of demoralisation among the men, a corpse was not always an essential requirement; the leader's mere absence sometimes had a similarly deleterious effect. This was well demonstrated at the battle of Raphia between Ptolemy and Antiochus the Great in 217, in which the right wing of each side routed the other's left wing and chased it off the field. The result so far was a stalemate in which the two phalanxes faced each other in splendid isolation. The big difference between the two sides lay in the behaviour of their commanders. Antiochus got so carried away in his pursuit of the enemy that he gave no thought to events on the field. Ptolemy, by contrast, took his place with his phalanx, exhorting and encouraging his men, while Antiochus' phalanx was leaderless. It is not surprising that Antiochus' troops lacked purpose, encouragement and direction, which cost them the battle.[6] A similar state of affairs arose at Ipsus in 301 (p. 165) when Demetrius drove the opposing cavalry under Seleucus off the field and pursued it for a considerable distance. In this instance Seleucus moved some elephants to block Demetrius' return, which left his phalanx leaderless and at the mercy of the enemy.[7]

A less common cause of impaired morale was witnessed during the Ionic Revolt in which the Ionians decided to put all their resources into their navy. The Ionian commander was a Phocaean named Dionysius, who inspired his men initially with considerable success. But he proceeded to institute a training programme which became so rigorous that the men became disgruntled and eventually rebellious.[8] At the start of the battle of Lade (494) the Samians deserted, followed by the Lesbians, leaving the Persian enemy with an easy victory.

On first thoughts it is not obvious why a body of men should become totally demoralised when they still retained numerical superiority, but this was the scene in the final battle of the Athenians' ill-fated Syracusan expedition in 413. Already depressed by two defeats within the year the Athenians began to give way and then beached and abandoned their ships. They had become so utterly dispirited that any attempt at breaking out of the harbour was out of the question even though they still had more serviceable craft than their opponents. However, the Athenians' state of mind was not just a reaction to this particular battle but to a build-up of despair. Their fortunes had deteriorated steadily ever since the arrival of the Spartan general Gylippus with reinforcements for the Syracusans. But the main cause of their loss of morale was the realisation that the enemy had become so much more proficient at sea. The idea that the Syracusans could defeat them three times in a row would have been previously unimaginable.[9]

The most bizarre event connected with morale occurred on the river Chares where a fierce battle took place in 235 between Aratus, the general of the Achaean League, and his arch-enemy Aristippus, the tyrant of Argos. Aratus' forces had gained the upper hand and had pursued the enemy for a considerable distance at which point Aratus withdrew to his camp in a fit of despair! He was upbraided by his indignant men, whose chagrin was enhanced when the enemy claimed the victory.[10] Plutarch offers no specific reason for Aratus' peculiar behaviour other than referring to it as a 'characteristically erratic' turn. That it occurred at such a strange moment, when his men were actually winning, does suggest a psychiatric quirk in an unstable personality. It had clearly subsided by the next day, when a shame-faced Aratus deployed his men and was prepared to fight again.

Almost as bizarre as the behaviour of Aratus were the mood and attitude of both the Samnites and the Romans at Luceria in 294, near the end of the third and final Samnite War. In the preliminary fighting the Romans fared so badly that they became utterly dispirited. Oddly, however, the Samnites too lost their martial zeal and wanted to depart without another fight but, unfortunately for them, their route led past the Roman camp. The consul struggled hard to put some life into his men and eventually both sides lined up, but nobody moved. A few squadrons of cavalry were sent in but they were either unhorsed or trod on the Romans who had gone to help them. This started a Roman rout back to their camp. The consul finally placed a cavalry guard on the gate and issued an order that anyone, be he Roman or Samnite, should be treated as an enemy if he made for the rampart. The Romans were prodded back to face the enemy and eventually hostilities broke out. This time the Romans gained the upper hand, but all in all both sides suffered badly in what would seem to be a state of mutual war-weariness.[11]

Physical Fitness

Like morale, physical fitness is not often mentioned as a predominant factor unless it is at rock bottom. Presumably fighting men are assumed to be fit unless otherwise stated. There is one glaring report of a body of men who were notoriously unfit for combat, namely the Sybarites, whose affluent and self-indulgent ways have made their name a byword. In spite of their huge numerical superiority they had not a hope of success against the healthy inhabitants of Croton, whose commander happened to be an Olympic athlete. But this was a unique case.[12]

At Acragas (307) the inhabitants had to defend their city against a lieutenant of Agathocles but they were disrespectful and rebellious against their own general who had already been defeated once before. At first he refused to fight, but when reproached with cowardice he led out his men who, though numerically equal to the enemy, were said to be greatly inferior to them in both morale and fitness. Not surprisingly, they were routed in a trice.[13]

Training

The Spartans were the first people to introduce training to their army. This certainly consisted of practising manoeuvres such as the countermarch whereby the whole phalanx was turned about virtually *in situ* to face in the opposite direction. Probably there was little emphasis at the time on tactical training. It was not until the fourth century that this became evident, notably on the part of the Thebans. It is said that in Athens where the phalanx was composed mainly of landed gentry, training was frowned upon as being beneath their station. The navy, on the other hand, was manned by the lower orders and training presented less of a problem. Indeed it is impossible to imagine oarsmen who had not received some training.

The effects of good training (by a Spartan) on a Carthaginian army at the Bagradas river (255) have already been cited above under 'morale'. So also have the effects of excessively rigorous naval training before the battle of the Lade (494) when it led to disaffection and ultimately desertion. In a third variation, in which hastily embarked half-trained crews were pitted against a Lacedaemonian fleet off Eretria in Euboea (411), the results were as might be expected. To add to their plight they were hungry at the start and had great difficulty finding any food in Eretria. Defeat came quickly with the loss of twenty-two of their thirty-six ships.[14]

Piety and Superstition

Piety and superstition are far-reaching topics which are considered here only in relation to their place in warfare. Both the ancient Greeks and Romans regularly performed ritual animal sacrifices to the gods before battle and examined the victim's entrails for auspices. If the omens were unfavourable the commander would repeat them, sometimes several times, until the omens augured a victory. This could present difficulties. When the omens were unfavourable at Plataea (479) the Persians were shooting arrows at the Spartans, many of whom were killed or wounded while Pausanias hesitated. In despair he raised his eyes to the temple of Hera and implored the goddess for help. While he was doing so the Tegeans sprang forward to attack and a moment later the sacrificial victims promised success.[15] At Tamynae in Euboea (348) the enemy advanced against Phocion while he was performing sacrifices in his camp. He insisted on being left undisturbed until he had finished, and he took a long time in the process! As soon as he was ready, the Athenians burst out of the camp and routed the enemy. The account says nothing about the results of the sacrifices but it suggests that the whole performance might have been a ploy to lure the enemy closer.[16] There is a well-known tale about the consul Publius Claudius Pulcher, who evidently had little respect for sacrificial portents. When told before the battle of Drepanum (249) that the chickens would not eat, he flung them into the sea where they could drink.[17] If this is true, he reaped the vengeance of the gods which he deserved by being utterly defeated, but it has to be said that the defeat was attributable to his appalling leadership. He was leading his ships from behind and failed to realise the impending chaos which was being created up front.

Apart from rituals, the Greeks in particular gave heed to other phenomena such as thunderstorms and eclipses, which often frightened them and guided their actions. During the last year of the Syracusan campaign (413) the situation of the Athenians was deteriorating rapidly and they were prepared to sail away, but an eclipse of the moon supervened. The soothsayer was adamant that come what may they would have to stay for 'thrice nine days'.[18] They obeyed the injunction but the delay ended in total disaster. Similarly, a total eclipse of the sun (13 July, 364) seriously disrupted the plans of the great Theban general Pelopidas. He had been given 7,000 troops for an expedition against Alexander, the brutal tyrant of Pherae, but the eclipse so dismayed the Thebans that Pelopidas had to depart without them and get reinforcements elsewhere.[19]

It seems that thunder and lightning could be regarded in whichever way you chose. A thunderstorm during the first battle in the Athenians' Syracusan campaign, at the Olympieion (415), was dismissed by the Athenians as a normal affair at that time of the year, but it dismayed the Syracusans and put them off their stroke.[20] In complete contrast, a similar storm before the 'Tearless Battle' near Melea (368) was regarded as a favour from the gods, possibly because it is said to have come from a clear sky. A sanctuary and statue of Heracles happened to be nearby and, in conjunction with the storm, these events filled the Spartans with strength and confidence. Heracles certainly rewarded them favourably as not one single Spartan was lost in the subsequent battle, hence its name.[21] On the river Anio (Aniene, 211), when Hannibal was making a feint attack on Rome, a torrential downpour washed out any thoughts of a battle. Both sides returned to their camps. They lined up again on the following day, but when exactly the same thing happened Hannibal saw it as an ill omen. He accepted it and withdrew altogether.[22]

Agathocles was undoubtedly the most histrionic general in the whole history of ancient warfare. During a battle against the Carthaginians at Tunis (310) he noticed that his men were cowed by the enemy's superiority in numbers. It is said that he released a number of owls which he had brought with him and which settled on the helmets and shields of his men. As these birds were sacred to Athena, they were regarded as a good omen, which restored the men's courage. At any rate, they won the battle.[23]

Favourable Characteristics

Traits favourable to victory, such as loyalty, obedience, courage, are reported less often than the losing streaks except perhaps by comparison with an enemy who lacks them or maybe because they are taken for granted in a military force. When they are reported it is often in global nonspecific terms such as 'they fought with great courage', typically patriotic slogans to which little significance can be attached. They are only noteworthy when they are attributed to a particular individual or group and under specific circumstances. Predominant among the favourable characteristics are initiative and

ingenuity, traits which can never be anything but winners. A display of
initiative, in particular, usually requires courage and bravery as well.

Ingenuity and Initiative

Ingenuity may be defined as the ability to devise something new or original.
It is undoubtedly possessed by those with military genius, and it is therefore
not surprising that the most ingenious piece of dissimulation in military
history was devised by Alexander the Great. Alexander, trapped in a valley
near Pelion (335), observed that a large horde of hostile tribespeople had
congregated on the surrounding high ground. Only one exit was available
to him, through a narrow defile. His problem was how to lure the
'spectators' down so that he could deal with them. His elegant solution was
to draw up his men and put them through a complex barrack square drill in
complete silence. This so amazed and intrigued the tribespeople that they
came down lower to have a better view. The drill routine then ended with a
wedge formation and the order to shout the war cry and charge, from which
the intruders fled.[24] General Fuller describes the incident well and cites
Colonel Dodge's assessment of it as unique in the annals of warfare.[25]

Among lesser mortals than Alexander, Philopoemen was a man who
displayed considerable ingenuity and inventiveness. This was demonstrated
in his chain-letter ruse to assemble a military force in secret, as recounted
later (p.98). But he was also a man with pronounced initiative, which came
to the fore in the battle of Sellasia (222). As a junior officer, he used his
nous and mounted a diversion which saved the day (p.76).

Initiative has a wider spectrum than ingenuity. Defined as an ability to get
things going, it is not confined to originality but principally to putting
standard practice into use at *opportune* moments. A man with a marked
ability in this direction was Diophanes, an Achaean commander who had
been sent with 1,000 veterans and 100 horse to Pergamum (Bergama) to
assist Eumenes' garrison (190). The reason was that Seleucus, the son of
Antiochus the Great, had been ravaging the surrounding territory and
virtually imprisoning the garrison within its walls. After entering the city by
night, Diophanes proceeded to watch the enemy, and he noticed that in the
absence of any opposition they had become contemptuous and ill-
disciplined. When Diophanes suggested to the garrison commander that
they should make a joint sally, the idea was dismissed as outright folly.
Undeterred, Diophanes marched his men out and lined them up quietly in
front of the walls, facing an enemy of at least four times his strength. After
some hours of inactivity the enemy adjourned to the grassy parkland, where
they lay about nonchalantly eating their lunch. At this point Diophanes, who
had been waiting for such a moment, suddenly ordered a charge and
created a panic among the enemy that was out of all proportion to their
numbers. Some of those who were lounging about on the periphery were

slaughtered; others were unable to catch their mounts before being struck down. The enemy returned on the following day and Diophanes again watched them quietly. The day was uneventful until sunset when they started to leave. Waiting until they were just out of sight, Diophanes charged their rear and drove them back to their camp. That settled it. Seleucus was forced to abandon his camp and give up his marauding activities.[26]

In the works of the ancient chroniclers initiative seems so often to be largely the prerogative of officers below the top level. It may be that the 'top brass' were assumed to have the ability to initiate outstanding events. Whether this was so or not, acts of great initiative in lesser individuals invariably stand out as meritorious deeds. It seems, also, that there may have been rather more Romans among them. If this was true, it is suggested here that it may have been attributable to the greater flexibility of the legionary army, which permitted and encouraged individuality, in contrast to the phalanx. In the latter, individual heroic deeds were frowned upon because they disrupted the unit.

In Roman military history there were two exceptional instances of initiative, both of which are recounted later in connection with the associated battles. In one, the stakes could not have been higher: Rome was saved from Hannibal by the personal initiative of one consul in the events both preceding and during the battle of the Metaurus in 207 (p. 191). In the other, the deeds of an unknown tribune turned impending disaster into a resounding victory at the battle of Cynoscephalae (Chalkodónion, the name means 'Dog's Heads') in 197 (p. 208). These are two of the most intriguing stories in the history of ancient warfare. Other examples are given below. Although they are less impressive, they display the same quality of initiative in more localised circumstances.

As a junior officer, a Spartan commander called Herippidas showed initiative during the campaign of Agesilaus in Asia Minor. He was also ambitious, and it is evident that his deed of valour was viewed by him as his great moment in which he could prove himself. When it was heard that Pharnabazus was camping about twenty miles away at Caue, this young officer asked Agesilaus for a force of 4,000 men and some cavalry with which to attack their camp after dark. By nightfall less than half of the detachment had reported for duty. Unwilling to call off his expedition, Herippidas set of with the force at his disposal and fell upon the camp. The outposts were killed, the Persians fled and the camp was captured together with large quantities of baggage and baggage animals (395).[27]

At Phalanna (Falanna, 171) during the Third Macedonian War some Romans were scattered around in the fields gathering harvests when king Perseus himself attacked them and seized 1,000 wagons and some men. He then turned his attention to a guard detachment of about 800 Romans under a tribune called Lucius Pompeius. With presence of mind this officer withdrew his heavily outnumbered force to a hill, where they were surrounded and were subjected to a barrage of arrows, javelins and darts. They were tormented in particular by the darts, which were fired from a new kind of dart-sling that had just been invented. Lucius formed his men into a tight circle protected by their shields, but they then had the problem of repelling any of the enemy who climbed the hill. When Perseus called out to Lucius and his men to surrender and even offered rewards if they did, they courageously refused. Nearing their end from exhaustion, they were eventually rescued by the consul, who had been told of their ordeal. It could be argued that the tribune was merely fulfilling his duty, but the combined refusal of all concerned to capitulate at a real risk to their lives adds another dimension to their bravery.[28]

There was no such doubt about the deeds of Cornelius Scipio Aemilianus in the Third Punic War. As consul, he was later responsible for the siege and destruction of Carthage. He had already received a high decoration for his fighting in Spain, and he was awarded another for his bravery in Africa before the siege of Carthage while he was still only a military tribune. The consul at the time of his present exploits was Manius Manilius, who undertook an expedition against Hasdrubal when he was holed up at Nepheris, now unknown, in wild and rugged territory (149). Scipio disapproved of the project because of the difficult terrain. A few hundred yards from their objective the force had to descend into a river bed and climb out on the other side. Scipio again remonstrated with the consul on the grounds that they could be cut off. He was accused of cowardice but events proved him right. After heavy fighting, Hasdrubal withdrew until the Romans were faced with recrossing the river bed whereupon he returned to the attack. At this point Scipio collected some cavalry, divided them into two groups and instructed them to use hit-and-run tactics, taking it in turn to advance, throw their javelins and retire. This diversion drew the enemy against him and allowed the main body to cross the stream, an operation which they themselves subsequently accomplished only with considerable difficulty. As if that was not enough trouble, four cohorts had got separated from the rest and, unable to cross the stream, had taken refuge on a hill. Once again Scipio set out to rescue them or perish, and once again he succeeded. Throughout the whole episode he showed not only initiative but commendable bravery and courage, in marked contrast to the cowardice of which he had earlier been accused.[29]

In two other reports military tribunes are said to have retreated to hilltops and drawn the enemy's attention to themselves so that the main force could escape.[30, 31] As with Scipio, initiative was again clearly to the fore in both cases. It may be noted that in all three of these people this trait was shown in the creation of diversions (pp. 74 ff) for which they were solely and imaginatively responsible.

Unfavourable Characteristics

The unfavourable aspects or human failings include traits such as impatience, over-confidence, complacency and contempt for the enemy, all of which are in the same broad category. Also included are matters of opinion such as misjudgement and disagreement, and general traits like laxity and incompetence. All of these receive much attention in the ancient chronicles, probably because they conduced to defeat and underlined some of the reasons for it.

The Athenian general Demosthenes was not only impatient but also gullible. In 426 during the Peloponnesian War he acted on bad advice and invaded Aetolia where, he was told, the opposition would be of no account. His impatience was such that he did not even wait for promised Locrian reinforcements. In the event, he did manage to capture Aegitium but his success was turned to disaster by the arrival of an Aetolian army of javelin men who virtually annihilated his force by means of repetitive hit-and-run attacks.[32] A similar disaster took place in Roman history through the impatience of Mark Antony in the prelude to his siege of Phraaspa (36). His impatience led him to march ahead in such a hurry that he refused to wait for his 300 wagons of siege engines, which were attacked and destroyed by an enemy force. When it came to the siege Antony bitterly regretted his folly which resulted in failure to achieve his goal.[33]

Although impatience usually stemmed from commanders, this was not invariable. Three years prior to Demosthenes' failure, the Spartan general Cnemus took an army to Stratus at the request of some Epirot cities. The army marched in three divisions which were proceeding independently to an agreed camp site, but the Chaonians got so far ahead of the others that they were out of sight. They were a hot-headed lot. When they arrived, they gave no thought to a camp but rushed straight forward to the attack. They were duly routed by the Stratians, leaving Cnemus to abandon all his plans.[34] Although the immediate cause of the failure was the headstrong behaviour of the Chaonians, Cnemus must clearly accept the ultimate blame for allowing his columns to proceed too independently and without adequate communications.

When a commander comes face to face with a bitter enemy, impatience – or more precisely impetuousness – of a purely personal nature may take over to the exclusion of everything else. This was seen in events at the battles of Cunaxa (401) and at Cynoscephalae (364). At Cunaxa, Cyrus was attacking the enemy centre when he caught side of his brother Artaxerxes, the king, whom he aimed to supplant. He made a suicidal dash with his 600 horse against the 6,000 who surrounded Artaxerxes. He managed to wound his brother with a spear but was then himself killed.[35] Events at Cynoscephalae presented a similar picture when Pelopidas saw his enemy Alexander of Pherae, the man who had thrown him into prison some years before. Pelopidas, full of hatred and venom, made a wild dash for the other, who retreated to the folds of his bodyguard while Pelopidas was struck by javelins and killed.[36]

Personal ambition was sometimes the cause of impatience coupled with haste. Pompey was an offender in this respect. In 75 he hurried to challenge Sertorius to battle and engaged him by the river Sucro (Jucar). The reason for his haste was simply that he wanted to get the credit for a victory before he was joined by Metellus, who was on his way.[37] The same discreditable emotions came to the surface again when Crassus asked that Pompey should be sent to assist him in the destruction of Spartacus and his slaves. When it came to the point, Crassus bitterly regretted his action and, in the words of Appian, tried in every way to come to an engagement with Spartacus so that Pompey might not reap the glory beforehand.[38] He eventually defeated Spartacus but Pompey, who had just arrived, dealt with the fugitives and claimed to have ended the war!

Common among human weaknesses in ancient warfare were complacency, over-confidence and contempt for the enemy. It is difficult to imagine human sentiments which would be more likely to injure oneself. In the Greek world, Agesilaus of Sparta occupied himself during the second year of his campaign of 396–395 by ravaging all the lands around Dascylium in Phrygia. It was here that the satrap Pharnabazus resided in a sumptuous palace in a well-stocked park. (The Greek word for such a setting is *paradeisos,* whence the word 'paradise'). The Greeks got so accustomed to hunting and foraging in this Garden of Eden without any molestation that they became just too complacent. They were scattered around one day when Pharnabazus suddenly appeared in person with two scythed chariots and about 400 cavalry. The Greeks, about 700 in number, rushed to band together, but when the Persians charged with their chariots in the lead they killed about a hundred of them.[39]

Similarly, the events outside Pergamum in 190 were also conducive to complacency, but in this case it resulted from boredom from a of lack of opposition. The more interesting aspect of this episode concerns the initiative of the man who was sent to deal with the problem, which has already been related above (p. 42). It is sufficient to remind the reader that Seleucus had been perpetually ravaging the territory around the city and virtually imprisoning the garrison within its walls, and that the garrison commander was too frightened to take any action against the perpetrators. Their complacency and indiscipline eventually led to their doom.

Complacency led many commanders to reject advice, but in every one of the following cases the 'brush-off' was to their detriment or disaster. At Gaza (312) the young Demetrius Poliorcetes was urged by his friends not to pit himself against such an experienced veteran as Ptolemy I. He rejected the advice and suffered a crushing defeat.[40] Second, when in 69 the able consul Lucullus was preparing to attack Tigranes, the latter was advised by

Mithradates not to come to close quarters with the Romans but to surround them and cut them off. The advice was scorned, Tigranocerta fell, and Tigranes fled.[41] Again, when Mithradates besieged Cyzicus in 74, Lucullus positioned himself across his enemy's supply route. Mithradates ignored all advice to call off the siege but pursued it with full vigour until famine started to take its predictable toll. His subsequent withdrawal was a costly affair.[42] But the most disastrous case was that of Crassus, whose ambitions, over-confidence and rejection of advice led to the destruction of his army at the battle of Carrhae in 53 (p. 228). Although these examples may be thought of as disagreements with advisers, they entailed much more than that. There was no apparent discussion, and all advice was scorned out of hand by commanders who 'knew best'. The operative words are surely complacency and over-confidence to a degree which allowed no room for doubt.

In the military history of Rome, Livy frequently mentions over-confidence either in commanders and their men or in the enemy. Little store can be set on the earliest instances in view of the absence of sources before the third century. The bare bones of available data were probably padded out and embellished into good stories. By contrast, the naval battle off Mylae (p. 169) in 260 was an historical event which was chronicled by Polybius, the most reliable chronicler of the era. He reports that the Carthaginians were fully confident of victory – and not without good reason. They were adept seamen, whereas the Romans had had no need of a fleet until they got involved in the First Punic War. Mylae was their first major nautical test. The Carthaginians, however, were unaware that the Romans, conscious of the inferiority of their ships, had invented and equipped them with *corvi* ('ravens'). The *corvus* consisted basically of a gangway in the prow where it was normally carried upright against a pole, but it be could be rotated and lowered onto the deck of an enemy vessel which it held fast by means of a large protruding spike. The sea battle was converted into a fight on deck in which the Romans excelled. In spite of their initial over-confidence which caused them to head straight for the enemy without caution, the Carthaginians fled when they saw the capabilities of the new contraption.[43]

Finally, at Lake Trasimene (217) it was the Romans who suffered a massive disaster, largely as a result of the consul's complacency. Hannibal knew that his opponent Flaminius was a vain and over-confident general and so he decided to play on it. He marched south, almost in front of the other's nose, ravaging the countryside as he went. Flaminius was so affronted that he followed Hannibal and camped near the defile leading to the lake. The next morning, in murky weather, he marched through the defile and straight into one of the greatest ambushes in military history.[44] With a total lack of forethought he failed to entertain any suspicions of the trouble ahead, which could have been prevented by a little judicious scouting.

Misjudgement, Disagreement, and Disobedience

Like most patriots Judas Maccabaeus had an unquenchable zeal. His fervour
for his cause was so pronounced that the Syrians under Antiochus IV
repeatedly underestimated him and sent ever larger armies against him and
his small band of followers, and yet Judas almost invariably triumphed. It was
not until they reputedly sent a mighty force of 100,000 men with 20,000
horse and thirty-two elephants against him at Bath-Zacharias (Beit Skaria) in
162 that Judas himself began to fear the odds and decided to withdraw.[45]
Misjudgements of people, distances or lapses of time are common in
everyday life. The distinct feature in the case of Judas was the Syrians'
repeated failure to get the measure of the man.

Pyrrhus of Epirus may have been a great military adventurer, but in
addition to being complacent and at times contemptuous he was a person
who seemed particularly prone to misjudge his enemy and disagree with his
ally. When Cleonymus of Sparta found himself at loggerheads with his
people, he invited Pyrrhus to help him sort matters out. That adventurer
arrived with 25,000 infantry, 200 horse and twenty-five elephants (272). As
Plutarch remarks, it was clear from the size of his army that Pyrrhus had no
intention of conquering Sparta for Cleonymus but the Peloponnese for
himself! He began by despising the apparent weakness of the defences and
ignoring Cleonymus' request for an immediate attack, postponing it until
the next day. However, during the night the Spartans, men and women, dug
a large trench and buried wagons in it up to their axles to impede the
elephants. On the next morning Pyrrhus attacked but failed to penetrate
the Spartan line or cross the trench, and the city was saved by the arrival of
reinforcements.[46] From Sparta he proceeded to Argos where hostilities had
erupted. In the middle of the night the gates were opened up to him and he
entered with his Gauls (272). But when it came to the turn of the elephants
with their howdahs, Pyrrhus had overestimated the height of the gateway
which was insufficient to allow them through. All the howdahs had to be
removed, resulting in chaos and confusion as the elephants ran amok.[47]

In the early days of Rome disagreements were apt to arise as a result of
the presence of two consuls for each year. It is reported that in 431 the two
consuls at Mount Algidus (Compatri) could not agree on anything, and the
problem was only solved by the appointment of a single overriding dictator.[48]
Likewise in 418 and again at Algidus there were two military tribunes who
could not reach any agreement. On this occasion the solution was an
agreement whereby the tribunes assumed command on alternate days.[49]
This was an arrangement between commanding officers which cropped up
from time to time in Roman military history and was apt to lead to defeats.
It was, in fact, the custom at the time of the disastrous Roman defeat at
Cannae (216, p. 180) when the consuls were the cautious Lucius Aemilius
Paulus and the hasty Gaius Terentius Varro. Hannibal, who made a practice

of sizing up his opponents, is believed to have waited to engage until a day on which Varro was in command. On that fateful day Varro led out the legions against the advice of his colleague.[50]

Personality problems were again to the fore in the great defeat of the Romans by the Northmen at Arausio (Orange) in 105. The commanders were the consul Gnaeus Manlius and a proconsul Servilius Caepio. The latter was jealous of the consul and refused to cooperate in a joint camp. Anxious to secure all the glory for himself, Caepio camped between the consul and the enemy. This stupid move allowed the enemy to take on the two armies one at a time and both were captured.[51] Naval warfare was not exempt from the effects of similar personality clashes and disagreements, as occurred at Embata in 356. A Greek fleet under Chares was reinforced by another one under two veteran admirals, Iphicrates and Timotheus, to help to deal with some rebellious islands. When these fleets arrived off Embata the weather was so stormy that the veterans said it would be folly to fight. Chares disagreed, accused the other two of treason, and proceeded alone to meet the enemy and a handsome defeat. In the aftermath, Timotheus and Iphicrates were found guilty and were fined. Accordingly Chares, although he behaved rashly under the circumstances, cannot be accused of failure to cooperate.[52]

In contrast to the events at Embata, frank disobedience was evidenced at Notium (406) in the last stages of the Peloponnesian War. When Alcibiades was in charge of the Athenian fleet, he was called away and left the fleet in the care of his deputy, Antiochus, with strict orders not to engage in any hostilities until his return. Egged on by ambition and vanity, Antiochus flagrantly disobeyed the order and sailed out with ten ships. He concealed eight of them in an ambush and then sailed across in front of Lysander's nose as this brilliant Spartan admiral lay in harbour. Lysander, knowing that Alcibiades was away, saw his chance and sailed out with his whole fleet. The ensuing battle escalated as the entire Athenian fleet came out in support. It ended in disaster for the Athenians with the loss of twenty ships. On his return Alcibiades was blamed and fell into disgrace in Athens.[53]

On a contrary and somewhat amusing note, similar circumstances prevailed at Imbrinium (place now unknown) in 325 during the Second Samnite War. When the dictator (sole supreme commander) in charge of managing the Samnite War had to pay a visit to Rome, he left his Master of Horse, Fabius Maximus Rullianus, in charge and adjured him not to engage the enemy. The latter, hearing that all was quiet on the Samnite front, marched out against the enemy and engaged them in a pitched battle. He scored an outstanding success.[54]

Laxity, Negligence, and Incompetence

An extraordinary coincidence surrounds two illustrative examples of laxity in that, apart from occurring under similar circumstance, both took place at Herdonea within two years and the culprits concerned were both named Gnaeus Fulvius. Although Hannibal joked contemptuously about this ('same name; same result') they were not in fact the same man. In 212 the Roman commander was the praetor Gnaeus Fulvius Flaccus; in 210 it was the proconsul Gnaeus Fulvius Centumalus. On the first occasion, Hannibal heard that the praetor had become slack and careless after some successes and that there was no longer any discipline among his men. That night he concealed some troops in the neighbourhood and, on the next morning, followed up their surprise attack with the rest of his army. The Romans, itching for a fight, fell in without any order and scrambled to take their places wherever they fancied. The whole line was shallow and grossly extended; the officers could not make themselves heard. The result was a foregone conclusion. Only 2,000 of the 18,000 escaped to live. Among the first to leave was the praetor, who jumped on his horse and galloped away.[55]

On the second occasion, two years later, in which Hannibal defeated the Romans at Herdonea they did at least put up a good fight. Laxity was less in evidence and was confined to the proconsul, who was described as a man who displayed a 'characteristic negligence'. The position which he held outside the town was inadequately defended. Moreover, his negligent streak was reinforced by his optimistic hopes of success. These were based on a report that the town had begun to waver in its support for Carthage, to which it had adhered after the Roman defeat at Cannae in 216. Hannibal, who controlled the town, was away in Bruttium when he heard about the proconsul's relaxed attitude. Seizing the opportunity for a quick victory, he made a lightning march back to Herdonea and appeared in battle order. A frontal charge followed by a double envelopment with his cavalry secured an easy victory, in which the proconsul did at least die fighting with his men.[56]

The consul Publius Claudius Pulcher has already been censured above for his alleged disregard for sacrificial portents before the battle of Drepanum (Trapani) in 249 (p. 40). He must now be taken to task for losing the battle through his incompetence. He had sailed up the west coast of Sicily by night with the object of making a surprise attack on the Carthaginians base at Drepanum. When they got there, the leading ships started entering the harbour at the southern end of its mouth. Adherbal, the Carthaginian commander had been caught off guard, but he hastily manned his ships and started leading them out of the harbour, clinging to the northern shore opposite the one by which the Romans were entering. Claudius, however, was leading his fleet from behind and was unable to see what was going on at the front. By the time he realised the truth some of his ships were in the harbour while others were either in the entrance or approaching it. His countermanding order to turn and put to sea resulted in pandemonium. Some ships fouled each other or even sheared off their oars. When they were eventually brought into line abreast close to the shore, they were in the worst possible position. The enemy fleet had gained the open sea, where they were able to manoeuvre and attack as they pleased. In the ensuing carnage ninety-three Roman vessels were captured with their crews and only thirty managed to escape, including the consul's.[57]

Notes

1   Plutarch, *Aemilius Paulus*, 2.5 & *Cato Major*, 11.1.
2   Livy, 8.13.6–8.
3   Polybius, 1.32–34.
4   Herodotus, 9.22–25.
5   Diodorus, 13.98.4–99.
6   Polybius, 5.85.5–13.
7   Plutarch, *Demetrius*, 29.3.
8   Herodotus, 6.12–14.
9   Thucydides, 7.59–71.
10   Plutarch, *Aratus*, 28.1–2.
11   Livy, 10.35–36.15.
12   Diodorus, 12.9–10.1.
13   Diodorus, 20.62.2–5.
14   Thucydides, 8.95.
15   Herodotus, 9.61–62.
16   Plutarch, *Phocion*, 12–13.
17   Livy, *Epitome* 19.
18   Thucydides, 7.50.
19   Plutarch, *Pelopidas*, 31.1–3.
20   Thucydides, 6.70.
21   Xenophon, *Hellenica*, 7.31.
22   Livy, 26.11.1–4.
23   Diodorus, 20.11.3–5.
24   Arrian, *Anabasis*, 1.5.11–6.4.
25   J. F. C. Fuller, *The Generalship of Alexander the Great*, Wordsworth, 1998, pp. 224–5.
26   Livy, 37.20–21.3.
27   Xenophon, *Hellenica*, 4.1.20–24.
28   Livy, 42.65.5–66.1, 9.
29   Appian, *Punic Wars*, 102–3.
30   Livy, 7.34–36.
31   Frontinus, 1.5.15; Livy, *Epitome* 17.
32   Thucydides, 3.97–98.
33   Plutarch, *Antony*, 38–39.
34   Thucydides, 2.81–82
35   Xenophon, *Anabasis*, 1.8.
36   Plutarch, *Pelopidas*, 32.5–7; Diodorus, 15.80.5.
37   Plutarch, *Pompey*, 19.1.
38   Appian, *Civil Wars*, 1.120–121.
39   Xenophon, *Hellenica*, 4.1.15–19.
40   Diodorus, 19.81.1.

41　Appian, *Mithridatic Wars*, 85.
42　Appian, *Mithridatic Wars*, 75.
43　Polybius, 1.22–23.
44　Polybius, 3.84.1–2.
45　I Maccabees, 6.28–47; Josephus, *Jewish Antiquities*, 12.9.4.
46　Plutarch, *Pyrrhus*, 27–30.1.
47　Plutarch. *Pyrrhus*, 31–34.3.
48　Livy, 4.26.1–11.
49　Livy, 4.45.7–46.3.
50　Polybius, 3.110.1–4.
51　Dio Cassius, 27, fragment 91; Livy, *Epitome* 67.
52　Diodorus, 16.21; Nepos, *Timotheus*, 3.
53　Diodorus, 13.71; Xenophon, *Hellenica*, 1.5.11–14.
54　Livy, 8.30.1–7.
55　Livy, 25.20.5–21.
56　Livy, 27.1.3–15.
57　Polybius, 1.49–51.

4

The Element of Surprise

Throughout the ages surprise has been the most important tactical element in warfare, involved in virtually every aspect of the tactical spectrum. Indeed Clausewitz[1] goes so far as to say that it lies in varying degree at the foundation of all undertakings without exception. By definition surprise will be evoked either intentionally or otherwise by any attack, event, or observation that is unexpected. However, on many occasions surprise is deliberately induced with the help of a deception which ensures that the attack is not anticipated. An example is the common ambush, in which the concealment of the attackers and secrecy surrounding the attack provide the deception. Under these conditions, the deception is merely the means to secure the fundamental objective of surprise. The same principles apply to tactics such as decoys, diversions, and large turning movements, in each of which a deception is employed as the means to the end. There is, however, another large group of events in which surprise is elicited without any intentional resort to deception. As both groups are large, the subject needs to be considered under two headings: first, surprise by itself in the absence of deception, and second, surprise induced by means of deception. This chapter is devoted solely to the first of these categories: surprise without any resort to deception, but it requires a further qualification. Clausewitz concludes that any attempt to create surprise must invariably embody an element of deception or stratagem, 'be it ever so small'. This clearly refers to secrecy, the most widely pervasive of all deceptions, for without some element of secrecy or concealment there can be no surprise. However, this element is so inherent in every attempt to surprise that it has to be accepted without further question. There remains the third permutation on the themes of surprise and deception, namely deceptions which are not primarily aimed at creating surprise. These are discussed in chapter 6.

Dictionary definitions of 'surprise' include such words as 'sudden' or 'startle', on the one hand, and 'unforeseen' or 'unawares' on the other. From this it is clear that there is a subtle yet considerable variation of meaning between these terms in regard to both the time scale of the stimulus and the intensity of the resulting emotion. 'Sudden' and 'startle' suggest an intense stimulus and a strong and almost instantaneous awareness of it; the other terms are suggestive of a more gradual dawning on consciousness which hardly demands a swift reaction. A commander might be said to be surprised at the enemy numbers or at his deployment, but he may have ample time to make compensatory adjustments to his own side. This and other similar instances of 'surprise' do not convey the shock emotion usually denoted by the word when it is used in a military connotation unless the alarm was sufficiently great to prompt an immediate withdrawal or equivalent response.

Many and diverse were the surprise attacks recorded by the ancient chroniclers. Probably the most successful were attacks which have one theme in common in that they were directed against an enemy who was otherwise engaged. This group is in itself diverse, depending upon the particular activity of the victim at the time. Then there were attacks of a totally different order which were related to deployments and manoeuvres and which were usually to be found in set piece battles. These include tactics such as flanking attacks and attacks while an enemy is in mid manoeuvre. All these tactics will be discussed below. First, however, there is a heterogeneous group of surprise attacks which have no particular element in common. They varied not only in the conditions under which they occurred but also in the intensity and time scale of the initial surprise and the response. Their number is legion, to use an inapt expression, but three examples will suffice.

The consul Gnaeus Manlius Volso had only just arrived in Galatia in 189 to subdue the Gallic hordes when he camped near a stronghold called Cuballum, now unknown.[2] His advance guards were suddenly attacked and thrown into confusion by Gallic horsemen, who inflicted some casualties. They were driven off by the Roman cavalry. Another example occurred during a Sicilian invasion of Italy by Dionysius, the tyrant of Syracuse. His opponent was a Syracusan exile called Heloris, who camped with his Italiots on the Elleporus river (?Callipari) in Bruttii (389). When Dionysius heard of his enemy's position, he advanced toward him and encamped nearby. Heloris, on the other hand, was unaware of his enemy's proximity. He was marching in the van of his army with only a few troops when Dionysius suddenly struck and virtually annihilated them, including Heloris.[3] Again, Aratus, the general of the Achaeans, provided an unusual background to a surprise attack. After a battle near Mount Lycaeus (Likaon) in 227 rumours circulated that he had been killed.[4] One might have expected that his opponents would be the ones to take advantage of the situation, but it was the irrepressible Aratus himself who made good use of it by launching a totally unexpected attack on the city of Mantinea, which he captured.

Sorties have one element in common, a sudden eruption of an armed body of men from a town, fort or camp to attack those outside. They were not unusual events. In 48, during Rome's Second Civil War, Marcus Octavius laid siege to Salonae (Split) with a ring of five camps. When the inhabitants became desperate from starvation, they made a sortie and stormed the nearest camp so successfully that they proceeded to attack the other four camps in succession and with the same success. They were rewarded with the complete evacuation of Octavius, who fled to his ships.[5] In 212 the Romans were bent on capturing Capua from the Carthaginians. They began by devastating the crops for miles around until the Capuans, supported by Carthaginian cavalry, made a sortie and overwhelmed the Romans before they could recall their troops.[6] Again, during the Gallic War the Romans at Octodurus (near Martigny, 57) awoke to find themselves surrounded by a dense horde of tribespeople covering the surrounding heights. When the enemy charged down the slopes, a bitter fight ensued for many hours until the Romans were forced to retreat within their camp to recoup. After a rest they suddenly charged out and surrounded the enemy who fled in panic after sustaining heavy losses[7]. It will be noted that this episode involved two sudden charges, one by the enemy followed later by the Roman sortie.

In each of these sorties the parties concerned were the inhabitants or occupants of the town or camp and no deception was therefore involved in their presence within the enclosure. The only element of deception was implicit in the secrecy of the operations which is an obvious component of all sudden sallies. This was in contrast to a sortie at Cleonae (Kleonai, 235) when Aratus, a rabid tyrant-hater heard that the tyrant of Argos was planning to attack the place next day. Making a wide detour to deceive the tyrant, he marched at great speed through the night and occupied the town in the dark. On the arrival of the enemy next day he and his men poured out and surrounded them.[8] As a sortie this is a good example, but the unexpected presence and concealment of Aratus in the town provide all the features of an ambush.

When allowance is made for the longer time scale in naval operations, surprise attacks at sea were just as numerous as those on land. After ten years of hostilities against the Persians, king Evagoras of Salamis (Gazimağuza, formerly Famagusta) equipped sixty new ships, bringing his total to 110 vessels. When a Persian fleet under their admiral Glos sailed past *en route* to Citium (Larnaca), Evagoras sailed out of his harbour and fell upon it (381).[9] The element of surprise and his orderly deployment secured some initial success, but Glos was reprieved by the time interval which enabled him to deploy, restore order and counterattack with devastating result. In another example, Gnaeus Scipio heard that a Carthaginian fleet of forty decked ships had sailed up the Spanish coast, paced by an army on shore, and was anchored off the mouth of the Iberus (Ebro). Scipio moved in against them with his thirty-five ships and caught the enemy totally unprepared (217). The Carthaginians did not resist but fell back on the shore where they beached their ships and sought the protection of their army on land. The

Romans then towed away every enemy ship that could be floated, all twenty-five of them.[10]

In attacks which are unexpected it is usually the attacker who creates the surprise, but this is not invariable. In 368, during the fourth Punic War of Sicily, Dionysius I, the tyrant of Syracuse, had collected a large combined force which included 300 triremes. As the Carthaginians had been severely hit by the plague, Dionysius decided that it would be a good time to strike. Accordingly, he invaded their territory and captured several towns. In the process he heard that the Carthaginian dockyards at Drepanum had been destroyed by fire – another excellent opportunity.[11] Anticipating no resistance, he sent only 130 of his 300 triremes to the naval base, where they anchored in the harbour. He must have sustained a nasty shock when 200 Carthaginian ships suddenly appeared and sailed against him. The Punic attack was such a complete surprise that the Carthaginians were able to tow most of Dionysius' fleet away. There is no suggestion that Dionysius was deliberately disinformed about the fire. Presumably he was just misinformed and was negligent in failing to obtain any confirmation of the gossip.

The time scales affecting surprise and response have already received some comment above, particularly when the surprise has not had a sudden impact and the response has been unduly delayed. A seemingly extreme case concerns the events leading up to the battle of the Aegates (Egadi) islands, which terminated the First Punic War in 241. From start to finish, these events developed over some nine months. After the fiasco of the battle of Drepanum in 249 (p. 50) the Romans had lost the war at sea. The trouble was that neither side managed to win the war on land. It was a stalemate. As the war approached its twenty-third year both sides were worn out and battle-weary. The Romans for their part realised that they could only win it by a victory at sea, and they decided to make one final effort. A fleet of 200 quinqueremes was built in secrecy to a design copied from a Carthaginian ship which had proved to be fast and manoeuvrable. On the other side of the coin, the Carthaginians 'never expected the Romans to dispute the sea with them again' as Polybius puts it.[12] They tended to neglect their naval force and became complacent. When the Roman fleet was fitted out, it sailed for Sicily in early summer 242. The news took the enemy by complete surprise. As soon as they heard it, they started to prepare their fleet, but according to a recent estimate[13] it seems to have taken them around nine months, with delays particularly in finding crews. Before they eventually sailed they loaded their ships with provisions for the troops on land at Eryx in Sicily. Even at this stage they had no intention of engaging the Romans until they had delivered the goods and taken troops on board. But a further surprise awaited them when the Roman fleet intercepted them and brought them to battle before they could land. The Roman victory at the Aegates islands which brought the war to an end is well known.

Attacks While an Enemy Is Otherwise Engaged

The chronicles tell of a number of specific conditions which were particularly conducive to success in that the enemy was caught completely off guard while being occupied in other activities such as sleeping. No deception was necessary apart from the small element of it which is invariably embodied in surprise itself and in any secrecy involved. It was simply a matter of taking advantage of an appropriate time and opportunity. For obvious reasons nocturnal attacks against an enemy camp were perhaps the most successful, but attacks at meal times or while the enemy was setting up camp were other often effective variations on the theme.

At Night or Dawn

These attacks were not only the most successful but also the most numerous. Herodotus relates what is probably the first recorded account of a nocturnal attack.[14] It took place 'not many years before Xerxes' invasion of Greece', at a time when the little state of Phocis was subjected to repeated attacks by her larger neighbour Thessaly. On one occasion the Phocians found themselves bottled up by the enemy on Mount Parnassus. Their resourceful leader Tellias waited until the moon was full to mount a nocturnal attack on the enemy. He whitewashed the armour and exposed parts of 600 of his men for the purpose of identification in the dark and sent them into the Thessalian camp. They were instructed to kill anyone who was not white like themselves. The abject terror created by these apparitions and the flight of the survivors can be left to the imagination.

The first campaign of Alexander the Great constitutes a veritable treasure trove of surprise attacks. Bent on subduing the unruly tribes that threatened the security of Macedon, he engaged in five consecutive assaults, three of which provide good examples of surprise attacks. One was at night and one at dawn. In the latter he crossed the Danube by night and opposed the Getae on the north bank at dawn (335). Their utter amazement stemmed not from somnolence but because they had been watching his movements on the far bank until dusk the day before. How he had managed to appear before them at dawn surpassed their comprehension. In their bemused and frightened state of mind a single charge routed them and their town was razed.[15] Later in the year (335) Alexander had attacked two Illyrian tribes, who thought that they had seen the last of him. He learnt, however, that they were camping nearby with such complacency that they had posted no sentries and erected no defences. It was a heaven-sent opportunity. In a nocturnal attack many of the enemy were killed in their beds and many more were slaughtered on the spot or as they fled. The only fugitives to escape had thrown away their weapons.[16]

During the early stages of the Maccabaean Revolt, the irrepressible Judas neatly turned the tables on his antagonists by means of an attack at dawn. He heard that a large Syrian force was planning to attack his camp by night from their position at Emmaus (Amwas). Accordingly he marched through the night to Emmaus and attacked the enemy camp at sunrise (166). The element of surprise was sufficient to allow him to slay 3,000 of the enemy, a number equal to his entire force.[17]

On two occasions enemy camps were set on fire at night. One was carried out by Philopoemen at Pleiae (near Asopus, 192) where the occupants were virtually annihilated.[18] The other incident involved a well-researched plan which was engineered by Scipio. In 203 both Hasdrubal and his ally Syphax had set up their camps near Utica close to Scipio's camp with the object of hemming him in with superior forces. Scipio employed spies who had access to the camps as attendants on emissaries and were in fact centurions in disguise. They reported back on matters such as the positions of entrances, layouts, and guard posts. In the ensuing attack both camps were fired simultaneously, killing most of the occupants.[19]

At Meal Times

These were less frequent than nocturnal attacks but one of them is note-worthy by virtue of an unusual ruse. It happened at Sepeia in Argolis. For two centuries Argos had been the undisputed leader in the Peloponnese until a rival emerged in the form of Sparta. In about 494 their armies met in what was to be the last round of the feud. King Cleomenes I of Sparta had been told by the Delphic oracle that if he made an assault on Argos, he would succeed in capturing it. The Argive generals had also consulted an oracle and had been told to beware of Spartan wiles. To forestall any trickery, they put their heads together and adopted a ruse. They instructed their herald to listen to the orders issued by the Spartan herald and then to repeat them on the Argive side. In this way, they argued, they could not go wrong. It was a stupid plan, and it did not take Cleomenes long to realise what was in the wind. He instructed his men that when they heard the next call to breakfast, they were to forego the meal and to pick up their arms and charge the enemy camp. The feasting Argives who were not killed on the spot fled to a sacred wood nearby, which Cleomenes promptly fired with utter ruthlessness.[20] This finally closed the chapter of Argive versus Spartan hegemony (leadership) over the Peloponnese. The Spartans now reigned supreme. It may be noted that Cleomenes' ruse did no more than initiate the attack by ensuring that the time was ripe. In principle the action was like all the other attacks on an enemy who was known to be otherwise engaged.

At Pergamum in 190 an Archaean commander called Diophanes launched a successful attack on a force of guerillas while they were having their midday meal. They had been sent by Seleucus to ravage the surrounding lands and, encountering no opposition from the frightened garrison commander, they did as they pleased. When Diophanes arrived, he stationed his 1,000 Achaeans outside the wall and waited patiently, allowing the enemy to become accustomed to his inactivity. Around midday the enemy lay down, scattered around the parkland, and proceeded to have their picnic lunch. This was what Diophanes had been waiting for, and he suddenly attacked them with devastating effect. This was only a part of the whole picture, which is related further elsewhere (p. 42).

While an Enemy Is Setting up or Breaking Camp

These were a fairly frequent variant on the theme of attacking a victim who was otherwise engaged. Once again Alexander's first campaign provides an example. On his route northwards to the Ister (Danube) in 335 he was following a horde of retreating Triballians when he heard that they had side-stepped him and detoured back to their haunts on the river Lyginus (?Yantra). He turned about and retraced his steps, catching the enemy off guard. Finding them setting up camp near dense woodland, he attacked and drove them into the forest. His problem was how to lure them out into the open. He achieved this by keeping his infantry and cavalry out of sight and sending his archers and slingers to discharge their missiles into the wood. The enemy decided that they could deal with these light troops, and they emerged to attack them. Alexander then led his infantry forward with the cavalry on both wings. A charge was too much for the lightly dressed and armed Triballi who turned and fled, leaving 3,000 of their number dead.[21]

In the above example Alexander compounded his attack with a deception in order to lure the enemy out of the woods. It was not a straight-forward case of simple surprise. To find such an incident one has only to look to the campaign of Timoleon, the liberator of Sicily. After landing on the island he was approaching Hadranum (Adrano) in 344 with his little band of mercenaries when he heard that the current tyrant, Hicetas, had arrived there with 5,000 men and was pitching his camp. Realising that this was the best time to attack, Timoleon immediately marched his 1,200 mercenaries as quickly as possible, getting there in four hours. The enemy were taken so completely by surprise that they fled at the mere sight of him.[22] (In Diodorus' version the enemy were engaged in eating, a different variation on the same theme).

When the Carthaginians tried this tactic before the battle of Ilipa in 206 (p. 197), their attempt was frustrated through the foresight of Scipio (Africanus to be). He had just arrived preparatory to the battle and his first consideration was to fortify his camp. With his customary prescience he foresaw the possibility of an attack and posted a squadron of cavalry out of sight behind a hill. When the attack came, Scipio's cavalry had little difficulty in scattering the advance guard, but the enemy came on in force and the engagement turned into a full cavalry battle. Eventually Scipio withdrew his work force and sent them into the fray, followed by some infantry who poured out of the camp. The tide was turned and the enemy was forced into a retreat which became a rout.

Attacks on an Enemy Loaded with Loot

These were infrequent occurrences. The opportunity did not arise every day, but a heaven-sent chance presented itself to the consul Volumnius during the Third Samnite War. While the Romans were engaged against the Etruscans, who had intervened to feather their own nest, the Samnites seized the opportunity to invade Campania and ravage the land. The consul Volumnius was on his way back to Samnium from Campania when news reached him that the Samnites were encamped on the river Volturnus. He changed course to intercept them and camped at a sufficient distance to keep them in ignorance of his presence. He learnt from spies that they were planning to leave for Samnium the next day and were so encumbered with booty that they were in total disorder. What an opportunity! Volumnius promptly charged their column and overpowered them without effort (296). Most of them were so totally overburdened with their spoils that they had elected to dispense with their weapons. The camp was then assaulted with predictable result. To add to the Samnites' problems, their prisoners escaped and captured the Samnite general, whom they led up to the consul still in his saddle. The Samnites are said to have lost 8,500 men killed or captured. The Roman losses (unstated) were probably minute, but they did recover 7,500 prisoners and a vast quantity of loot.[23]

Surprise in Battle

There were three manoeuvres which were specific to battles, notably the larger set piece affairs, and which could evoke varying degrees of surprise in the enemy. Although they are discussed in turn, they may be interdependent in that one may lead to another. A turning movement, for instance, might lead either to an inviting gap in the enemy line as he extended his wing to prevent being outflanked or to an attack on him while he was manoeuvring to fill the gap. In theory these manoeuvres might have been open for all to see, in which case deception was not usually applicable and the element of surprise might have been minimal even if the event had not already been anticipated. In practice, however, matters were sometimes very different. If the lines were very extended and if visibility was poor as at the battle of Magnesia-ad-Sipylum (Manisa, 190, p. 213), the two wings often had no idea of the situation at the other end of the line. Alternatively, at the battle of Gabiene (316, p. 161) the dust cloud created by elephants and horses' hooves was so dense as to allow Antigonus to charge unseen through a gap in the enemy's line and capture his baggage train. In effect, the murk provided secrecy and ensured a large measure of surprise.

Turning Movements on the Battlefield

Turning in the military sense is defined as manoeuvring so as to attack an enemy in the flank or rear. This covers a wide variety of eventualities. Clausewitz[24] refers to 'tactical turning movements *great and small*' (the italics are mine), but he does not expand on the differentiation between his two groups. They may not have been the same as those encountered in classical warfare. It would seem that turning movements in the classical era can be divided fairly sharply into two groups depending upon whether they occurred in battle on the field or as more remote events such as turning enemy positions on obstacles like mountains, rivers or ravines. The latter, usually larger examples, invariably involved deception to ensure that the manoeuvres were carried out in the strictest secrecy, which was an absolute requisite for success. On the battlefield, on the other hand, a turning movement could usually be seen or anticipated. If it was not foreseen, the extent of the resulting surprise would depend upon the suddenness and speed with which the manoeuvre was executed. The larger movements, which involved wide detours away from the battlefield and were dependent on both surprise and deception (secrecy), are matters for the next chapter.

Turning was particularly prone to occur in set-piece battles when a wing extended beyond the end of the opposing line during the deployment. If the threatened wing was then extended to counteract the threat of being outflanked, one of two things was likely to happen or even both. Either a gap would appear in what was the shorter line or, if the commander attempted to repair the gap, the enemy would seize the opportunity to attack while the manoeuvre was in progress and the line was in disorder. Both of these eventualities are discussed with examples in the next sections.

Assuming that the opposing lines were of the same length, there was a particular reason why in their deployment they should not have ended up facing each other without any overlapping of the wings. Thucydides has pointed out that when a hoplite phalanx advanced it tended to incline to the right because each man sought to gain protection for his unshielded right side from his neighbour's shield.[25] When this happened down the line, the whole line shifted gradually to the right so that the right wing of each line extended beyond the opposing wing. This state of affairs was peculiar to the hoplite phalanx because hoplites marched in close order and each carried a large round shield in front of him fastened to his left forearm. The projection to the left provided protection for his neighbour's right side. In contrast, the Macedonian pikemen advanced in open order with their small shields slung from the neck and carried over the left shoulder. Examples of a shift to the right and its consequences are seen in the hoplite battles of First Mantinea (418, p. 126) and 'the Nemea' (394, p. 131).

Attacking an Enemy in Mid-Manoeuvre

Attacking an enemy in mid-manoeuvre was not unlike penetrating a gap in his line. The gap was merely replaced by a disorganised force which was in no position to defend itself properly. This was well shown in the battle of Leuctra (371), in which the Spartans under Cleombrotus confronted a Theban force under Epaminondas. The battle is described fully elsewhere (p. 136) and only the relevant details will be recounted here. Epaminondas created history by massing his phalanx fifty men deep and placing it on his left, opposing the Spartan command centre which was traditionally on the right. He slowly advanced his phalanx obliquely, edging always further to the left in order to draw Cleombrotus away from the rest of his force and to create a gap in his line. Cleombrotus, however, divined his opponent's motives and started to extend his wing further to the right in an attempt to outflank the enemy wing with his own superior numbers. When his men became disordered in the middle of this manoeuvre, Pelopidas and his Sacred Band of 300 charged and were followed by the phalanx. They created a breach and turned to attack the enemy in the flank. Cleombrotus himself was killed and his army was routed.

The risks attending a major manoeuvre in the middle of a battle were clearly well known to the commanders in ancient warfare as evidenced by the relative paucity of reported instances. Even a well-planned manoeuvre was at risk of disruption by enemy action, but if the manoeuvre was being clumsily executed even before the enemy intervened, disaster was a certainty. The Roman proconsul Marcellus discovered this to his cost when he faced Hannibal at Canusium in 209. Marcellus had been asked to dog Hannibal and divert him away from Tarentum, but he eventually got too close to his enemy and could not resist an almost inevitable engagement. The struggle persisted for two hours by which time the Roman right wing was beginning to falter through exhaustion. Marcellus decided to bring up the 18th legion into the front line to relieve the stricken wing, but the manoeuvre went awry. Half of the army was withdrawing while others were moving up until the whole lot were flung into confusion and the turmoil turned into a rout. It was a costly move, which left 2,700 men dead, including four centurions and two military tribunes.[26]

In the First Mithridatic War the Pontic army under Mithridates' general Archelaus confronted Sulla and the Romans in 86 at Chaeronea. According to Appian the Romans were outnumbered about three to one. Unfortunately neither of the accounts is very lucid. The action took place in a narrow plain surrounded by craggy hills where the two armies deployed opposite each other. Sulla placed cavalry on both wings and positioned a force in reserve on high ground in the rear. He himself took charge of the right wing. The action started when the enemy unleashed his scythe-bearing chariots in a charge which proved futile. The distance was too small to allow the chariots to gain an effective speed and they were easily side-stepped. Archelaus then extended his right wing with the object of outflanking the Roman left by virtue of his superior numbers. Sulla's reserve flying squad then charged to the assistance of the beleaguered wing but found itself being hemmed in against the cliffs. At that point the opposing wings on the other side of the field had not engaged and Sulla himself was idle. He crossed the field from his post on the right to rally his left, where he managed to turn the tables. Archelaus then abandoned his attempt to outflank Sulla's left wing and turned his attention to his opponent's right wing which, in Sulla's absence, was leaderless. Sulla observed the move. Leading the pick of his cavalry and collecting two reserve cohorts *en route*, he rode back across the field and charged Archelaus before he had completed his manoeuvre. Creating confusion, he broke the enemy lines and put them to flight. Seeing both their wings giving way, the Pontic centre refused to hold its ground and fled *en masse*.[27]

A Gap in the Line

A gap in the line of deployment was an obvious invitation to the opponent to make use of it. 'If there is no gap, make one' seems to have been the motto of some commanders, notably Alexander the Great. One of his re-curring tactics, at the Granicus (Kocabas, 334)[28] and notably at Gaugamela (331)[29], was to attack the enemy left wing so hard that more men were drawn in from the centre until a gap, or at least a weakness, appeared. Through this he charged, aiming straight for the enemy's command centre which in the Persian army was always in the centre.

The first battle of Mantinea (418, p. 126) is noteworthy here by virtue of a gap in the line and the ensuing tactics. The Spartans and their allies under Agis II confronted a confederate army of Mantineans, Argives and Athenians. As the armies approached each other, the right wing of each side became unduly extended for the reasons given above by Thucydides. To counteract the trend, Agis ordered his entire left wing to move further to the left to forestall an outflanking movement by the Mantineans on the opposing right wing. This created a gap in the Spartan line. At the same time Agis ordered two polemarchs on the right wing to move their *morae* (about 600 men each) across to fill the gap, but they refused to do so at such short notice. When the armies closed, the Mantineans and a force of Argives swept into the hiatus in the Spartan line and surrounded their isolated wing, chasing it off the field. In the centre, king Agis and his Spartans launched a furious attack against the confederate centre and drove it into headlong flight. This left the Athenians and their cavalry on the confederate left wing in a state of total isolation. The Spartan right wing already extended well beyond them as a result of the initial shift of both lines to the right, and there seemed to be nothing to stop them not only from outflanking the Athenians but encircling them completely. They were only saved from annihilation because Agis, triumphant in the centre, wheeled to the assistance of his beleaguered left wing. This relieved the pressure on the Athenians and gave them time and a loophole for escape.

Tegyra was the site of a true chance confrontation between two Spartan *morae* (around 500 men each) on the one hand and Pelopidas with his Sacred Band[30] of 300 lovers and a few cavalry on the other (375). The ensuing encounter is detailed here because it involved a gap in the line which, however, contained some rather unusual features. When the two sides met near Tegyra, Pelopidas ordered his cavalry to charge the enemy centre. After causing disruption he himself immediately followed it up with the Sacred Band. Both of the Spartan polemarchs were killed. The fact that both polemarchs were killed shows that they must have been commanding their respective *morae* side by side in the centre, one on the right side of his unit and the other on the left of his. This is unusual. Possibly they did not want one of the polemarchs to be out on a limb but preferred to facilitate communications between the units. Following the deaths of both polemarchs the Spartans are said to have been terrified and to have parted their ranks to make a corridor for the Thebans to pass through and proceed on their way. Plutarch is inconsistent here, adding later that the Thebans had forced their way victoriously through the whole Spartan army. In the unlikely event that the gap was created voluntarily Pelopidas evidently chose not to pass through it. He turned aside and hacked at the enemy until they fled.[31] The action is of particular significance because it was the first occasion on which a Spartan force had been defeated by a force inferior in numbers to their own. The effect on Theban morale was great. Some of the lessons learnt at Tegyra were subsequently adopted a few years later at Leuctra (371, p. 136) and again at Second Mantinea (362), at which Epaminondas was killed.

The combat at Tegyra had a naval counterpart at the battle of Myonnesus (C. Doğanbey, 190) in that in both engagements the enemy line was penetrated in the centre. At Myonnesus the Romans had formed up in line abreast while the Rhodians under Eudamus brought up the rear. It was only then that they sighted the enemy ships, which were approaching in a double line astern. When the enemy under Polyxenidas deployed into line abreast, their line was so long as to be capable of surrounding the opposing Roman wing. Seeing this, Eudamus promptly rectified the imbalance by bringing the Rhodian ships forward to equalise the lines. The action was then started by Eudamus who proceeded immediately to direct his own vessel straight at the enemy flagship on their left wing. His prompt action was like a starter's gun, and in no time the fleets were engaged along the whole line. The Romans had eighty ships, twenty-two of which were Rhodian; the enemy boasted eighty-nine ships. Although the Romans were inferior in number, they had one immense advantage. Most, perhaps all, of their ships were equipped with fire apparatus consisting quite simply of a cauldron full of blazing material. The cauldron was mounted outboard at the end of a long pole and it could be tipped to pour its contents onto any ship that ventured too close. The device had been used on a small scale during Polyxenidas' treacherous attack at Panormus (190, p. 68) and it had proved its worth. The present encounter provides the best and possibly the only other recorded example of its use. It struck terror into the enemy, who were forced to keep their distance and were unable to close or ram. On the other hand, when they turned away they presented their broadside and could themselves be rammed. The device undoubtedly proved to be the decisive factor. With the enemy in terror of it, the Romans had little difficulty in breaking through their centre and they then turned to attack their left wing in the rear. Already under a frontal attack by the Rhodians, the enemy left was surrounded and many of their ships were sunk. Polyxenidas managed to escape. The enemy right wing was still intact, but when the men saw their admiral deserting his colleagues and fleeing, they also took to flight. The king's fleet lost forty-two ships captured or sunk. It is said that only two Roman vessels were destroyed.[32]

Gaps in a military formation did not necessarily arise as a result of tactics and manoeuvres. The nature of the terrain sometimes played a part. The phalanx was a formidable weapon but it had two well-known disadvantages. First, it was not flexible and was unable to turn abruptly to face an adversary. Second, it required level terrain for its cohesion. During the final battle in the Third Macedonian War, at Pydna (p. 220) in 168, the phalanx of Perseus progressed relentlessly forward. The Roman legions, armed with swords, were unable to hold their ground against the hedgehog of long pikes (*sarissae*) wielded by the enemy. The outcome looked ominous indeed to the consul, Aemilius Paulus. He subsequently admitted that he had never felt so anxious in his life until he noticed that gaps were appearing in the normally unbroken front ranks of the phalanx. Approaching the lower slopes of the foothills below Mount Olocrus it had started to move onto rougher terrain where the men could not maintain an orderly formation. Aemilius immediately divided his men into small groups and told them to penetrate the gaps in the phalanx and attack the enemy in their flanks. The Macedonians, unable to turn, were forced to discard their pikes and resort to their short swords, which were no match for the longer Roman weapons. As a result, the phalanx was gradually broken up into small segments which were attacked on all sides until the Macedonians fled. About 25,000 of them were killed, rather more than half of the total force.

The battle of Pydna also featured a more 'conventional' gap in the line.

It is told in full later (p. 220), as also are the battles of Paraetacene (317, p. 155) and Gabiene (316, p. 161) which provide further examples.

Notes

1   Clausewitz, *On War*, 3, 9.
2   Livy, 38.18.5–6.
3   Diodorus, 14.103.4–104.
4   Plutarch, *Cleomenes*, 5.1; *Aratus*, 36.1–2.
5   Caesar, *Civil War*, 3.9.
6   Livy, 25.18.1.
7   Caesar, *Gallic War*, 3.1–6.
8   Plutarch, *Aratus*, 29.1–4.
9   Diodorus, 15.3.4–6.
10   Polybius, 3.95–96.6; Livy, 22.19–20.3.
11   Diodorus, 15.73.3–5.
12   Polybius, 1.61.5.
13   J. F. Lazenby, *The First Punic War*, UCL Press, 1996, pp. 152 ff.
14   Herodotus, 8.27.
15   Arrian, *Anabasis*, 1.3–4.5.
16   Arrian, *Anabasis*, 1.6.9–11.
17   1 Maccabees, 4.1–15; Josephus, *Jewish Antiquities*, 12.7.3–4.
18   Livy, 35.27.1–9; Plutarch, *Philopoemen*, 14.4.
19   Polybius, 14.4–5; Livy, 30.3.8–30.6.
20   Herodotus, 6.77–78.
21   Arrian, *Anabasis*, 1.2.
22   Plutarch, *Timoleon*, 12; Diodorus, 16.68.9–10.
23   Livy, 10.20.
24   Clausewitz, *On War*, 6, 2.
25   Thucydides, 5.71.
26   Livy, 27.12.13–17; Plutarch, *Marcellus*, 25.4.
27   Appian, *Mithridatic Wars*, 43; Plutarch, *Sulla*, 19.1–4.
28   Arrian, *Anabasis*, 1.15.2–3.
29   Arrian, *Anabasis*, 3.14.
30   Plutarch, *Pelopidas*, 18.1.
31   Plutarch, *Pelopidas*, 17.2–5.
32   Livy, 37.30; Appian, *Syrian Wars*, 27.

5

Surprise with Deception

Many of the surprise confrontations recorded by the ancient chroniclers were compounded with an element of deliberate deception, usually in the form of secrecy. The most obvious of these is the age-old ambush, which can be defined as a surprise attack from a place of concealment, in which the act of hiding constitutes the deception. Although the deception is a vital part of the trap, it is only the means to secure surprise when the force in hiding breaks cover to attack. The surprise resulting from the secrecy remains the principal element. Feints are in the same category. A feigned withdrawal is only the preliminary act prior to a sudden about turn and an unexpected lunge, giving rise to surprise. When an obstacle such as a pass or a river is turned by means of an unobserved detour, the end result is a surprise attack on the enemy's rear. The secret turning movement is only the means to the final surprise attack. Again, when one army establishes a routine by confronting another on several successive days without offering any action, the object of the exercise may be to catch the opposition off guard on the day on which battle is unexpectedly offered. Other tactics included under this heading are decoys and diversions. All of these tactics which are intended to conceal the true intention are dissimulations of one sort or another.

Before discussing these tactics, it is convenient first to consider the use of *disinformation* as a means to securing a surprise attack. Disinformation is commonly used for other purposes, only remotely connected with surprise, and these belong in the next chapter. In tactics which did employ disinformation to put the enemy off guard, the deceit often took the form of blatant lies and broken pledges which must have contravened the 'rules of war', vague as they were in those days. Diodorus cites the case of Agathocles, tyrant of Syracuse, who offered a truce to several thousand infantry who had sought refuge on a hill.[1] When they descended, he disarmed and then surrounded them before butchering the lot.

Whereas all is said to be fair in love and war, it is hard to tolerate falsehoods such as those uttered by the Galatians who, at Ancyra in 189, asked for a conference. After two fruitless appointments, on one of which they failed to appear at all, they kept the third one in the form of an armed body of 1,000 horsemen charging down at full tilt. The Romans only escaped with their lives thanks to the help of an outpost which had been stationed near the camp to protect some foragers. Under the circumstances, it is forgivable that the Romans took no prisoners and that few of the Gauls survived.[2] In 170 an affair at Uscana (now unknown) in Illyria in the Third Macedonian War was rather more acceptable under the dictates of war. The legate Appius Claudius Cento was sent to Uscana against Gentius, the oppressive king of the Illyrians and an ally of Rome's enemy, king Perseus. The inhabitants of Uscana sent secret messages to Appius declaring that they wanted to betray the city to him. He was too naive, fell for the bait and named a day. When his troops arrived outside the apparently deserted city, the gates were flung open and the inhabitants sallied out *en masse*. The Romans, unsuspecting and in disorder, failed to stand up to the charge and were slaughtered in flight. But the Illyrians can perhaps be permitted their deceit, a not uncommon one. The fault would seem to lie with the Roman commander for his naivety and lack of any caution.[3]

One of the most dirty pieces of deceit in the annals of classical military history was perpetrated by one Rhodian on another. Admittedly the perpetrator, Polyxenidas, had been exiled from his native land for criminal activities. He had subsequently gained employment as the commander of Antiochus' fleet. In 190 a fleet of ships under the command of the Rhodian Pausistratus, an ally of the Romans, sailed into the Roman naval base at Panormus, the port of Ephesus. Polyxenidas had a grudge against him and he devised a ruthless plan to get his revenge. While the consul was away at the Hellespont, he (Polyxenidas) contacted Pausistratus to tell him that he wanted only to return to his home country. He would be willing to hand over the king's fleet to him if the latter could arrange his return home. By devious methods he managed to convince the other of his sincerity and to cause him to relax his vigilance. He then attacked the harbour with mercenaries by land and blocked the entrance with his ships. After a hurried embarkation Pausistratus attempted to force a way out of the harbour, but only seven of the Rhodian ships were saved. These were the ones which were fitted with fire-containing cauldrons which could be emptied on to an attacker (p. 119). Pausistratus' own ship was sunk, taking him with it.[4]

The use of false witnesses to spread fallacious gossip was another variant on the theme of disinformation. On occasions this led forces into complete disaster as in the classic ambush of a whole army and two consuls at the Caudine Forks in 321 in the Second Samnite War (pp. 73–4). The Samnite chief had been busy spreading rumours that the Samnites were far away besieging Luceria in strength whereas in truth they were close at hand. These mutterings were reinforced by 'shepherds', in fact soldiers in disguise, who confirmed their truth. The Romans were intent on marching to

Luceria to help their allies and, having accepted the rumours as true, they decided to take the shorter route through the Forks. The ambush was so effective that there was no battle; not a sword was raised. It was one of the most galling days in Roman history.

Tactical Feints

The chronicles of ancient warfare are replete with accounts of feints and ambushes, which were undoubtedly the most common tactics aimed at catching the enemy off guard. Taken together they must have accounted for the overwhelming majority of all tactics.

A feint in its most common form consists of a mock retreat while feigning fear in preparation for a sudden about turn and surprise attack. It has to be distinguished from the hit-and-run tactic in which the attack precedes the retreat, and in which the process is repeated again and again without any element of either surprise or deception. The hit-and-run sequel is therefore the opposite of a feint withdrawal in which the retreat precedes the attack.

Herodotus tells us that at the pass of Thermopylae (480) the Spartans became expert at feigning defeat and running away only to turn and attack their pursuers.[5] There were numerous similar examples. In some instances the pretenders were in the position of being able to retreat uphill before turning to attack, as at Satricum (Conca, 381). In addition to surprise it gave them the bonus of attacking from higher ground.[6] There were many variants on the basic theme. When the consul Sempronius Gracchus was encamped near a place called Complega (179), the inhabitants came to him bearing olive branches and professing peace. As soon as they had been received, they perfidiously set about attacking the camp. Feigning fear, the consul pretended to abandon the camp and he then turned and fell on the horde while they were burdening themselves with loot. This failed to teach them a lesson, and so later in the same year he started harassing their camp every day. By gradually increasing the scale of his activities he eventually brought them out in force. At this point he ordered his skirmishers to feign surprise and alarm and to flee back to the Roman camp. As they were entering through one gate, Gracchus himself emerged with his whole army through the other gates. The enemy were taken completely by surprise and their camp was captured.[7] The prize for the longest feigned withdrawal probably goes to the brilliant Numidian general Saburra. When the Roman consul Scribonius Curio marched out against King Juba's forces and encountered Saburra on the Bagradas river (49), the latter was waiting for him. He had instructed his force, mainly cavalry, to withdraw gradually as if in fear. He led the Romans on for sixteen miles until he had lured them on to a plain. Here he turned to face the Romans with his cavalry to the fore and proceeded to annihilate them (p. 114).

There was no restriction on the numbers involved for feigned retreats. Early in the battle of Chaeronea (338, p. 142) Philip II of Macedon ordered the whole of the right wing of his phalanx to retire slowly. Not a man to act without good reason, the withdrawal was a feint to lure the Athenians on. This would lengthen their line until ultimately a gap would appear through which his son Alexander on the opposite wing would be able to break through with his cavalry. But it is said that there was also another motive in that the withdrawal would take his right wing onto higher ground, giving his men the advantage when they did attack.[8]

Feints are not confined to warfare on land. The first movement by the Greek fleet at the battle of Salamis (480) was to back water in a feint withdrawal almost to the shore. The purpose of this was to lure the Persian ships on into the narrow part of the bay where their large numbers would be at a positive disadvantage.[9] Again, in the harbour at Syracuse in 413 the Athenian and Syracusan fleets confronted each other without any action for two days. At the end of the third day of stalemate the Syracusans sent a message ashore asking for food to be brought to the jetty. When they backed water to the jetty they gave the impression that they were retiring for the rest of the day, but after a quick snack they sailed out again and caught the Athenians off guard and in confusion.[10] A similar event took place off Ephesus (*c.*246) in the Third Syrian War when the Rhodian admiral Agathostratus withdrew to his moorings as if he was anxious to avoid a fight with an Egyptian fleet. He sailed out later and took the enemy by surprise as they were joyfully disembarking after their 'victory'.[11]

When an enemy is anxious to avoid a fight for good reason, such as his gross inferiority in numbers, a well-planned feint can force him into an action. This was seen in the entrance to the Gulf of Corinth when in 429 the Corinthians were sailing eastward along the southern shore and the Athenian admiral Phormio was pacing them along the northern shore. The Corinthians had seventy-seven ships against Phormio's twenty, and so the latter was loath to venture out into mid-stream. The Corinthians decided to lure him out by feigning an attack on his base at Naupactus (Lepanto) further east on the north shore. Putting their fastest ships in the lead, they suddenly turned and bore down on him across the gulf. It was a challenge that Phormio could not afford to ignore because he had left Naupactus undefended. Eleven of his ships hurriedly put out and managed to escape the net and reach open water. The rest were hemmed in against the shore. The eleven Athenian escapers were chased by the fastest twenty Corinthians but ten of them managed to reach Naupactus and turned to await their pursuers. A little later the eleventh Athenian came in sight, hotly pursued by an enemy vessel, but a merchant ship was moored in its way. The saga ended in a deft manoeuvre as the Athenian ship sailed round the merchantman in a tight circle and rammed its pursuer amidships, sinking it. The other pursuers were taken aback and were uncertain what to do until the

Athenians fell on them, capturing six of them.[12]

All these feints involved simulated actions, sometimes associated with a pretence of fear or defeat, but there were other variations on the theme. During his campaign to subdue the Thracian and Illyrian tribes before he embarked on his great anabasis, Alexander the Great first encountered a group of Thracians who threatened to block his passage over what is believed to have been the present Shipka Pass in the Balkan range (335). They had assembled at the top of the pass together with all their wagons in what appeared to be a defensive laager. However, Alexander realised that the laager might be a deception and that the wagons could have a more ominous purpose as missiles which could be sent careering down the slope into an attacking force. He instructed his men that in this event they should lie down flat on the ground in close formation with their shields interlocked over their backs. His interpretation was proved correct. The wagons were sent down, thundering over the shields, and not a single man was seriously hurt. The 'laager' clearly had been a feigned affair intended to disguise an unusual form of sudden attack, which was only rendered innocuous by Alexander's foresight.[13]

There were other objectives to feints such as luring an enemy away from a target or diverting his attention away from events. The luring of an enemy into abandoning his target is well illustrated by Hannibal's feint attack on Rome in 211. At that time Hannibal was in possession of Capua, which he wanted to retain, but pressure by the Romans was intense. To draw them away he marched to Rome, hoping that this would have the desired effect. When he presented himself at the Colline Gate, he threw the city into panic. It was the sang-froid of Fabius Maximus Cunctator which restored the Roman nerve by pointing out that Hannibal's action was only a feint. Without a siege train he had no hope of harming the city. Hannibal's move succeeded only in effecting the precautionary withdrawal of 15,000 Romans from Capua. All the rest were left to continue their attacks.[14]

Feint hostilities to divert the enemy's attention were put to good effect by Aemilius Paulus in the Pydna campaign (168, p. 220). Encamped opposite the Macedonian king Perseus with a dried-up river bed about a mile wide between them, Aemilius devised a large turning movement by some of his men to outflank the enemy's impregnable position. To divert the prying eyes of Perseus, Aemilius detailed some men to cross the river bed and attack the Macedonians who were continually patrolling on the other side. They persisted in these attacks for two days at a cost of several Roman lives, but they served their purpose. Perseus knew nothing of the Roman diversion until it was too late to interfere successfully.

Ambushes

An ambush is defined as a surprise attack from a place of concealment. It is the most primitive of tactics and yet it has also proved to be with little doubt the most universally successful tactic throughout the ages. In the whole history of warfare in the Greek and Roman worlds down to the first century BC ambushes have been recorded in over one tenth of those engagements which have been chronicled in any detail. Very few were foiled or failed, less than half a dozen failures being reported by the ancient historians. In 314 Cassander sent an expedition into Caria to deal with the troublesome Ptolomaeus, a general of Antigonus. A force of 8,000 infantry was detached from the force to lie in wait for the enemy near Caprima (now unknown), but the intended victim was told about the plan by deserters and turned the tables in advance. He fell upon the enemy's camp at night, taking them by surprise as they slept.[15] Among the other few failures an ambush at Tifernum (297) was detected by the intended victim,[16] as also were some movements in an ambush at Mutina (Modena, 193),[17] while at Athacus in 200 during the Second Macedonian War some peltasts posted in hiding between the opposing camps broke cover too early and were ineffectual.[18]

Ambushes tended to follow a general pattern, illustrated by one set up by Agesilaus during his campaign in Asia in 396/5. He had already out-witted the Persians and was well in the lead on his way to Sardis when he noticed tell-tale dust in the distance. Realising that the enemy were catching up, he planted a force in some woodland by the roadside and then proceeded to march ahead, decoying the enemy into the trap. As soon as the enemy had passed the site of the ambush, the men in hiding broke cover and attacked the Persians in the rear while Agesilaus turned and delivered a frontal attack with predictable result.[19] A variation on the theme was to plant an ambush before an impending battle, siting it close to the field and in a position to attack the enemy in the flank or rear. Such was the successful ambush set by Hannibal before the battle of the Trebia (218, p. 175). A third variation was possible if a commander knew that his enemy was proposing to attack a particular town or camp. By secretly getting there first, he had only to throw open the gates and disgorge on the unsuspecting victim, as happened at Cleonae (235, p. 55) and Gindarus (38, p. 86). But perhaps the most unusual ambush was created by Pompey even though it was not his primary aim. In 65 he was on the river Abas (Alazani) when he heard that Oroeses, the king of the Albanians, was coming against him. Pompey was anxious to conceal the size of his army, which might have caused Oroeses to withdraw. To this end, he placed his cavalry in the front and instructed his infantry to kneel motionlessly behind them under their shields. When Oroeses contemptuously sent his cavalry forward to attack, the Roman cavalry turned in simulated flight and withdrew through the ranks of the now upstanding infantry, who proceeded to confront the pursuing enemy horse. The Roman cavalry then turned and attacked the enemy in the flank.[20]

Ambushes are usually thought of as events on land but this is by no means invariable. In 315 during the Wars of the Diadochi (Successors of Alexander the Great) Polycleitus inflicted a successful double ambush – by land and at sea – on the same enemy. He was sailing eastwards along the southern coast of Asia Minor to Aphrodisias in Cilicia when he heard that Theodotus, the admiral of Antigonus, was sailing some way behind him in the same direction and that a land force was pacing him along the shore to protect him. Polycleitus disembarked his soldiers and concealed them somewhere along the enemy's route. He then anchored his ships behind a promontory and out of sight. The enemy army was the first to fall into the ambush, in which many were killed and others taken captive. When the fleet went to the assistance of their colleagues on shore, Polycleitus' ships broke cover and routed them, capturing all the ships and many of the crews.[21] He was subsequently honoured by Ptolemy as the author of a great victory.

The frequency of ambushes suggests that generals were tuned to the possibility of inflicting one on the enemy if a suitable opportunity presented itself. However, it seems that there was less awareness among commanders that they might be the victim of such an occurrence even if the circumstances were propitious. Pompey the Great suffered such an indignity in 76 during the Sertorian War. Sertorius was besieging Lauro (near Ondara) in Spain when Pompey marched to relieve it. Spying a hill nearby which seemed to offer an advantageous position, he moved to take it. So also did Sertorius, who got there first. Pompey's chagrin at losing the race was tempered by the realisation that he had trapped the enemy between the city and himself, but he had failed to look over his shoulder. His exuberance subsided like a burst bubble when he saw that Sertorius had left 6,000 men behind in his camp and that he, the great Pompey, was now the victim of an ambush. He did not dare to attack with the enemy in front and behind and had no alternative but to watch Sertorius besiege the town while he was unable to lift a finger.[22]

The victim of an ambush usually marches blithely into the trap but sometimes he was driven into it with an even greater certainty of success. During the Peloponnesian War the Athenian general Demosthenes heard that an enemy army was marching southwards toward Olpae (426) on the Ambracian Gulf. Their route would take them past the twin peaks known as Idomene, and when they reached them they camped on the smaller one. Anticipating this, Demosthenes had previously left some of his men concealed on the larger peak. At nightfall he set out with the rest of his army and, after sending a part of his force into the mountains behind, he fell on the enemy camp. Most of the occupants were killed in their sleep, but those that escaped fled into the arms of the second contingent – an unusual combination of nocturnal attack and ambush.[23]

Undoubtedly the biggest and best-known ambushes of the era were those at the Caudine Forks (321) and at Lake Trasimene (217). Both were unusual in that they involved complete armies, and both were major blots on the Roman escutcheon. The ambush at the Forks took place during the Second Samnite War when the Samnite chief spread rumours around that he and his army were in Apulia besieging Luceria. The rumours were reinforced by 'shepherds' who were in fact agents in disguise. The Romans were keen to go to the assistance of their staunch Lucerian allies. Deceived by the rumours and unaware that the Samnites had camped nearby at Caudium (Montesarchio), the Romans decided to take the shorter but more hazardous route through the Caudine Forks in Samnium. This consisted of a valley which was approached by a defile at each end and was surrounded by mountains on all sides. When the Romans reached the eastern defile, they found that their exit was blocked by felled trees and boulders. On returning to the western end, they found that it too had been similarly blocked and that the enemy occupied all the heights and passes. Any attempt at escape was fruitless and they had no alternative but to capitulate. Everyone from the two consuls downwards was sent under the yoke in one of the most galling days in Roman history. The confrontation cannot be called a battle because no sword was raised; it was just a simple but perfect ambush, and it could have been forestalled by some scouting in advance.[24]

The ambush engineered by Hannibal at Lake Trasimene (217) was similar in many respects but it was also a bloodbath which cost many Roman lives. Hannibal, a good psychologist, knew that Gaius Flaminius was a vain and overconfident individual, and he played on his opponent's weaknesses. When the Romans entered the narrow plain with the lake on one side and the enemy among the foothills on the other, the defile by which they had entered was blocked behind them by Hannibal's cavalry.[25] This disaster, too, might have been avoided by preliminary reconnaissance.

Decoys and Diversions

Both diversions and decoys are concerned with drawing the attention of the enemy, but the similarity ends there. By definition the aim of a decoy is to lure someone into a trap or danger. In the world of sport the decoy will be in the trap as the lure; in military matters it is the lure into danger that constitutes the decoy. In ambushes, for example, a force is frequently decoyed into the trap as it is lured past the concealed foe, who breaks cover and launches an attack in its rear. Thus, in a decoy the person who sets the trap draws the attention of the enemy *toward* himself as he beckons on the victim. Diversions, by contrast, are usually concerned with drawing the attention of the enemy *away* from particular events. The military tribune at Saticula (343) who exposed himself and his men by climbing to the top of a hill was essentially drawing the attention of the enemy away from the main force to allow it to escape unmolested.[26] Drawing attention to himself and his men was the means to the end but not the primary object of the exercise. A similar eventuality might arise if it was desired to draw the enemy off a threatening attack to oneself by instigating an attack on him elsewhere, as at Sellasia (222, p. 76). Alternatively, a diversion might be created to draw the attention of the enemy away from an operation such as a large turning movement in order to preserve its secrecy. Good examples of this occurred before the battles of Pydna (168, p. 220) and the Hydaspes (Jhelum, 326, p. 149) where they are described in detail.

During the Peloponnesian War the Spartan admiral Mindarus besieged and captured the town of Cyzicus on the Propontis (Sea of Marmara). Later in he same year (410) the Athenians sent out a large fleet in secrecy under Alcibiades and two other admirals. They disembarked their marines on land out of sight of the town and divided the fleet into three squadrons, one under each admiral. According to the account of Diodorus and in accordance with their plan Alcibiades sailed well ahead with his twenty ships and lured the Lacedaemonians out to battle with their fleet of at least sixty ships. When they approached, he lured them even further out by feigning a withdrawal before turning and confronting them. The other two Athenian squadrons then sailed in along the coast behind the enemy and cut off his retreat. Caught off guard, Mindarus had to land wherever he could and the battle continued on land.[27] This was clearly a decoy initially, with Alcibiades and his ships acting as the bait. However, it also led to a diversion when the decoy drew the attention of the enemy away from happenings in their rear. The incident shows that decoys and diversions are not mutually exclusive and that a decoy can in fact be the operative factor in both. Xenophon's more confused account of the incident differs in one fundamental respect. He says that the Lacedaemonians were out on naval exercises and were well offshore when Alcibiades cut them off.[28] In this version Alcibiades neither lured the enemy out nor needed to distract their attention from events behind them because he had already cut them off from the shore. In consequence, there was no no decoy and no diversion.

The treatment of a Roman legate, Triarius, by Mithradates conforms to the definition of a decoy. According to Dio Cassius, Mithridates had previously camped opposite the legate and had tried to provoke him into a battle but his efforts met with no success. He decided to lure the other out by attacking the town of Dadasa in which the Romans stored all their baggage. The ruse worked. As Triarius was advancing toward the place, Mithridates fell on him near Zela (Zile, 67) and surrounded his force, killing most of his men. Unfortunately Dio does not tell us precisely how the encounter came about. Mithradates may have simply marched out of Dadasa when he heard that his enemy was approaching, but the statement that 'he fell on' Triarius suggests that he may have decoyed him into an ambush.[29]

Among many reported diversions, one that is best known for its sequel occurred at the battle of Cynoscephalae (197) which ended the Second

Macedonian War. When King Philip's Macedonian phalanx drove the Roman left wing inexorably downhill, the consul Flamininus decided that his only hope of salvation lay in creating a diversion. He ordered the whole of his right wing, including the elephants, to charge up the hill against the enemy left wing which had only just arrived on the summit. The enemy was still in column formation and was caught completely off guard, presenting the consul with an easy rout and pursuit. By itself this success would have done no more than equalise the score, in which each side would have destroyed the opponents's left wing. In the event the result was turned into a glorious Roman victory by the initiative of an unknown tribune who collected a few cohorts from among the pursuers and attacked the victorious enemy phalanx in the rear. But that is another story. The whole episode is told in full in connection with the battle (p. 208).

A couple of other diversions will suffice here as illustrative examples. The first took place at the battle for the pass of Sellasia (222) between the Spartan king Cleomenes III and the Macedonian king Antigonus Doson. Here the road and the river Oenous (Inus) pass between two hills, both of which were held by Cleomenes. We are only concerned here with one of the hills, called Evas, on which Cleomenes had posted some allied troops under his brother. The cavalry of both sides were stationed by the river where they opposed each other. When Antigonus arrived he placed his Illyrians with some light troops at the base of Evas where, on the night before the battle, the Illyrians concealed themselves in a river bed. The next morning they began the battle by springing into view and attacking up the hill. At this point some of Cleomenes' mercenaries noticed a gap in Antigonus' lines through which they charged the Illyrians in the rear. This would have brought disaster for Antigonus had it not been for the initiative of a young cavalryman called Philopoemen, who later rose to fame. He rallied his colleagues and caused a diversion by charging the Spartan cavalry. This move brought the Spartan mercenaries back in defence, which left the Illyrians free to complete their assault. Philopoemen's diversion saved the day for Antigonus.[30]

The diversion at Sellasia was motivated by the initiative of an alert junior officer, as often seems to be the case. In contrast, a diversion at Gergovia (52) was ordered by the commander-in-chief, Julius Caesar, in whom such initiative might reasonably be expected. In a perverse way the seniority of the source seems to detract from the brilliance and gloss of the operation. Moreover, the affair at Gergovia was conceived by Caesar as a means of getting himself 'off the hook' without loss of face. He had just heard of an insurrection elsewhere which demanded his attention and made him anxious to disengage himself from his present commitment. Caesar's advance camp lay on a hill opposite the almost impregnable town of Gergovia, which was situated on the summit of a steep mount. Within the enemy's lines there was a wooded ridge at the other end of the town, and the enemy had been working hard to fortify it. To divert attention from his activities Caesar sent some men in that direction with instructions to make themselves conspicuous and to move around as if they were surveying and drawing up plans. This brought all the Gauls to the area to complete their fortifications, giving Caesar the opportunity he needed. He advanced his legions and told them to climb up to the ramparts. In the process they found that the upper slopes were covered with numerous enemy camps, which were protected by a high stone wall. The Romans proceeded to climb the wall and to capture three of the camps. This was considered to be a sufficiently bellicose gesture to allow Caesar to withdraw from the area without any semblance of cowardice. The diversion had served its purpose.[31]

Turning Movements (*Large*)

The distinction between 'small' outflanking movements in battle and their larger counterparts off the field has already been drawn (p. 61). Concern here is only with the larger ones, which showed a general pattern. It involved detaching part of a force from the main body to outflank an enemy position by making a wide detour. Attacks were then directed simultaneously from the front and rear. Secrecy was essential for success.

The turning of the pass of Thermopylae in 480 to entrap Leonidas and his band is too well known to warrant repetition. The first example here took place at the same time as the events at Thermopylae and not far away, as part of the same Persian invasion of Greece by Xerxes. Greek and Persian fleets were confronting each other off Artemisium (480) in the north of Euboea when the Persians decided to turn the Greek position. They detached a squadron of 200 ships to sail out to sea and when they were out of sight to turn south and sail around the island of Euboea, taking the Athenians in the rear. The Greeks had warning of this and so there was no element of secrecy. They waited for the turning force but to no avail. Chance (p. 104) in the form of a tempest had done their work for them by driving the squadron on to the rocky southwest coast of Euboea and destroying every ship.[32]

A turning on the island of Sphacteria (425) was a smaller event but one which still conforms to the pattern of 'large' outflanking movements. The island, about three miles long, stretched across the mouth of the Bay of Pylos, leaving only channels between it and the mainland at its northern and southern extremities. During the battle for Pylos the Spartans ferried 420 hoplites across to the island to prevent the Athenians from occupying it. When the Athenians subsequently got control of the mainland, the Spartans were trapped. After a prolonged and unsuccessful siege of the island the Athenians landed hoplites, archers and peltasts, and the Spartans were steadily driven back to the northernmost point where they took refuge in a

fort. Behind it steep cliffs fell away to the sea. Stalemate ensued until a
Messenian offered to take a few men and climb around the cliffs to take the
Spartans in the rear. When they succeeded, their appearance was so unex-
pected by the Spartans that they knew they were beaten and surrendered.[33]

Alexander's turning of the river Hydaspes in 326 must have been the
largest and most complex operation of its kind in classical history. It is
described later in conjunction with the battle (p. 149). It has been suggested
that Hannibal may have taken a leaf out of Alexander's book when he
turned the Rhodanus (Rhône, 218) over a century later. Hannibal, however,
was confronted by a horde of tribesmen, not an organised army, and his
turning operation was less complex. Moreover, his biggest problem was in
transporting his elephants across the river whereas Alexander was faced with
the threat of the enemy's beasts on the other side.[34]

Another major operation was the turning of the heavily defended valley
of the Aous (Vijose) in Epirus. In 198 the consul Flamininus had set out to
invade Macedonia, but instead of using the long circuitous route he chose
the more direct but hazardous route along the course of the river Aous.
Philip anticipated his choice and was ready for him. The river flows through
a narrow valley between two mountains, both of which were fortified and
occupied by the Macedonians. Flamininus hesitated for six weeks before
proceeding. The crest on one side of the valley or defile was occupied by
light-armed troops; the king's camp was pitched on top of the other and
catapults abounded on many of the crags. While the consul was pondering
the almost impregnable position a shepherd, who had been sent by a friend,
offered to guide him around the obstacles to a point in the enemy's rear
which overlooked his position. Flamininus had no choice but to accept the
offer and trust the man, with promises of a large reward. To avert suspicions
on the part of the enemy, he maintained harassing attacks for a couple of
days and then sent out a force of 4,000 infantry with 300 cavalry. They were
to proceed as far as the horses could go up the valley, where the cavalry were
to stay put. The infantry were to proceed with the guide by night,
fortunately helped by a full moon at the time. When the party reached their
destination they were to send up a smoke signal but must not engage until
they heard sounds of a battle. On the third day the smoke signal was sent up
and the consul divided his men into three columns, one to advance up on
each side of the valley while he proceeded in the middle. As they advanced
up the valley, the fighting became progressively more difficult and
dangerous. The Macedonians had little difficulty in finding cover among
the rocks and in niches and crevices. Matters were reaching a critical point
when shouting was heard from above. The effect on the enemy was electric;
they scattered and fled. Fortunately for them, pursuit in that terrain was well
nigh impossible, which accounts for the low number of only about 2,000
enemy casualties. When Philip realised this, he ceased his flight and rallied
his men for another day.[35]

The turning in 330 of the Susian (or Persian) Gates by Alexander was a similar operation. The only significant differences lay in the obstacle, which in this case was a rocky ravine strewn with boulders, and the force holding the heights which has been put at 25,000 at the lowest and allegedly up to 40,000 men.[36]

One turning movement which was executed during a battle but was largely outside it took place at Delium (Dilessi) in 424. In the winter of that year some Boeotians hatched a plot to overthrow the Boeotian regime in favour of a democracy. They were aided by the Athenian general Hippocrates, who seized the town of Delium. Meanwhile the Boeotians were rallying to Tanagra about four miles (six-and-a-half kilometres) away. They were commanded by Pagondas, who led them out and took up a position at the base of a hill against the Athenians, who were stationed on the other side of the hill. The engagement was started by the Boeotians, who crested the intervening hill and saw the Athenians deployed in line of battle below them. As the Athenians were already prepared and deployed there was no sudden attack. Both commanders took their time to address and deploy their troops. In the ensuing engagement the Boeotian right got the better of the Athenians but their left was being badly mauled. Pagondas responded to this by taking advantage of the cover afforded by the hill and sending two squadrons of cavalry round to engage the Athenian left in a totally unexpected attack. The sudden appearance of these reinforcements created panic in their ranks and the whole army fled, pursued by the enemy. The Athenians lost nearly 1,000 of their 7,000 hoplites, including Hippocrates.[37] (A noteworthy feature of this engagement was the Boeotian formation, in which the Theban hoplites were massed twenty-five deep in contrast to the Athenians eight per file. This is probably the first report of a phalanx twenty-five deep, suggesting that it may have been the beginning of the Theban trend which extended later to forty-eight or fifty files under Epaminondas in the period of Theban hegemony.)

This turning has all the features of the 'large' examples cited above, secrecy being provided by the hill. A similar manoeuvre was engineered by Scipio in a narrow valley hemmed in by mountains at an unnamed place north of the Ebro. Confronted by the Spanish chieftains, Mandonius and Indibilis, he sent some of his cavalry in secrecy round behind a mount to take them in the rear while he made a frontal attack.[38]

Establishing a Routine

It is said that familiarity breeds contempt. By the same token, familiarity can also be fostered and encouraged in order to lure an enemy into acceptance of a routine which, once established, can suddenly be changed, leaving the enemy floundering. For want of a name this could aptly be termed the

Repetition Tactic. There can be no doubt that the most masterly example of this tactic was provided by Scipio Africanus as a preliminary to the battle of Ilipa (206). It is told in all its detail later in connection with that battle (p. 197). There were, however, at least three other instances in which the same basic principle seems to have been employed, although they lack Scipio's finesse.

In 405 the Athenians under Conon moored their fleet of 180 ships by the creek of Aegospotami in the Thracian Chersonese. The enemy fleet under the brilliant Spartan admiral Lysander was already moored at Lampsacus across the Hellespont. The next morning the Athenians sailed out and presented themselves at the entrance to the enemy's harbour. They hung around there all day but Lysander declined the challenge. However, after the Athenians had departed he sent fast ships to spy on them and report back on what the crews did after they disembarked. For the next four days the same things happened; the Athenians challenged the Spartans but obtained no response. The fifth day passed like the earlier ones until the Athenians retired contemptuously, but the spy ships had received special instructions. As soon as they saw that the Athenians had disembarked and were foraging near and far, they used a shield to send a signal back to their base. Lysander immediately ordered his whole fleet out at top speed with the hoplites on board. When Conon saw them coming he attempted to recall his men, but they were too scattered. Only nine Athenian ships managed to escape; all the rest were captured and most of the crews were rounded up.[39] The virtual loss of the entire Athenian fleet brought Athens to submission and an end to the Peloponnesian War.

Again, when war broke out in Hither Spain in 181 it fell to Quintus Fulvius Flaccus, the praetor in charge of the province, to deal with the insurgent Celtiberians. He was camped in the vicinity of Aebura (probably Cuerva) when a large horde of them arrived and set up their camp about two miles away at the base of a hill. They were said to be about 35,000 strong, a force which Fulvius could not possibly match, and so he put all his efforts into showing them that he was afraid of their numbers and would not risk a major encounter. He sent two troops of cavalry up to their ramparts to reconnoitre with instructions to withdraw if the enemy emerged. This was repeated on several successive days after which the enemy came out and lined themselves up midway between the two positions. They stayed there for four days. When Fulvius made no move, they tired of the inaction and returned to their camp. When the praetor judged that the enemy no longer expected any action, he sent some troops up to the enemy rampart. This brought out the whole army whereupon the Romans retreated as instructed, luring the enemy on in pursuit. What the enemy did not know was that during the preceding night Fulvius had sent out a squadron of cavalry and 6,000 auxiliaries in secrecy to the back of the hill behind the enemy's camp. As the Spaniards were approaching the Roman ramparts in ignorance of the ambush, Fulvius sallied out with his army and signalled to the men on the hill. They charged down and set the enemy camp on fire before proceeding to attack their army in the rear with great success.[40]

The battle of Callinicus (or Larissa as it is sometimes called) in 171 gives a less tortuous illustration of the deliberate establishing of a routine. It took place during the Third Macedonian War when king Perseus confronted a Roman army near Larissa. Their respective camps were about twelve miles apart. The initiative was taken by the Macedonians, who suddenly appeared in force while the Romans were conferring about their plans. After some skirmishing in which neither side had the advantage, the Macedonians withdrew. For several days running the same things happened. The Macedonians always appeared at the same time of day and withdrew when the challenge had failed to bring the enemy out. Livy states that the object of these feint withdrawals was to lure the Romans out to attack them in the rear, but it seems from what follows that they had another purpose in mind. Perseus moved his camp to within five miles of the enemy and on the next day arrived unexpectedly at dawn, catching the Romans off guard. He drew up his line in battle order near a hill called Callinicus less than half a mile away, forcing the Romans to assemble and deploy their forces in great haste and some disorder. Both sides placed their elite cavalry squadrons in the centre, flanked on the wings by more cavalry interspersed with light-armed troops. The Roman infantry were drawn up behind the rampart. At the outset a vigorous charge by the Macedonian left wing threw the Roman right into confusion, while Perseus himself forced the Roman centre back and routed it. Livy attempts to put a good Roman face on these events but the outcome was clearly a disaster. The Romans were only saved from near total destruction when Perseus' attention was drawn to the sight of the legions advancing from the rampart. He was advised to be content with his resounding success and to call off the pursuit.[41]

Notes

1   Diodorus, 20.89
2   Livy, 38.25; Polybius, 21.39.
3   Livy, 43.10.
4   Livy, 37.10–11; Appian, *Syrian Wars*, 24.
5   Herodotus, 7.211.
6   Livy, 6.24.
7   Appian, *Spanish Wars*, 43.
8   Polyaenus, 4.2.2.
9   Herodotus, 8.84.
10 Thucydides, 7.39–40.
11 Polyaenus, 5.18.
12 Thucydides, 2.90–91.
13 Arrian, *Anabasis*, 1.1.6–10.

14 Livy, 26.10.
15 Diodorus, 19.68.5–7.
16 Livy, 10.14.5–6.
17 Livy, 35.4.
18 Livy, 31.36.1–3.
19 Diodorus, 14.80.1–4.
20 Dio Cassius, 37.4.1–2.
21 Diodorus, 19.64.4–7.
22 Plutarch, *Sertorius*, 18.3–4; *Pompey*, 18.3.
23 Thucydides, 3.112.
24 Livy, 9.2–6.2.
25 Polybius, 3.83–84; Livy, 22.4–7.1–5.
26 Livy, 7.34–36.
27 Diodorus, 13.49.2–50.4.
28 Xenophon, *Hellenica*, 1.1.11–18.
29 Dio Cassius, 36.12.
30 Polybius, 2.67.
31 Caesar, *Gallic War*, 7.44–46.
32 Herodotus, 8.7, 13.
33 Thucydides, 4.35–38.
34 Polybius, 3.42–3, 46; Livy, 21.27–8.
35 Livy, 32.5.8–6.4; Plutarch, *Flamininus*, 3.4–5.1.
36 Arrian, *Anabasis*, 3.18.1–9; Curtius, 5.3.16–5.4.
37 Thucydides, 4.90–96.
38 Livy, 28.33.
39 Xenophon, *Hellenica*, 2.1.18–28; Plutarch, *Lysander*, 9.4–11.
40 Livy, 40.30–32.
41 Livy, 42.57–60.1.

6

The Element of Deception

The last chapter has amply illustrated the huge overlap between the elements of surprise and deception in military tactics. From time immemorial the two elements have frequently been compounded in tactics in which deception is the means whereby an enemy is caught off guard and surprised by an unexpected attack, as in ambushes, feints and similar ruses. In these tactics the two elements are clearly inseparable. In chapter 4 surprise was considered by itself when it was gained without any intentional resort to deception. The concern now is with the converse category in which deceptions of one sort or another were the prime object of the exercise and were devoid of any *intended* element of surprise. However, it has to be remembered that a deception inevitably arouses some intrinsic surprise when it comes to light, but this may be regarded as a secondary effect and one which may not even manifest itself until later. Today the potential for intricate and sophisticated deceptions abounds, but when the word 'technology' was unknown they were limited and in short supply. When they did occur they provided some of the most intriguing episodes in the history of classical warfare.

Disinformation

Disinformation is deception by means of the spoken or written word for the purpose of conveying false information. It differs from misinformation in being deliberate as opposed to an unintentional falsehood.

Devoid of any element of surprise, disinformation can be a useful tool when employed as propaganda to boost the morale of the troops. A case in point occurred at Mycale (Samsun), a promontory in Asia Minor to which a Greek fleet had chased a Persian fleet in 479. It is said that the ensuing battle took place on the same day as the battle of Plataea in Boeotia, and that the minds of the soldiers were preoccupied with thoughts of their kinsmen confronting the Persians on the mainland. Suddenly, a rumour circulated through the troops at Mycale to the effect that the Greeks had won a great victory at Plataea. Naturally this put heart into the men and gave a great boost to their morale. It is said that the coincidence that the battles really did take place on the same day only became known later (if indeed it was true). To account for the rumour Herodotus expands on the work of the gods, but Diodorus hits the nail on the head when he declares that the Greek commander Leotychides must have thought of the ruse and initiated the rumour.[1]

Disinformation in the form of false propaganda was likewise resorted to by Agesilaus just before the battle of Coronea (394). He had just received news of the Spartan disaster in the battle of Cnidus, in which their allies had deserted without a fight and the Spartan admiral Peisander had lost his life. The news depressed Agesilaus himself and he decided that he would have to alter it for consumption by the troops. Preserving the gallant death of the admiral, he announced that Peisander had died after winning a glorious victory. At the time of the announcement he also offered sacrifices 'as though giving thanks for good news'.[2]

Livy reports similar events in the early days of the Roman Republic. Usually the propaganda was simply a lie, to put it bluntly. At Antium (Anzio) in 468 the Romans were faring badly against a superior force of Volscians, and they would have fallen back if the consul had not told one wing – falsely – that the other wing was winning. This earned him a sufficient reprieve to withdraw his men to their camp in good order. It may be noted *en passant* that in view of their superior numbers the Volscians anticipated that the Romans might try to slip away. To forestall this they made preparations to attack the Roman camp at night. When the consul heard about this, he responded by instructing a body of mounted trumpeters to move around outside the defences making as much noise as they could until dawn. This dissimulation not only deceived the enemy concerning the Roman motives but it also kept them on tenterhooks during a sleepless night, facilitating a Roman victory next morning.[3]

Sometimes bad news was withheld altogether in what might be termed negative disinformation, as at Trifanum (340) in the Great Latin War. When the Latins raised a second army against the Romans, it was not told about the disaster recently suffered by its first army at Veseris earlier in the same year.[4] But it did not help. The second army suffered an even bigger defeat at the hands of the Romans, in which they sustained enormous losses. Another variant on the theme of disinformation involved the employment of false witnesses to spread fallacious gossip. On occasions this led forces into complete disaster as in the classic ambush of a whole army at the Caudine Forks (p. 74).

One of the earliest reported deceptions was created by Themistocles just before the battle of Salamis (480). He was adamant in his conviction that the Greeks must fight the Persian fleet in the narrow straits between the island and the mainland, but after bitter controversy among the Greeks it seemed that his plan might still be outvoted. In that event the Spartans would withdraw to the Isthmus. To obviate this disaster Themistocles sent a trusted slave in a boat with a message for the Persian commander to the effect that the Greeks were demoralised and were set on withdrawing from the straits. As the Persians were already aware that the Greeks were bitterly divided, they accepted the message at its face value. Xerxes then ordered his whole fleet to block all the entrances to the straits, trapping the Greeks where they lay as Themistocles had intended.[5] The sequel is well known and Themistocles' strategy was utterly vindicated.

The Spartan king Agesilaus was a master of shrewd disinformation with a sharp insight into his opponent's mental processes. This was well shown during his campaign in Asia Minor in 396–395. In the autumn of the first year he made all the necessary preparations for an onslaught into Caria, openly informing all the towns along his intended route of his forthcoming needs. When this reached the ears of the Persian satrap Tissaphernes, the latter responded by leading all his infantry across the river Maeander into Caria. Agesilaus promptly fulfilled his real intentions by marching in the opposite direction into Phrygia, where he was largely unopposed.[6] As if this was not enough, he perpetrated a superb double bluff at the beginning of the next campaigning season when he proclaimed his intention of marching to Sardis in the heart of Lydia. Tissaphernes was determined not to be caught out again. In his conviction that this time Agesilaus really would attack Caria, he again crossed the Maeander, leaving Agesilaus free to do exactly as he had proclaimed by marching into Lydia.[7] One might call this psychological pseudo-disinformation. Although Tissaphernes must have experienced some surprise at these reverses, his emotions were undoubtedly those of chagrin, frustration and fury. Any surprise that was elicited was hardly the object of the exercise. Although irrelevant in the present context, Agesilaus added insult to injury by setting an ambush for the satrap when the latter eventually caught up with him near Sardis. This was the real surprise, evident in any successful ambush. In the ensuing confrontation the Persians are said to have lost 6,000 men against the 600 casualties sustained by the Spartans. The Persian king was so outraged by these reverses that he ordered the decapitation of Tissaphernes.

More than three centuries later Publius Ventidius was responsible for a bluff of which even Agesilaus might have been proud. Ventidius had been assigned the task of driving the Parthians out of Syria and Asia when, in 38, he heard that Pacorus, the son of Orodes of Parthia, was advancing with a large army to invade Syria. Ventidius was caught off guard because his troops were still in their winter quarters and there were no preparations in place to confront the enemy. He resorted to a subterfuge by approaching a high-ranking acquaintance who was friendly with Pacorus and was sympathetic to the Parthian cause. To this man he expressed his view that Pacorus would do better to cross the Euphrates by his usual hilly route rather than further

down the river where it ran through a plain. The latter was in fact the route
which Ventidius hoped he would take. He was certain that this 'confidence'
would reach the ears of Pacorus and, furthermore, that the latter would be
deceived by what he would regard as a piece of deliberate disinformation. In
the event Pacorus did cross the river lower down against the 'advice', as
Ventidius had intended. This was the longer of the two routes, which gave
Ventidius time to assemble a force, cross the river by the shorter route, and
reach the Roman camp at Gindarus before the enemy. When Pacorus
encountered no opposition, he attributed his apparent lead to Roman sloth
and attacked the fort immediately, expecting an easy victory. His expectation
was shattered by a sudden Roman sally in which Pacorus was killed and the
Parthian survivors fled.[8] It may be noted that the actions of Ventidius did in
essence embody a distant outflanking movement followed later by a surprise
attack from a place of concealment, in other words an ambush. The entire
ruse consisted therefore of two distinct deceptions: the unusually tortuous
disinformation which enabled him to get in front of his opponent secretly,
followed later by the ambush from the Roman camp. The story is virtually a
carbon copy of events at Cleonae in 235 (p. 55) in which Aratus, hearing
that his enemy the tyrant of Argos was planning to attack the place, got
there first by a nocturnal forced march and occupied the town. Next day he
and his men disgorged onto the unsuspecting enemy. But there is one major
difference between the two episodes. Whereas Ventidius employed
disinformation to get in front of his enemy, Aratus resorted to dissimulation
(below). He began his march in an unexpected direction away from
Cleonae before turning to the place.

Dissimulation

Dissimulation is defined as the act of concealing or disguising an intention
or action. In other words, it may be thought of as a pretence in regard to
one's identity, intentions or deeds. Such a deception is often the end in itself
with no suggestion of surprise, at least in the short term. If such a ruse does
give rise to some surprise, this is not the primary objective nor will it have
the same instantaneous and forceful quality as in a true surprise attack. It is
argued that in these ruses any surprise that was elicited was incidental and
irrelevant in the present connection. For example, Philopoemen's objective
in 201 was to assemble a force in secret (p. 98). What he eventually did with
it was another matter. It must have caused some surprise to the enemy when
they discovered to their cost that he had a force at all, but the assembly of
the force was the prime object of the exercise rather than any attack at a
later date.

Impersonation as a form of dissimulation would appear to offer a fertile
field in the tricks of warfare, but only rare cases seem to have been reported

in the ancient chronicles. During the First Punic Invasion of Sicily in 480 Hamilcar asked the people of Selinus (a dependency of Carthage) to send some cavalry to his camp near Himera. The reply, which stated a date for their arrival, fell into the hands of Gelon, the tyrant of Syracuse and an enemy of Carthage, who decided to turn it to his own advantage. He sent some of his own men to the camp, and when they had been admitted to the dockyard they set fire to the enemy ships.[9] It sounds as if it had been all too easy in the days before high-tech security measures.

The ruses cited below show considerable variety in their ingenuity. No two are alike and there are no common threads apart from their reliance on deception in one form or another. They are so individual in character that the only course open is to describe them separately as such.

Early in the Hellenistic era and within a few years after the death of Alexander the Great the rivalry between Antigonus and Eumenes led to the two great battles in Paraetacene (317) and Gabiene (316) respectively. In both battles there were some interesting tactics which will be recounted elsewhere (pp. 155, 161). Of interest here is the saga of machinations comprising both disinformation and dissimulation in the periods both before the first battle and between the two battles as the opponents jockeyed for the advantage.[10] It began after Eumenes' victory over Antigonus at the river Coprates (Dez) in July of 317.[11] Antigonus retired to Media to lick his wounds; Eumenes moved to Persepolis. While he was there, Eumenes heard that his enemy had broken camp and was moving against him. When they were one day's march apart, both men prepared for the fray. But deserters from Antigonus' army came to Eumenes to tell him that his adversary intended to break camp that night. Eumenes was certain that he would make for Gabiene, which was unplundered and could supply ample provisions. In fact, it gave him the idea that he would do better to move there himself – and to get there first. Accordingly he, in his turn, sent 'deserters' to tell Antigonus that he would fight that night, while he had every intention of decamping immediately (disinformation). Antigonus decided to stay and fight but he failed to find his rival, who had a head start on him. Clearly, Antigonus with his army would be unable to catch up with the other, and so he resorted to another ruse. He left his army to follow at leisure while he himself took the cavalry and pursued Eumenes at top speed. He caught up with his adversary in the district of Paraetacene near Susa. When he saw Eumenes descending onto a plain, he showed himself on the high ground, giving Eumenes the impression that he had his whole army with him (dissimulation). Eumenes started preparing for battle while Antigonus earned a brief respite to bring up his army and rest the men.

After the battle Antigonus wintered in Media, while Eumenes moved south-eastwards into the lusher land south of Gabae (Esfahan). Here his troops were scattered around in their winter quarters as much as six days' march apart. As Antigonus' army was inferior in numbers to his rival's, the idea occurred to him to make a winter march to Gabiene and to take the other by surprise while his army was scattered. There were two routes to Gabiene. One was easy but would involve a twenty-five days' march through inhabited country in which Antigonus would be readily observed. The other route was over a waterless desert, a march of only nine days. Antigonus opted for the latter course. He gave permission to his men to build camp fires by day, but they must extinguish them completely at night so that they would not be seen from the heights surrounding the plain (dissimulation). After a few days the men became so cold at night that they ignored the order, and their fires were duly seen and reported to Eumenes. It was his turn to adopt a ruse which would delay his enemy for a few days and give himself time to assemble his army from their quarters. He took some of his men, each one carrying a jar containing combustible material, and chose a place on the high ground facing the desert. He ordered the men to light the fires at distances of about thirty feet (ten metres) apart during the first watch, to dim then in the second watch and thereafter to leave only a few burning (dissimulation). The ruse succeeded. Some shepherds saw the 'camp' in the hills and hurried to tell Antigonus, who abandoned his advance and turned into unplundered country to give his troops a break. A few days later the two armies encamped near each other and prepared to fight the second round.

One of the best-known pieces of dissimulation in classical military history was Hannibal's famous ruse to escape from a noose set by Fabius Maximus. Appointed dictator after the Roman disaster at Trasimene (217), Fabius adopted delaying tactics which earned him the appellation of Cunctator (he was also called the Shield of Rome). His strategy was to dog, delay, harry and wear down Hannibal wherever he went while avoiding any active engagement. In this way they passed into Apulia, then through Samnium and entered Campania. Here Hannibal descended through a pass near a mount (called Callicula by Livy and Eribianos by Polybius) and down into the inviting fertile and lush Falernian Plain around Capua. It was Hannibal's hope that the sight of him pillaging and devastating this region would entice Fabius to go down and attack him. But Fabius resisted the temptation, stuck to his plan and hovered around on the ridges. It occurred to him that if he sealed the other exits from the plain, which he did, Hannibal would be forced to return by the same route by which he had entered. Fabius then sent a force up Mount Callicula and he himself camped on a hill overlooking the pass. It began to look as though the master of traps might himself be trapped, but not so Hannibal. Realising his position, he sent his men to collect dry faggots and to round up 2,000 strong oxen from those which they had captured. After dark the oxen were driven up the pass and the faggots were attached to their horns. The faggots were then ignited and the oxen with their lighted 'torches' were driven up to the top of the hill. To the Romans in the pass it seemed that the enemy was escaping over the top.

When they went up to investigate, they were puzzled, terrified and forced to keep their distance. While Fabius remained in his camp, also puzzled and fearing a trap, Hannibal led his army through the pass unopposed.[12]

Although this action of Hannibal's is a good example of a diversion, it is not included under that heading in the preceding chapter (p. 74), which is devoted to surprise coupled with deception. Hannibal's ruse was solely a matter of deception, devoid of any element of deliberate surprise. When the Romans did inevitably experience surprise, it reflected only their belated awareness of the completed coup. It is evident from these remarks that diversions in general involve a variable admixture of surprise and deception. Their common ground is their ultimate purpose – to divert the attention of the enemy away from other events.

In 195 a masquerade was acted out to resolve a moral dilemma.[13] The consul Marcus Porcius Cato was at Emporiae as governor of the province of Hither Spain when some delegates from the Ilergetes, who were friendly with Rome, implored him to help them. Their walled towns had been under repeated attacks by neighbouring hostile tribes. The consul explained that with many hostile tribes around he could not afford to divide his forces. Once again they implored him, saying that if he could not help them they would be forced with the utmost reluctance to join the enemy. Porcius was in a cleft stick. He was loath to turn friends away, but at the same time he genuinely could not afford to do otherwise. The next day, while the delegates were still in town, he gave them a gesture of hope by openly embarking a third of his men. He then sent the delegates home with messages for their chief. The Ilergetes inhabited an area between the river Iberus (Ebro) and the Pyrenees but it was some way inland. It was therefore reasonable to imply that help would come by ship, presumably up the river. When the delegates had left, Porcius proceeded to disembark his men, assemble all his forces and march against a neighbouring hostile town. The attack was so successful that one by one the surrounding tribes sued for peace wherever he marched. By the time he reached Tarraco, the whole of Spain north of the Ebro had submitted. Nothing more is said about the Ilergetes, but their problem clearly ceased to exist.

In the campaign leading up to the battle of Pydna (168, p. 220) the consul Aemilius Paulus used dissimulation as a distraction to divert the prying eyes of his enemy, king Perseus, away from other happenings. Perseus was encamped in a highly fortified position on the banks of the Elpeus river, which at that time was dried up. When Aemilius arrived with his army, he set up camp opposite Perseus on the other side of the river. It was obvious to Aemilius that a frontal assault across the river bed was out of the question, and he sent out a force to turn the enemy's position and establish a camp in his rear. To divert attention from these activities he sent some of his men onto the river bed to attack enemy detachments. These fights persisted for a couple of days during which the Romans lost a number of men. They were in fact feints, but unlike those referred to elsewhere (p. 69) the object was not to generate surprise. It was solely to divert attention and in this the fights served their purpose. Perseus knew nothing of the turning movement until it was revealed to him, too late, by a traitor.

Alexander was a man who so often devised a unique solution to a problem. The obstacle in question here was the mountain stronghold called the Sogdian Rock. It was obviously a feature of considerable size judging from the fact that a large number of Sogdians had sought refuge on its summit. A garrison said to be 30,000 strong is almost certainly a gross exaggeration but it does at least give a vague idea of its proportions. The rock faces were precipitous on all sides with only one narrow track to the top which was held by the residents. It had a store of provisions sufficient for two years and water was provided by the snow. It looked impregnable, a word which did not exist in Alexander's vocabulary as he decided to add it to his conquests. In his mind the operation would be a public relations exercise destined to show the world that nothing was impregnable to the invincible. In a parley with the chief's son, Alexander asked him to surrender and was derided. He was told to wait until he had found men with wings. And so he did. Asking his men for volunteers with climbing experience who would be well rewarded, he got 300 candidates. Armed with ropes and iron tent pegs for use as pitons, they set about climbing by night up the steepest face which would be the least liable to observation. Thirty of them fell to their deaths, but by dawn the rest reached the top of the rock just as the inhabitants below were beginning to stir. They signalled their triumph with white flags, as previously instructed. Alexander got a herald to shout to the defenders that they must surrender immediately as men with wings had been found and were now in possession of the summit. He pointed upwards. When the defenders looked up, they were stunned and surrendered.[14]

What made the Sogdians give in so readily? The inevitable surprise alone seems quite insufficient to discourage opposition. It is difficult to know how serious the natives were about 'men with wings'. Were they being facetious, or did they, in the light of their beliefs and superstitions, mean what they said? If so, Alexander's winged men were a gigantic deception. Polyaenus[15] says that the chieftain surrendered in the belief that Alexander's power was more divine than human, which supports the contention. However, there is no suggestion of this in the principal chronicles. Arrian says only that the Sogdians' immediate reaction after the initial surprise was alarm at the small number of invaders who, they imagined, must have been part of a larger well-armed force. Alexander had a pronounced ability to divine his opponents' thought processes and he probably guessed that this would be their reasoning and encouraged it as a deception to discourage opposition. Much has been written here in an earlier chapter about surprise attacks with deception in which the two elements were closely intertwined. At the Sogdian Rock, by contrast, there was no attack and the surprise and deception were separate and independent factors. If the supposition that Alexander encouraged a deception to discourage an attack is correct, the deception was the all-important element.

Secrecy is a form of dissimulation in which the players pretend that they are not performing the actions in which they are actually involved. Like most of the ruses described above, Scipio's famous capture of New Carthage (Cartagena, 209) depended entirely on secrecy and meticulous planning. Publius Cornelius Scipio was a strong contender for the title of Rome's greatest strategic and tactical genius. When, at the age of twenty-five, he landed in Spain and set up his headquarters at Tarragona (Tarraco), he found himself opposed by no less than three Carthaginian armies. They were all in the interior, separated from each other, but all were at least ten days' march away from the coast. Scipio could not afford to attack any one of them for fear that they would unite and outnumber him. Instead he adopted an ingenious strategy, ignoring all the enemy armies and making his attack against their largest base and most important port and arsenal, New Carthage. The stroke, unexpected by the enemy, was planned to a nicety. During the preceding winter Scipio had carefully questioned every arrival from New Carthage concerning every aspect of the place. Among many other things, he learned that there were only a thousand trained soldiers in the garrison because, as Polybius says, no one dreamt that while the Carthaginians were masters of nearly the whole of Spain it would enter anyone's head to besiege the city.[16] As none of the enemy forces was within ten days' march of his objective, he did precisely that, reaching it on the seventh day and capturing it by land and sea after one day of fighting. The unexpectedness of his move was secured by utter secrecy; only his lieutenant who commanded his ships was told the objective. The prime object of the secrecy was to keep the enemy armies in the dark. If they had got wind of his strategy beforehand, the whole plan would have been vitiated. Once he had left Tarraco, time was on his side and there was perhaps less need for secrecy. On his arrival he cleverly set up his camp at some distance from the walls and arranged to have the initial battle with the inhabitants in front of the camp. They had to exert and tire themselves to get there before engaging. In addition, Scipio was able to send out further fresh reserves from his camp when needed. On the following day his attack on the citadel took the enemy by surprise when his men erected ladders from a large lagoon, which lapped the northern walls. Scipio had ascertained from informants that it was fordable at low tide. To draw the enemy's attention away from this operation he had previously reinforced the scaling party who were attacking from the expected direction. The city fell into his hands, causing immense damage to the Carthaginian cause.[17] It is worth noting that his treatment of the Spaniards was not only exemplary but good diplomacy into the bargain. It reaped dividends in the form of recruitment and new allies, including three powerful chieftains and many tribes – the beneficial effects of good strategy.

The final entry in this list relates to a deception which led to one of the greatest disasters in Roman history – at Carrhae in 53 (p. 228). Marcus Licinius Crassus Dives was an ambitious man who yearned to excel both Caesar and Pompey in reputation. When he acquired the province of Syria as consul, he entertained the idea of subduing the Parthians. The resulting campaign was not instigated by the Senate and was entirely his own private war. He crossed the Euphrates with an army of seven legions and 4,000 cavalry and with no knowledge of the country or of the Parthian army with its distinct and highly effective method of fighting. At an early stage he had been accosted by a wily Arab chieftain, called Ariamnes by Plutarch (Abgarus by Dio Cassius), who set about worming his way into Crassus' confidence. He had had a friendly relationship with Pompey which provided a good reference. This treacherous double-agent advised haste and persuaded Crassus that he would save much time and effort by leaving the Euphrates and launching out across country to catch the Parthians before they decamped. His quaestor Cassius did not trust the Arab and repeatedly advised the consul to stay by the river with all the attendant advantages of a supply line and protection. Crassus would have none of it and marched into the countryside and into what became a boundless, treeless and waterless desert. When he first caught sight of the Parthians puny-looking force, he was emboldened, but this was another deception. The Parthian force was commanded by their formidable general Surena, who had concealed his main force behind his advance guard and had ordered them to cover themselves with skins to prevent any reflection from their armour. When they approached the Romans and were signalled to drop their coverings, they revealed themselves as a formidable body of cavalry in gleaming helmets and breastplates on horses clad in glittering plates of bronze and steel. The transformation was accompanied by a loud and eerie spine-chilling drone. After the Parthians had surrounded the Romans, Crassus and his men were subjected to persistent long-range fire from adept mounted archers, against which Crassus and his men stood no chance. These and the ensuing events are detailed in the description of the battle. Surena's ruse of concealing his main force initially is reminiscent of Pompey's similar tactic on the river Abas, which aimed at concealing his full strength from the enemy to prevent him from withdrawing in fright (p. 72). Surena's object may have been similar, but the unmasking also evoked sheer terror in the enemy. In the two accounts of these events by Plutarch and Dio Cassius respectively, the basic pattern of deception is similar but Plutarch's account is the clearer and more detailed.[18]

Cryptography

Cryptology is the science which covers every aspect of secret communication by any means. It includes not only the methods involved in the sending of secret information but also the interception and deciphering of information sent by others. Cryptography in its literal sense covers a narrower field and is confined to the written word. For present purposes it can be considered under two headings:

1 Messages written in plain text which are merely hidden from unauthorised eyes. This is clearly the most primitive method of conveying written information in secret.
2 Written communications which are encoded in one way or another.

Whatever method is used, anything happening in the field as a whole constitutes a deception by virtue of the inherent secrecy involved.

Hidden Messages

The first known treatise on cryptography was written in Greek by Aeneas Tacticus in the fourth century.[19] It covers all of the methods described in this section in chapter 31. The earliest and most obvious way of sending a message in secret is by concealing it, sometimes on the person. There is a considerable literature on ways in which this was achieved, such as sewing the message into the sole of a sandal or other garment, or sending a book in which appropriate letters on an agreed page had been marked discreetly with a tiny dot. But one illustrative incident deserves further mention. Herodotus tells the story of Histiaeus of Miletus, who wanted to send a secret message to his son-in-law Aristagoras, instructing him to rebel against the Persians (in what was to become the Ionic Revolt). He sent for his most trusted slave, shaved his head and pricked the message on his scalp. When the hair had grown again he was sent to Aristagoras, who was told to cut off the slave's hair and examine his scalp.[20] It may have been an ingenious idea, but it was exceedingly slow and hardly a practical procedure for purposes other than that for which it was devised.

One of the more involved procedures involved writing a message in ink mixed with glue on an inflated bladder. When the writing was dry, the bladder was deflated and pushed into a flask of suitable size, leaving the neck of the bladder just protruding from the mouth of the flask. When the bladder was reinflated and filled with oil, the flask was corked, so that nothing could be seen apart from the oil. The recipient would pour out the oil, remove the bladder and reinflate it to reveal the message. When washed, it could be used again to send a reply.

The method which Aeneas Tacticus describes as 'the most secret of all' was probably devised by himself. It involved drilling twenty-four holes (the number of letters in the Greek alphabet) through a wooden disk, each hole representing a different letter. A thread is then drawn through the holes in the order of the letters in the message. When it is unthreaded by the recipient, the message will appear in the reverse order. It is evident that the recipient would have to be given a key showing the arrangement of the letters.

Although not quite so secure, a much simpler method of sending a message in secret was used by Demaratus. As an exile in Persia, he wanted to convey to the Greeks the information that Xerxes was planning to invade them. He scraped the wax off a wooden writing tablet, wrote the message on the wood and then covered it again with wax.[21] The dissimulation was further improved if an innocuous message was written on the wax.

Frontinus in his *Stratagems* tells of some basic Roman methods of conveying information in secret, but he adds nothing significant to what has already been said with the one notable exception of an incident in which pigeons were used.[22]

Ciphers

Evidence from stone inscriptions, cuneiform tablets, and papyri shows that the ancient Egyptians, Hebrews and Babylonians devised primitive methods of concealing the meaning of information. But it was the Spartans who developed the first recorded method of enciphering messages, which they used for conveying information from one commander to another. They used an instrument called the *scytale*, which is described by Plutarch. It consisted of a wooden rod around which the sender wrapped a long narrow strip of parchment and proceeded to wind it spirally around the rod in such a way that each turn abutted the one above, leaving no gap. On this the message was written and the rod was then removed. The message could only be deciphered by winding the scroll around a rod made at the same time to the same exact dimensions. This was in the hands of the recipient.[23] The method was unusual, if not unique, in that the encoding and decoding were performed automatically.

In the most elementary form of cipher, the vowels were simply omitted from the plain text message. As an alternative, the vowels were replaced by dots, the number of dots denoting the number of the vowel in the alphabet, ranging from one for alpha to seven for omega.[24] Slightly more advanced forms of cipher were sometimes used in Roman times, notably by Caesar and Augustus. They were monoalphabetic substitution ciphers in which each letter of the alphabet was replaced by another one. The cipher used by Augustus was the simplest, each letter of the plain text being represented by the next one up. Caesar went one better (or to be precise three or four!) by substituting the third or sometimes the fourth higher letter in the alphabet. It would not take long today to crack these ciphers. A considerable advance was devised by Polybius in what has been called the Polybius chequerboard. It consisted of a biliteral substitution in which a pair of symbols replaced each letter of the text. It was the forerunner of many later systems, which illustrate the principles involved but which are outside the scope of this work.

Notes

1   Herodotus, 9.100–101; Diodorus, 11.35.
2   Xenophon, *Hellenica*, 4.3.13–14.
3   Dionysius of Halicarnassus, *Roman Antiquities*, 9.57.6.
4   Livy, 8.11.10–11.
5   Herodotus, 8.75.
6   Xenophon, *Hellenica*, 3.4.11–12.
7   Xenophon, *Hellenica*, 3.4.20–21.
8   Dio Cassius, 49.19–20.3.
9   Diodorus, 11.21.3–22.
10   Diodorus, 19.26, 37–39.
11   Diodorus, 19.17–18.
12   Polybius, 3.92.8–94.6; Livy, 22.15–18.4.
13   Livy, 34.11–16.
14   Arrian, *Anabasis*, 4.18.4–19.4.
15   Polyaenus, 4.3.29.
16   Polybius, 10.8.4–5.
17   Polybius, 10.6.9–15; Livy, 26.42–7.
18   Plutarch, *Crassus*, 20 ff; Dio Cassius, 40.20 ff.
19   Aeneas Tacticus, *On the defence of fortified positions*, 31; see especially 31.1–3, 10–13 and 21–22.
20   Herodotus, 5.35.
21   Herodotus, 7.239.
22   Frontinus, *Stratagems*, 3.13, especially 13.8.
23   Plutarch, *Lysander*, 19.5–7.
24   Aeneas Tacticus, *On the defence of fortified positions*, 31.30.

7

The Element of Secrecy

Surprise and deception are two of the most important elements in warfare. But what about secrecy? Secrecy is such a pervading element in warfare and so intimately connected with surprise and deception that it tends almost to be taken for granted. It has already received so many mentions here in connection with planning, the human element, surprise and deception as to be overlooked in its own right. In fact, secrecy is with little doubt the fundamental element underlying perhaps most of the human acts in warfare. It is now time to reassess and summarise its influence in the light of what has been said up till now.

The relationship between secrecy and deception is abundantly clear because secrecy is in itself a deception, a pretence that what is said or planned or is happening does not exist. As such, it is a component which pervades and underlies the majority of strategies. No disinformation can achieve its purpose if it is not a secret; no ambush can succeed if the secrecy concerning the place of concealment has been revealed; and no feint can achieve the desired result if the motivating thought behind it is patent. In short, any plan or strategy will lose its impact if it ceases to be a secret and becomes common knowledge or is even merely surmised correctly. A good example in practice was provided by Alexander the Great's foresight at the Shipka Pass in 335. When he was confronted by a lot of wagons which the tribespeople had dragged up to the top of the pass, the ensemble had all the appearance of a defensive laager. Alexander's mind penetrated the dissimulation and he realised that the wagons would be used as weapons rolled down the hillside onto his men. His preventative measures prevented a disaster.[1]

It follows from what has been said that without an element of secrecy or concealment there can be no successful deception. What about surprise and how does it fit into this scheme? By definition surprise arises from the unexpected and, in the military world, this implies an element of secrecy or concealment. Secrecy is the cause and surprise the result. Hence, it is axiomatic that without secrecy there can be no surprise. As pointed out earlier, Clausewitz maintained that in every attempt to elicit surprise there was invariably an element of 'stratagem',[2] by which he was presumably referring to secrecy. It appears, therefore, that some degree of secrecy is invariably at the foundation of both deception and surprise. In chapter 4 a variety of surprise attacks were described which had one thing in common. They were made when the enemy was otherwise engaged, e.g. at night or at mealtime. This timing or other specific condition for an attack amounts to a ruse, albeit a simple one. By comparison with an ambush, the trickery involved in a night attack appears to be much smaller than the deliberate concealment of a force. Nevertheless, the principle is the same in both instances and the difference is only one of degree. It is pertinent therefore to ask whether any sudden attack by an enemy can be regarded as totally free of secrecy and deception. Clausewitz would say 'No'. There will always be an element of secrecy inherent in the sudden and therefore unexpected nature of the move and also an equally inevitable element of surprise arising from the unexpectednes.

These conclusions refer specifically to the military situation. They are hardly applicable in general to surprise occurring outside warfare and in an everyday setting. It is a common experience that ordinary events may occasion surprise if they are totally unexpected and perhaps accidental, as exemplified by a loose tile falling on an unsuspecting passer-by. Such events no doubt happen in warfare also but they are clearly in a different category to those discussed in this work. Intentional surprise, secrecy and deception are not involved in any way, and such happenings are most likely likely to come under the heading of 'chance'. The roof tile which hit Pyrrhus on the back of the neck and knocked him out at Argos in 272 can be excluded from these remarks.[3] It was a deliberate attempt to kill, and it is doubtful if Pyrrhus was in a fit state to experience any surprise!

Evidence of the widespread involvement of secrecy in other factors in warfare is shown, paradoxically, by the brevity of this chapter. For the most part secrecy has already been mentioned repeatedly in earlier pages. Nevertheless, a reassessment of the subject as a whole is indicated. To recapitulate a few salient points, secrecy is the absolutely essential element for success in all ambushes, sorties and decoys to mention but a few. It is the fundamental *sine qua non* in all instances of disinformation and dissimulation, and it is quintessential in many tactics such as large turning movements aimed at circumventing obstacles, e.g. defiles, hills and rivers. In all these examples and many more it is a case of 'no secrecy, no success'.

With the exception of a few instances of disinformation for the purpose of propaganda, virtually all the secret activities listed above were precursors to attacks and were the means to take the enemy by surprise. Of several large turning movements which illustrate the point, one was the turning of the Susian (or Persian) Gates by Alexander the Great in 330. His aim was to get from Susa to Persepolis as quickly as possible before the Persian treasure could be evacuated. Faced with a choice of two routes, a long detour by the main road or a direct track over the mountains via the pass known as the Gates, he predictably opted for the latter. Leaving his lieutenant Parmenio to take the heavy-armed troops and baggage by the road, he himself set off with the rest to the pass. Here he was confronted by Ariobarzanes who had built defences across the pass, which he held with 25,000 men (Arrian says 40,000). Any direct assault was met with such a barrage of boulders that even Alexander had to admit defeat by that route. Among their prisoners was a man who offered to lead them by a track to the far side of the pass. The main body of the force was left at the bottom with instructions to light many fires and act as if the whole force was there until they heard sounds of a fight, when they were to make a frontal assault. Alexander's party set off after dark and Curtius gives a graphic description of the obstacles, ravines and hidden snow traps which they encountered.[4] He reports that the trek took two nights and a day before they encountered outposts, who were either slain or fled. Fortunately, none of them thought to warn the main body, which was taken completely off guard. Attacked from both front and rear and with no escape route open to them, they were massacred.[5] It is hardly necessary to expound on the essential role of secrecy in this operation (as in all major turning movements), but it is highlighted here by the failure of the outposts to perform their duty. It was a close shave at the end.

In this episode, like most of the others mentioned above (e.g. ambushes, sorties and decoys), the ultimate object was a surprise attack on the enemy. Examples of 'pure' secrecy, unalloyed with any element of intentional surprise, seem to be rare occurrences, but one fascinating exploit in particular leaps to the fore. In 201 during the Wars of the Achaean League, its General, Philopoemen, needed to amass a military force for use against his arch-enemy, Nabis the tyrant of Sparta. To this end he devised an ingenious plan. Secrecy was essential in order to prevent any knowledge of the plan reaching the ears of the tyrant's spies and secret police. Philopoemen's collection point was to be Tegea, from which a number of roads ran radially to the outlying towns. Philopoemen sent a letter to the chief in the most distant town along each road telling him to collect all the men of military age and to proceed with them to the next town in the direction of Tegea, which was named in the letter. Here he was to hand in a similar letter enclosed with the first one but which named the next town on the chain. Philopoemen had calculated the time taken for each of the human chains to reach the final destination so that he could arrange for them to converge on Tegea at about the same time. Until that point they had no knowledge of the broad plan or of its purpose.[6] Philopoemen's ruse had achieved his aim of assembling a force in secret; how and when he chose to use it was another matter. The force was subsequently used to ambush the enemy, which must have caused them acute surprise, but that is a different story. The enemy's surprise was hardly the object of the exercise. It was merely a late by-product of an operation which relied for its success entirely on secrecy.

The operation conducted by the consul Gaius Claudius Nero preceding the battle of the Metaurus (p. 191) in 207 was not dissimilar in motive from Philopoemen's ruse just described. Unlike the latter, Nero did not have to raise an army; he already had one in the south of Italy where his brief was to keep Hannibal at bay. But he did want to move a part of his force secretly from the south to the north to reinforce his consular colleague. The tale began when Hannibal's brother, Hasdrubal, crossed the Alps and descended on Italy with the object of reinforcing his brother. He sent a letter to Hannibal proposing a meeting place, but the letter was intercepted and sent to Nero, the consul in the south. Nero was alarmed. Hasdrubal would be confronted by the consul in the north, who was thought to have adequate forces at his disposal to deal with the situation, but Nero was unhappy and wanted to ensure that success was a certainty. With superb initiative he planned to march the length of Italy with 6,000 of his men in the strictest secrecy to reinforce his colleague in the north. He informed the Senate of his intentions, but he could not afford to wait for a reply. In his absence his second-in-command was deputed to run the camp as if it was fully-manned to avoid rousing any suspicions in Hannibal. Other measures were also adopted to preserve secrecy. For instance, when Nero and his force left their camp they marched southwards in the 'wrong' direction before turning toward the north. It was only at this point that Nero informed his men about the purpose of their expedition. At the end of their march, Nero entered the consul's camp after dark and arrangements were made for the two consuls to share all the facilities. The object of the secrecy was to ensure that Hannibal in the south knew nothing about it and that Hasdrubal in the north remained in ignorance until it was too late for him to effect a successful withdrawal. The plan succeeded admirably, and the success of the various deceptions and other measures taken to safeguard the secrecy is a striking tribute to the efficiency of all concerned. Hasdrubal only became suspicious that all was not well when his men were already drawn up in battle order. Although he withdrew immediately, it was too late for him to effect an escape. Hannibal in the south had no inkling that anything was amiss until his brother's head was deposited at the gates of his camp.[7]

Another episode of particular relevance here is Hannibal's ruse to extricate himself from the Falernian Plain around Capua in 217. To all intents and purposes he had been blockaded in by Fabius Maximus and seemingly prevented from leaving by his intended route over the pass near Mount Callicula. The story is well known and has already been recounted in more detail (p. 88). It is sufficient here to remind the reader that Hannibal collected 2,000 oxen and tied faggots to their horns. After dark the faggots were ignited and the oxen were driven to the top of the hill, suggesting to the Romans that the enemy were escaping that way. Hannibal, in fact, was creating a good example of a diversion, drawing the attention of the Romans away from the pass over which he marched his men with impunity.

The essential secrecy had been conveniently provided by the darkness of night. The episode is included here briefly because, like the two above, it exemplifies almost 'pure' secrecy and deception and is devoid of any intended element of surprise. No doubt the Romans were surprised – and bitterly disappointed – but this was only a late side-effect of a *fait accompli*. After he had escaped Hannibal did send back some Spanish troops but their sole purpose was to rescue the Carthaginians who had been herding the oxen up the hill.

Notes

1   Arrian, *Anabasis*, 1.6–13.
2   Clausewitz, *On War*, 3.10.
3   Plutarch, *Pyrrhus*, 34.2.
4   Curtius, 5.3.16–4.
5   Arrian, *Anabasis*, 3.18.1–9.
6   Polybius, 16.36.
7   Livy, 27.43–9, 51.11.

8

The Element of Chance

The goddess Tyche must have been a busy lady in time of war (much
of the time), influencing the course of events for good or bad. In
ancient times it was common to ascribe events such as victories to the
gods or good fortune while paying little tribute to the excellence of a
commander. However, Tyche's interventions were for the most part probably
on a small scale and passed unrecognised as such. It is not easy to be certain
what or how much did occur by chance. (Polybius has much to say on this
point).[1] What happened, for instance, when a commander was taken ill in
the early stages of a battle. Plutarch reports sources which hold that it
happened at Thapsus (Ras Dimas, 46) when Caesar drew up his forces but
then felt ill and failed to put in an appearance for the infantry engagement.[2]
It was thought likely that he might have had one of his epileptic turns. If so,
the timing of the turn must have been a chance affair? It does not seem to
have been influenced by any undue psychological trauma or other obvious
factor. As it happened his men were so eager for battle that they persuaded a
trumpeter to sound the charge and they carried on without their
commander to win a great victory, but it could well have been otherwise.

One area of reasonable certainty concerns chance encounters. An
encounter which occurred entirely by chance was one in which neither party
had any inkling that the other was in the vicinity. It was totally unexpected
on both sides, and nothing could be more calculated to elicit astonishment
bilaterally. It was also an infrequent, if not a rare occurrence. During his
campaign in Asia in 396 Agesilaus had so outwitted the Persians by luring
them into Caria that his advance into Lydia was unopposed. The only
incident in his otherwise uneventful progress occurred when his cavalry
went ahead and breasted a hill to reconnoitre. They were taken aback when
they came face to face with the cavalry of Pharnabazus, who were ascending
it from the other side.[3] This led to a minor skirmish in which the Greeks
fared worst until Agesilaus went up with his hoplites and forced the Persians
to withdraw. A somewhat similar incident is said to have occurred at
Camerinum (295) when the Romans climbed a hill to spy out the land,
unaware that the enemy had already occupied the ridge from another

direction. The Romans ended up by being attacked from both front and rear.[4] The principal difference between these two events lay in the fact that at Camerinum the two parties were intent on fighting each other and both were aware that the other was somewhere in the vicinity. The meeting cannot therefore be said to have taken place entirely by chance. A lack of reconnaissance was the real cause.

Perhaps the best example of a truly chance encounter in the strictest sense took place near Tegyra (375) between Theban and Spartan forces (p. 64). It occurred only a few years before Sparta was forced to yield her hegemony to Thebes. At that time the Thebans were occupied in driving Spartan garrisons out of Boeotian cities. On one expedition the brilliant Theban general Pelopidas was returning to Thebes from Orchomenus with his Sacred Band[5] of 300 and a few horsemen. Near Tegyra he encountered two *morae* of Spartans, totalling around 1,000 men, who were marching in the opposite direction as they returned to their base at Orchomenus. Pelopidas ordered his cavalry to charge the enemy centre and he himself followed them up with the Sacred Band, killing the two Spartan polemarchs and routing the whole force. The encounter is of historical significance in that never before had the Spartans been beaten by a force inferior in numbers to their own. It was the precursor on a small scale to the ten-year period of Theban Hegemony.

The 'Tearless' Battle, as it is called, took place in 368 near Malea ('Melea') in Arcadia, close to the Laconian border, during the Era of Theban Hegemony. Dionysius of Syracuse had sent a force to help the Athenian-Spartan alliance in its opposition to Thebes. These troops had joined Archidamus and his Spartans on a campaign in Arcadia. They were engaged in devastating the land when the Arcadian and Argive forces came against them, and Archidamus withdrew and camped in the hills above Malea. The Sicilian contingent, however, had served its term abroad and was due to return home. They set off on the road to Sparta, but in a narrow pass they encountered a road block which had been set up by some Messenians. A plea for help brought Archidamus to the scene. The next to appear were the Argive and Arcadian forces. They were also on their way to Laconia, with the aim of preventing Archidamus from returning there. Archidamus drew up his troops by the roadside and a battle ensued in which heavy losses were inflicted. But the remarkable feature of the battle, from which it derived its name, was the lack of any Spartan casualties. Not one of them was killed. It seems clear from Xenophon's account that neither side was aware of the position of the other and that this was a true encounter by chance.[6]

The following two encounters were both chance affairs but with a proviso. On both occasions the parties concerned knew that their opponent was somewhere within a few miles and that they had the same end in view – a battle. Nevertheless, in both instances the encounter when it happened occasioned surprise all round. The first concerned the movements of the

Spartan and Argive armies before First Mantinea (418, p. 126). War had broken out between Epidaurus and Argos. As Epidaurus was an ally of Sparta, the Spartan army under king Agis II marched out to her defence against Argos. The contestants were on the point of engaging when the Argive commanders made proposals to Agis for a truce. This was granted. The Argives then took up a virtually impregnable position in the hills where Agis could not get at them. He adopted a cunning ruse and began to divert the water courses from Tegea (his ally) over the territory of Mantinea (an ally of the Argives), flooding it and hoping that this would bring the enemy down to the plain. The Argives did so and formed up in battle array with no enemy in sight. At that time the Spartans were returning from their aquatic operations when suddenly, and to their great astonishment, they found themselves confronted with a full army in battle order. As Thucydides says, they were more startled than they had ever been and they had to form up and deploy in record time. The Argive generals had led their army into the plain, where they camped with the intention of advancing on the enemy, but he was nowhere to be seen at the time. It was on the next day that the Argives formed up in the order in which they meant to fight *if they made contact with the enemy*. It can be deduced that although the meeting did not occur entirely by chance, it caught the Spartans completely off guard and was at least not expected by the Argives at that particular moment. They were however prepared for it when it did happen. It is perhaps surprising that in their state of deployed preparedness the Argives were unable to capitalise further on their gain. The distance between the armies was probably too great to catch the enemy in complete disarray although the Spartans did have to deploy with urgency. The ensuing battle of Mantinea is detailed in Part Two.

The second of these chance encounters took place in 197 on Mount Cynoscephalae during the Second Macedonian War between the Romans and Philip V. Both armies had camped a few miles apart near Pherae and they had independently concluded that the terrain was totally unsuitable for battle. They marched off and, without ever setting eyes on each other, eventually pitched their camps several miles apart. Unknown to them, they were separated by a ridge of high ground known as Cynoscephalae. Philip seized the initiative and sent out a force which reached the summit of a pass between the peaks, where he left a strong outpost. In a more leisurely fashion the Romans sent out a scouting party. On ascending to the pass from the opposite side to the Macedonians, they were startled when they were confronted by the enemy at the top. After some see-sawing in which each side sent back to its base for reinforcements, the affair developed into a full battle (p. 208). It is clear that the two sides were intending from the start to have a battle, but it is also obvious that neither side knew the exact position of his adversary.

If one wants to know about events which might have been distorted by chance, a good start would seem to be to consider the effects of such a chancy affair as the weather. A case in point was the great storm which hit the Persian fleet as it lay at anchor off the coast of Magnesia (480) in the early stages of Xerxes' invasion.[7] It is said that this catastrophe (or blessing to the Greeks) destroyed 400 ships, but the ultimate effects of this loss in subsequent naval events are hard to conjecture. The material effects of a second storm not long afterwards are easier to assess. It forced a Persian squadron of 200 ships onto the rocky coast of Euboea (Evvoia), destroying every one of them (480).[8] As these ships had been despatched to round the island and take the Greek fleet off Artemisium in the rear, the threat was totally removed by the intervention of nature.

Of all the military events which were influenced by the weather the battle on the river Crimisus (Fredolo) in Sicily must be the best example. It took place in 339 when the Carthaginians landed an army reputedly of 70,000 men at Lilybaeum (Marsala). Timoleon, the liberator of Sicily, decided to attack them as soon as possible and on territory in the west which they controlled. He had with him only 11,000 men, mostly mercenaries. When he ascended a hill he got his first view of the enemy as they were crossing the Crimisus. The chariots had crossed first, followed by about 10,000 heavy infantry, and Timoleon realised that this was the time to attack when the enemy was divided. He and his men were unable to dent the infantry until they discarded their spears and resorted to swords, with which they were more skilled. At this point activities were interrupted by a violent storm accompanied by thunder, lightning, torrential rain and hail, which drove into the faces of the Carthaginians. In no time the river was overflowing its banks and the plain became a sea of rivulets coursing through a bog. The enemy's chariots were utterly useless, and the heavily armoured Carthaginians floundered around in the mud. If they fell, they could not get up again. Many of those who were crossing the river were washed away by the torrent. A similar fate met some of those who tried to flee, but many of them were despatched by the Greek light-armed troops who pursued them into the hills. It is reported that 10,000 met their deaths one way or another and that 15,000 were taken prisoner.[9] The hand of fate (or fortune for the Greeks) cannot be doubted. The storm apparently burst with little warning and could not even have been anticipated.

A very different climatic change put paid to the fleet of the Veneti in the Gulf of Morbihan (56) during Caesar's Gallic War. Their boats were strongly made of oak with flattish bottoms for negotiating shallow waters and with high sides for protection against high seas. Ramming them would do more damage to the rammer than the enemy. Against them the Romans had but two advantages – speed and oars. The enemy ships were too heavy to be rowed and they depended solely on sail. With forethought Decimus Brutus had equipped his ships with long poles fitted with a hook at the end by means of which the enemy's halyards could be severed, bringing the sails down with them. The Romans had achieved some limited success with these implements when nature intervened with a providential lull in the winds. This left the enemy ships becalmed like sitting ducks and ripe for boarding at Roman leisure. Very few of them survived to reach land in a battle which lasted all day.[10]

In the next and final episodes in this section, the role of chance is more problematic than that occasioned by climatic events. In the course of a skirmish with Hannibal on the river Ticinus (218), Publius Cornelius Scipio (the father of Africanus) had been severely wounded.[11] Not long afterwards he was camped at Placentia when the consul Tiberius Sempronius Longus, who had been recalled from Sicily, arrived with his legions. As Scipio was too ill to command, Sempronius assumed the lead. He was a hasty and ambitious man who was lusting for a fight with Hannibal, and he allowed himself to be enticed by the latter into a disastrous confrontation on the river Trebia (218, p. 175). The question arises as to whether Chance or Fate had thrown in her hand in a bad mood against the Romans. It all depends upon Scipio's wound but we have no details as to how it was sustained. Had he been in a slightly different position, he might have escaped altogether or sustained only a graze. Surely there was an element of chance in this? If he had escaped a serious injury, a very different man from Sempronius would have been commanding the Romans. He would not have allowed himself to have been lured so easily into battle or probably into the ambush that Hannibal had set. He was anyway in favour of delaying battle for several reasons and, according to Polybius, Hannibal would have agreed with Scipio if he had been in his position.[12]

Again in the Second Punic War, there was one occasion in the events preceding and leading up to the battle of the Metaurus (207, p. 191) when chance undoubtedly intervened in a bid to alter the course of history. A second incident later is more problematic. Hannibal's brother Hasdrubal had left Spain in a bold attempt to join his brother, who at that time was penned up in the south of Italy. Hasdrubal had crossed the Alps into Italy and had made his way down to Sena Gallica (Senigallia) in Umbria, where the consul Marcus Livius Salinator had been sent to oppose him. Hasdrubal wrote a letter to his brother to arrange a meeting in Umbria and he sent it on its way with six horsemen. They had ridden unmolested down most of the length of Italy, but near the end of their journey they took the wrong road and ended up in Tarentum. There they were picked up by a Roman foraging party and taken before the propraetor. Failing to give a satisfactory account of themselves, they confessed to their purpose under the threat of torture. The letter, still sealed, was taken to the consul Gaius Claudius Nero, who had been allotted the task of shadowing Hannibal in the south. Realising the overwhelming importance of the letter's contents, Claudius set in motion the actions for which he became renowned and which led ultimately to the defeat of Hasdrubal. There can be little doubt that chance played the trump card in this saga. The bearers of the fatal letter simply lost their way and took the wrong road.

The second, and less definitive, intervention by chance took place just before the battle on the Metaurus. Claudius and his force had entered the camp of Livius secretly at night and unbeknown to Hasdrubal. Hasdrubal remained in ignorance of them until he heard two trumpet calls in the consul's camp, instead of the usual single call. When he realised that the army of Livius had been reinforced by another consul, Hasdrubal's own army was already drawn up for battle whenever it was offered. He hastily sounded the retreat and decided to withdraw during the night and to get across the river. He had two local guides with him, but during the night march both of them ran off independently, one of them to a place that he had previously picked for the purpose. In their absence Hasdrubal and his men were unable to find a ford. They floundered around along the twisting river bank until Claudius appeared on the scene with his cavalry. He was soon followed by Livius with his heavy infantry already formed in battle array. That was the beginning of the end for Hasdrubal. The outcome of the episode's final stages had been largely dependent upon the escape of the two guides. There is no suggestion that they were bribed to default or that they acted on anything but their own personal motives. If they had anti-Carthaginian sentiments, they would probably not have allowed themselves to be engaged in the first place. Our ignorance of the thinking and motives of these two men precludes any certainty, but it would seem that in all probability chance may have lent a helping hand.

Notes

1   Polybius, 36.17.
2   Plutarch, *Caesar*, 53.3.
3   Xenophon, *Hellenica*, 3.4.13–14.
4   Livy, 10.26.7–11.
5   Plutarch, *Pelopidas*, 18.
6   Xenophon, Hellenica, 7.1.28–32.
7   Herodotus, 7.189–191.
8   Herodotus, 8.7, 13.
9   Plutarch, *Timoleon*, 25–29; Diodorus, 16.77.4–81.1.
10 Caesar, *Gallic War*, 3.7–16.
11 Livy, 21.46.7.
12 Polybius, 3.70.1–10.

9

Other Themes

Pursuit

Pursuit of a defeated enemy is normally an extension of the battle. It only becomes of intrinsic interest when, for one reason or another, the pursuer himself runs into trouble. The two 'classic' examples in which a pursuit was extended to the point of losing the battle took place at Raphia (217) and at Ipsus (301) respectively. At Raphia the armies of Antiochus III the Great and Ptolemy IV confronted each other with similar deployments. When the right wing of each side drove the opposing wing off the field, the two phalanxes faced each other in unsupported isolation and prepared for the final assault. Ptolemy took his place with his phalanx and was engaged in exhorting his men. Antiochus, on the other hand, had extended his pursuit of the enemy left wing and was nowhere to be seen. His phalanx was leaderless and, devoid of any encouragement and guidance, lost the fight and with it the battle.[1] At Ipsus (p. 165) events were in general similar to those pertaining at Raphia but with one major difference. After Demetrius had routed the cavalry of Seleucus and was in hot pursuit, Seleucus moved some of his abundant elephants across to block the return of Demetrius. It is well known that horses studiously avoid the beasts. In consequence his phalanx, like that of Antiochus at Raphia, was left leaderless. Seleucus chose not to attack the phalanx but instead he rode around it exhorting the men to desert to his cause, which many of them did. Again, Antiochus III was faring badly in the battle of Magnesia (Manisa, 190, p. 213) when he spotted a weak point where the Roman line rested on the river Phrygius. The Romans had put so much reliance on the river that they had not posted any auxiliaries there. Staking everything on this one manoeuvre, Antiochus charged along the bank and outflanked the Romans. He pursued some of them through to their baggage camp, where the guard and some reinforcements stopped his progress. Meanwhile his phalanx had been attacked and driven behind their ramparts where they eventually succumbed. Antiochus had not been there to help them in their hour of need, and he fled.

These are three instances in which a commander abandoned his phalanx and lost the battle, but there were other endings. At Cunaxa the Greeks on the right wing easily defeated their opponents and pursued them off the field. The extended pursuit was a great mistake as the barbarians needed no incentive to make a quick exit. If the Greeks had wheeled to the left they would have caught the Persian centre in the flank and might have altered the whole course of the battle.[2] Another similar example occurred in the Wars of the Achaean League at Mantinea (207), where Philopoemen was pitted against Machanidas, the tyrant of Sparta. Here, the tyrant broke through the Achaean left but instead of outflanking the enemy line he pursued the defeated enemy into the city. This gave Philopoemen the opportunity to fill the gap left by Machanidas and cut off his return.[3] The saga ended with a personal confrontation (p. 110) in which the tyrant was despatched by Philopoemen himself.

The tendency to pursue a fleeing foe was a frequent practice in the ancient world although the Spartans in particular did not generally subscribe to it. The following brief sketches are intended to illustrate various endings to pursuits. At Olpae (426) a successful wing pursued their opponents off the field, but by the time they returned to join the main body there had been a reversal of fortunes and they found themselves under attack. Many of them were killed.[4] In Diodorus account of a naval encounter off Mytilene (406) the Athenians lured the Peloponnesians on and then turned to attack them. However, the Athenians on the left wing were over-zealous and, having routed their opposite numbers, they pursued them too far and found themselves surrounded by the main body of the enemy fleet. They were driven ashore.[5] Again, at Ottolobum (200) in the Second Macedonian War the Roman cavalry fared badly in a skirmish with the Macedonians. The cavalry were routed and chased back down the road with excessive zeal until they encountered their own cohorts, who had been sent to follow them. After much slaughter of the Macedonians, it was their survivors turn to flee.[6] Last, at Ilerda (49) the Roman Ninth legion under Caesar forced the Pompeians to withdraw right back to the walls of the town but the Romans pursued them too far. They found themselves on a flat ridge with steep sides while missiles showered down on them from the enemy on the walls. If they turned to withdraw, the enemy were on them. After several hours of this they drew their swords and charged uphill at the enemy in desperation, killing some and forcing the others back into the town until at last they could retire.[7]

Baggage Trains

There was little that was more detrimental to the enemy's morale than the capture of his baggage train. Not only did it contain the reserve supplies, it usually also carried the mens' wives and families and all the non-combatants. The amount of valuable Carthaginian booty captured by Timoleon and his men after the battle on the river Crimisus (339, p. 104) was immense, but this loss to the enemy was small compared to the losses in some other cases. At Edessa (Vodena, 286), for example, Pyrrhus lost the whole of his baggage and was forced to abandon his campaign altogether and withdraw back to Epirus.[8] Still worse were the effects at Gabiene in 316 (p. 161) when Antigonus took advantage of the cloud of dust raised by the elephants and cavalry to outflank Eumenes' wing and capture his baggage train about half a mile in the rear. This so upset Eumenes' veteran Silver Shields and other Macedonian infantry that they refused to carry on fighting for him. They negotiated secretly with Antigonus and handed their leader Eumenes over to him. He was executed. Among other instances involving baggage, one at Tigranocerta (?Silvan) in 69 is notable. The consul Lucullus had noticed that behind Tigranes and his forces there was a hill. Leading his infantry in a detour, he took possession of it unobserved by the enemy and then instructed his cavalry below to make a feigned withdrawal. Waiting until the enemy were in disorderly pursuit, he charged down the hill onto their baggage train directly below. This caused chaos as the baggage personnel fled into the midst of the assembled horde, disrupting them as the Roman cavalry turned and hacked them all to pieces. It is said that in excess of 100,000 of the enemy were slain in contrast to 100 Roman casualties, but the enemy losses are probably greatly exaggerated.[9]

Personalised Encounters

In the early days of classical warfare conflicts not infrequently tended to become personalised affairs between the opposing commanders. As the general decided the course of events for his army, so he became the enemy's chief target. If he was put out of action, the action itself usually ground to a halt and the leaderless army withdrew and lost the fight. At Aricia in 506 Aristodemus, the Cumaean leader, slew the Etruscan leader with his own hand and gained a glorious victory.[10] Likewise, at the river Larissus (Mana) in 209 the general in command of the Elean cavalry charged against the person of Philopoemen, the leader of the Achaean cavalry. The latter deflected the blow and killed his adversary, causing the Eleans to lose heart and flee.[11] It seems that in these and other similar cases there was usually no personal antipathy or grudge. If one or other was killed or wounded, it was simply because he was in command of his team. This was certainly the aim of Alexander the Great at the battles of Issus (333)[12] and Gaugamela (331)[13] when, having broken through the enemy lines, he headed straight for Darius himself. The Great King, however, managed to beat a cowardly retreat on both occasions. As always, there were exceptions to this rule in which there was bitter enmity between the opposing leaders. The *bête noir* of the famous Theban general Pelopidas was the brutal tyrant, Alexander of Pherae, who had cast him into prison some years before. When Pelopidas caught sight of this monster on the summit of Cynoscephalae in 364, he lunged toward the other in a mad suicidal dash and was struck down by the tyrant's bodyguard[14]. In this instance the death of the leader did not bring the hostilities to an end. Pelopidas' cavalry were so enraged at the fate of their beloved leader that they attacked and routed the enemy phalanx, cutting down many in the pursuit. But no amount of enemy blood could assuage their grief and fury. Other similar bitter feuds culminated in single combats in the field, as when Eumenes slew Neoptolemus[15] at the Hellespont in 321 and Philopoemen personally despatched Machanidas[16], the tyrant of Sparta, at Mantinea in 207.

All the personalised encounters just mentioned occurred in the Greek world. In the Roman world such encounters were somewhat different, taking the form of challenges to single hand-to-hand combat by a champion. The idea did not in fact stem from the Romans themselves; the challenges were invariably issued by the enemy, who on three of the four occasions were Gauls. In 361 a Gallic incursion was met on the river Anio (Aniene) by the dictator Poenus at the head of an immense army. After a number of skirmishes for the possession of a bridge had proved futile, a Gaul of gigantic proportions bellowed out a challenge to the Romans to send out a contestant to fight him in single combat. Titus Manlius accepted the challenge and killed the Gaul. He then removed a torque from around the dead man's neck, earning for himself the soubriquet of 'Torquatus'. The Gauls were so stunned by his performance that they departed.[17] A near carbon copy of this event took place at Nola as late as 89. The only significant difference lay in the tiny size of the man who volunteered to try his strength against a challenger, again a Gaul of huge proportions. The Gaul was killed by the little man whereupon all the other Gauls fled, closely followed by the rest of the army.[18] In the exceptional, non-Gallic, encounter the challenger was an inhabitant of the Spanish town of Intercatia. The people of the town bitterly resented the aggressive consul, Licinius Lucullus, with his record of perfidy, and they refused to cooperate when he attempted to come to terms with them. Angrily he attempted to provoke a battle but the only response came from a distinguished looking citizen in splendid armour who challenged the Romans to single combat. The challenge was taken up by Lucullus' deputy, who triumphed in spite of his small stature.[19] His name was Cornelius Scipio Aemilianus, soon to be renowned as the destroyer of Carthage (146).

Although all these instances of single-combat 'jousts' took place in the Roman world, they are reminiscent of an event which occurred much earlier in the Greek world in the spring of 545. It has become known as the Battle of the Champions. It was part of the long feud for superiority between Argos and Sparta in the sixth and seventh centuries and concerned the disputed territory of Thyrea halfway between the two cities. When the two armies confronted each other it was agreed that 300 picked men from each side should fight it out. In the event only three men survived – two Argives and one Spartan. The Argives claimed the victory on simple numerical grounds; the Spartans claimed it because their champion had been the only man to remain on the field and to strip the equipment from the dead. The Argives had gone home. The dispute led to blows and, ironically, to a full-scale pitched battle between the armies, which the Spartans won.[20]

Unusual Tactics

Tactics which are out of the ordinary generally arose because an unusual situation demanded an unusual, perhaps ingenious, response. The report by an anonymous author of the action at Ruspina (Monastir) in 46 describes two unusual tactics, one used by the enemy and the other devised by Caesar himself. The enemy had a vast numerical superiority. When they extended their line it was obvious that they could easily encircle the Romans, which they proceeded to do. To counteract this trend, Caesar extended his line by deploying his men in a single line instead of the usual three lines (*hastati, principes* and *triarii*) and then getting the alternate cohorts to turn about and face the enemy in the opposite direction. The end result was one line in front of the standards and one behind them facing the other way, so that they could attack both ways and could not be taken in the rear. By showering the enemy with missiles in both directions they managed to keep them at bay while they themselves slowly fell back to their defences. The enemy's tactics soon became clear as they took on a form which was new to Caesar, who had no previous experience of Numidian warfare. Unfortunately, the account is not as clear and a little interpretation is necessary. It tells us that when the cavalry charged, they were interspersed with light troops who would rush forward and throw their javelins. When the cavalry retired, the light troops held their ground and prevented the Romans from pursuing the horse, which recouped and returned to the attack. It seems clear that it was the cavalry who threw their javelins in a typical hit-and-run attack, while the light troops stayed put. Any Roman who advanced in pursuit was then attacked by the light troops with their javelins in the flank. This prompted Caesar to issue an order that no man was to advance more than four feet in front of the standards.[21] Another unusual tactic by Caesar was devised in his deployment before the battle of Pharsalus (48, p. 232). In this tactic he withdrew one cohort from the third line of each legion to make a fourth line which he stationed beyond his right wing. Its specific purpose was to protect his wing against a flank attack by the enemy's numerically superior cavalry and light-armed troops. Caesar's special instruction to his men was to unnerve the enemy by aiming their javelins upwards at their faces. The tactic was so successful in routing the enemy's force that the fourth line carried on to outflank the enemy's wing and attack it in the rear.[22] Tactics such as these are good illustrations of the flexibility of the legion in warfare in comparison with, for example, the inflexibility of the phalanx.

On the subject of unusual tactics, the reader is reminded that the most ingenious tactic in the whole of military history was Alexander's unique barrack square drill at Pelion in 335, which has already been described (p. 42). Cited below are only those unusual tactics which are not referred to elsewhere.

In the early days of Roman warfare a novel tactic was introduced in the battle of Lake Regillus (496). When the consul saw that his men were flagging, he seized the standard and hurled it into the enemy ranks, ordering the men to recover it. No ploy was more calculated to spur a Roman soldier into a frenzy of effort.[23] Livy recounts a few instances in which this ruse was copied, all in the early days. It is astonishing, therefore, that the last time this ploy was apparently used was in 168 at the battle of Pydna (p. 220). According to Plutarch a commander of the Pelignians by the name of Salvius hurled the standard into what seems to have been the Macedonian phalanx. He was truly an optimist if he expected good results under those circumstances and, in fact, many of his men were killed in the attempt to recover it.[24]

'Devotion' in battle was an act of self-sacrifice on the part of a commander. After a spiritual act of self-consecration he devoted himself and his enemies to the gods of the Underworld and to death before charging headlong into the enemy ranks. Only two instances are recorded by Livy, the first by P. Decius Mus at the battle of Veseris[25] (340); the second by his son and namesake at Sentinum[26] (295). On both occasions the Romans were facing disaster, and the act of devotion was aimed at inspiring the men and restoring their morale. On both occasions it succeeded and paved the way to victory.

Probably the most grizzly piece of black comedy was performed in battle in 214. This was at a time soon after the Roman disaster at Cannae (216, p. 180) when almost every able-bodied male was enlisted. Sempronius Gracchus was in command of an army which was composed largely of slaves who had volunteered to serve in exchange for their freedom and were wondering when that day would come. When this force came face to face with a Carthaginian army under Hanno at Beneventum (Benevento, 214), hostilities ensued. Gracchus, sensing the slaves' resentment, proclaimed that freedom would be granted immediately to any slave who brought him a Carthaginian head. This nearly cost him the battle. The slaves were so busy decapitating corpses that they were quite unable to fight the living. Alerted to the risk, Gracchus told the slaves to forget about heads and proclaimed that no man could hope for freedom unless the enemy was utterly defeated. At this, the onslaught became so furious that only 2,000 of Hanno's force survived out of 18,000, or so it is said. Gracchus kept his promise and liberated every one of the slave-volunteers.[27]

Incendiary attacks can be regarded as unusual for the simple reason that they were both infrequent and unorthodox. When the Athenians set fire to Sardis (*c.*498) during the Ionian revolt, the incident was particularly noteworthy in providing Darius with an excuse for revenge, which took the form of the first invasion of Greece.[28] Less than a score of years later the tyrant of Syracuse sent some impersonators into the Carthaginian dockyard at Himera (480) to burn all the ships (p. 87). Much later, Philopoemen landed a force by night close to the camp of Nabis, the tyrant of Sparta at Pleiae (192). They attacked the camp 'with a new form of warfare' by flinging firebrands into it. Everything in it and nearly everyone was destroyed.[29] In the Roman world there were instances at Pometia (502)[30] and Fidenae (Castel Giubileo, 426)[31] in which it was the inhabitants who emerged carrying the firebrands, in the former case to burn the siege engines. But the best-known incendiary episode in Roman history must be Scipio's well-researched simultaneous attacks on the camps of Hasdrubal and Syphax at Utica (203). Most of the inmates of both camps perished. The episode is described in more detail elsewhere (p. 58).

Long-Range Warfare

In the classical era fighting at a distance was a tactic which was commonly practised, notably by many tribes, as their standard method of warfare. It usually consisted of a repetitive hit-and-run procedure of charging toward the enemy, throwing their missiles before actually closing, and then retreating to a safe distance before returning to the attack. If this was carried out on an individual basis or by small groups in turn, the enemy could be harassed by a continual stream of missiles. The attackers did not close with the enemy, and the absence of a direct man-to-man contact was of the essence of the tactic.

In 426 the Athenian general Demosthenes marched against the Aetolian town of Aegitium. He succeeded in capturing the place but in the meantime the Aetolians had amassed an army with contingents from every tribe in the area, near and far. When they arrived, they joined the inhabitants and proceeded to attack the Athenians from high ground, running down to throw their javelins and then retreating to a safe distance before returning to the attack. The Athenians had no answer to this harassment. If they advanced, the Aetolians immediately withdrew to keep their distance.[32] Similar events took place at the start of the battle of Paraetacene (317, p. 155). When Antigonus noticed that Eumenes had strengthened his right wing with elephants and his best cavalry, he opposed them with his lightest mounted troops. These included archers and lancers from Media and

Parthia who were expert at wheeling movements. There were also Tarentines equipped with javelins, and several other mounted contingents from Phrygia, Lydia and elsewhere. These groups took it in turn to make hit-and run-attacks, in which they kept inflicting wounds and injuring the elephants without suffering any harm themselves. To deal with this threat Eumenes was obliged to bring up his lightly equipped cavalry from his other wing and send them against the enemy in an outflanking movement.

In 200, early in the Second Macedonian War, an engagement at Athacus (place unknown) between Philip and the Romans provides an interesting twist on hit-and-run tactics. Philip sent some Illyrians and Cretans with cavalry support to harass the Romans in this way. However, the attackers knew no other form of warfare and were disconcerted by the static hand-to-hand fighting of the Romans who put up a stubborn defence. When the Romans attacked them, they fled.[33]

The Numidians, also, were renowned for their hit-and-run tactics, as seen at Ruspina (46) and described above (p. 111). Three years previously they had gone so far as to annihilate an entire Roman army near the river Bagradas (Medjerda, 49). The consul, Gaius Scribonius Curio, was besieging Utica when he heard that King Juba was approaching with a large army. He had decided to withdraw to Castra Cornelia and to reinforce his camp and lay in supplies when he heard from deserters that Juba had been called away by other troubles. Curio accepted the news without hesitation and changed his plans, but the 'news' was undoubtedly disinformation. Juba was only a few miles away, but he had sent a modest force ahead under his general Saburra. Ascertaining that Saburra was encamped on the Bagradas with his Numidian cavalry, Curio sent out all his cavalry to attack the camp at night. The surprise ensured a success in which many were killed. In the meantime Curio marched out with his whole army during the night and came to the enemy camp, leaving his cavalry to recuperate and follow later. Saburra expected this confrontation and had planned for it. Feigning fear he and his Numidians withdrew steadily, luring Curio into following him for a distance said to be about sixteen miles until they descended onto a plain. Here, Saburra drew up his cavalry in battle array. If a group of Romans attacked, the Numidians would withdraw, to the delight of the Romans who imagined that they were winning. Instead, they found themselves cut off in small groups and subjected to attacks from the rear in which they were trampled down under the horses' hooves. As the Roman numbers were whittled away, the enemy was being reinforced by fresh arrivals from King Juba. As a last resort Curio ordered the whole body of his troops to retire to a nearby hill but Saburra got there first. Some of the Romans were killed as they tried to escape; others just gave up and lay down waiting to be slain. Every one of the infantry was killed.[34] It is curious that in all this there is no mention of hit-and-run tactics, the Numidian *tour-de-force*. It is unbelievable that in the encounter on the plain the Numidians merely presented themselves to the Romans to lure them out and did not throw some javelins to make their point. It is equally difficult to believe that when they had isolated groups of them, they contented themselves with trampling some of them from behind while not making attacks frontally. The losses through trampling would hardly account for the fact that not one single Roman infantryman survived.

Among the tribal warriors who specialised in fighting at a distance the most devastating were almost certainly the Parthians. Their methods were apparent in full force in the battle of Carrhae (53, p. 228). The Parthian army was largely composed of mounted archers, who were adept at both aspects of their trade, including shooting arrows while they were riding away from their target. Their method cannot be termed hit-and-run since they did not normally venture to close with the enemy but remained at a considerable distance. In that era it was truly a matter of fighting at long range. This was made possible by the strength of their bows which imparted an unusually high velocity to their barbed arrows. In consequence, they contented themselves with riding around the enemy and subjecting him to a continual stream of arrows. If the enemy tried to break out of the circle, he was met by mailed cavalrymen (*cuirassiers*, also called *cataphracti*) armed with long spears, who either killed or sent them back to join their colleagues in the circle. At Carrhae the Romans' only hope was that the enemy would run out of arrows, but this thought was seen to be a mirage when a camel train arrived with a fresh supply. The Romans were utterly powerless and became resigned to their fate.

Natural Elements

It is hardly surprising that both military and naval operations have not infrequently been disrupted by the elements of nature. One has only to remember that in the First Punic War at least three Roman fleets were destroyed by storms. In the Greek world an estimated 400 of Xerxes' ships were destroyed by a violent gale off the coast of Magnesia,[35] and a further 200 ships from the same fleet were battered on the rocks of the Hollows of Euboea as they rounded the island in an attempt to turn the Athenian position off Artemisium (480).[36] Off Embata in 356 two veteran admirals decided it was too stormy to venture out to battle; the younger Chares was undeterred and sailed out with his fleet to lose many ships and, of course, the battle.[37]

A thunderstorm, floods and mud were the order of the day during the battle of the river Crimisus in 339, when Timoleon and his 11,000 followers opposed a huge Carthaginian force. Timoleon attacked when only half of the enemy had crossed the river. He was hard pressed until fortune lent a hand in the form of a violent thunderstorm with lightning, deluges and hail.

It came from behind him and drove into the faces of the enemy. The river overflowed its banks and the plain became a sea of mud, rendering the chariots useless. The heavily armoured enemy floundered around and, unable to rise to their feet, were slaughtered. Many others were swept downstream in the river which had become a torrent. It is said 10,000 lost their lives (p. 104). Somewhat similar climatic conditions prevailed when Alexander the Great turned the Hydaspes river (Jhelum, 326, p. 149) and was confronted by an enemy force as he landed on the far bank. There had been heavy rains during the night of his crossing and, as at the Crimisus, the chariots that came to meet him became stuck in the mud. It was much later, however, that climatic conditions exerted a more profound influence on Alexander's anabasis when, in what is now Pakistan, his men refused to take another step. They undoubtedly wanted to go home to their families whom they had not seen for many years, but the appalling weather was probably the last straw. They were expected to carry on into the unknown under monsoon conditions, permanently wet and with totally unsuitable clothing. For the first time in his life Alexander was forced to give in.[38]

Mist and fog also played their part in influencing the course of war. During the Peloponnesian War an Athenian fleet was patrolling near the island of Syme (Simi, 411) in poor visibility when it spotted a few Spartan ships approaching. With only a part of his fleet the Athenian admiral sailed against them, little knowing that the Spartans had become scattered in the murk. He had started the fight well, sinking three of the enemy ships, when he suddenly found himself almost surrounded by the whole Spartan fleet and had no alternative but to flee.[39] It was also misty and murky around Lake Trasimene when Flaminius led his army into Hannibal's classic ambush (217). Hannibal's camp was at the other end of the lake and the bulk of his men were sheltered in folds in the ground, unseen in the murk. If visibility had been normal the ambush would doubtless have still taken place, but the Romans might have had a little more warning of the impending onslaught and a better chance of defending themselves.[40] Again, it was a similar morning at the battle of Magnesia (190, p. 213) and the mist was such that neither wing of Antiochus' grossly extended line could be discerned from his centre. The situation was not so bad for the Romans with their shorter line and in fact was rather to their advantage. They dealt easily with a charge by chariots and then proceeded to roll up the whole disordered enemy left wing as far as the centre. In the mist the enemy right wing can scarcely have been aware of these events, but they left part of the Roman right wing free to cross the field and go to the assistance of their left wing when it was attacked by Antiochus himself.

The examples just cited illustrate the disadvantageous or even disastrous effects of fortuitous inclement weather on one or other side in an engagement. In contrast, there were times when a commander managed to harness the elements to his own advantage. At Salamis (480) before the battle commenced Themistocles ordered the Greeks to back water, which they did almost to the point of grounding themselves. A withdrawal such as this was commonly used as a feint to lure the enemy on, but Plutarch has advanced another possible reason.[41] Themistocles, he writes, was intent on delaying the engagement until the time of day which always brought a fresh breeze from the sea and a swell through the straits. This, he said, would upset and slew the taller Phoenician ships but would have little effect on the Greek ships. Plutarch's report is open to doubt, but it does raise a somewhat similar and better attested incident which occurred under like circumstances almost exactly half a century later. At Chalcis in 429 an Athenian squadron under the redoubtable Phormio engaged a Corinthian convoy of transport ships. The Corinthians were not prepared to fight and formed themselves into a defensive circle with their ships in a radial formation, prows outward. Phormio lined his ships up in line astern and proceeded to sail closely around the enemy, forcing them into an ever tighter circle. He was waiting for the wind to blow up as it usually did in that area and at that time of day. By the time it came the Corinthians were left with no space for manoeuvre and were in complete confusion. At this point Phormio launched his attack, sinking every ship that was encountered in the battle and capturing twelve more which managed to escape the net.[42] These events seem to provide some support for Plutarch's version of events at Salamis.

There were of course more direct ways of taking advantage of climatic conditions if they happened to be favourable. In 101 the king of the Cimbri challenged Marius to make an appointment for a battle! On the chosen day Marius lined his men up on the east side of the Campi Raudii, near Vercellae, so that the enemy were fighting with the morning sun in their eyes. Moreover, as the wind was also from the east they got the full blast of the cloud of dust which was raised by the horses. This was, in fact, so great that when Marius advanced he failed to make any contact with the enemy, leaving his consular colleague to bear the whole brunt – a disadvantage which had not been anticipated.[43] The sun was also a factor at Pydna (168, p. 220) where the consul, Aemilius Paulus, delayed the start of the battle until the afternoon when the sun would be in the eyes of the Macedonians. At Cannae (216, p. 180) it was the enemy, namely Hannibal, who chose the prime position with the wind behind him, blowing the dust cloud into the faces of the Romans. Although the patriotic Livy is the only source for this fact, he makes a great point of it, presumably offering it as an excuse for the catastrophic Roman defeat.

Finally, it was rain not wind that was responsible for the cancellation of a combat on the river Anio in 211. In fact the true cause was superstition as much as the weather. Hannibal was making a feint attack on Rome to draw the Roman forces away from Capua. He was opposed by the consul Fulvius Flaccus. As the two armies lined up, a torrential downpour washed away all thoughts of battle and the two sides retired to their camps. When the same thing happened again on the following day, Hannibal accepted the rains as an omen and withdrew altogether.[44]

Naval Antics

Ships are the 'hardware' of warfare at sea and are outside the scope of this work, as defined at the beginning. Tactics, on the other hand, are the 'software', the elements most prone to influence the course of events on a day to day basis. The accounts of naval tactics in the chronicles are somewhat patchy, and the following remarks aim to bring them together.

In the early days of naval warfare an engagement resembled a battle on land. The ships were crowded with light troops and hoplites, and when the opponents came within range they would pelt each other with javelins, arrows and other missiles while the vessels remained stationary. The issue was determined not by naval tactics but by the number and quality of the soldiers and their weapons. If a ship collided with another, boarding would take place and the battle would further assume the appearance of a battle on land. Thucydides describes just such a battle which took place in 433 between the Corcyraeans and the Corinthians off the Sybota islands. [45] It must have been about the last naval engagement to be fought in the old-fashioned way. Although warships had been fitted with rams since Homeric times, Thucydides makes no mention of deliberate ramming in this battle.

Early in the fifth century warfare at sea underwent two major changes. The trireme became the standard warship and with it the old method of fighting gave way to the new. The ship itself became the missile, dependent upon new tactics and the seamanship of the crews, while the hordes of soldiers were replaced by a small number of marines. Ramming and boarding became the standard order of the day, supplemented by further tactics and manoeuvres such as the *diekplous* and the *periplous*. Of these the *periplous* is the easiest to understand; it was simply an outflanking movement whereby a ship or ships at the end of an extended line sailed forward and turned to attack an enemy vessel amidships. The *diekplous* is also known as 'breaking the line'. In its basic form it occurred when a ship sailed between two enemy vessels to be in a better position to attack. Relying on its superior agility, it commonly executed a sharp turn behind the victim's stern and proceeded to ram it amidships or in the stern. If the attacker possessed sufficient skill, the manoeuvre could be improved by first shearing the victim's oars in order to immobilise him. This technique was perfected by the Rhodians. It was effected by confronting the victim prow to prow, then veering to one side at the last minute and passing close alongside him while the attacker shipped his oars.[46] There is a paucity of accounts dealing with naval tactics, and certain aspects of this manoeuvre are still a subject of debate, notably concerning the conditions necessary for execution of the manoeuvre. The tactic could be forestalled by deploying in two lines abreast but this would shorten the line and open the fleet to a *periplous*. Another ingenious tactic which was developed by the Rhodians involved dipping their prow just before ramming a vessel. The object was to inflict damage to the victim below the water line whereas the rammer would only sustain its scars high up. Polybius[47] reports that this tactic was used in the battle of Chios (201) between Philip V of Macedon and Attalus I of Pergamum, but it appears to have been little used even then for a good reason. The Macedonians were excellent fighters on deck, and the Rhodians were taking every step to avoid being boarded as a result of an inextricable tangle with the enemy. There appears to have been no other report on this particular tactic.

The circle (*kyklos*) was a defensive measure applied to a fleet, in which all the ships were stationed radially with their prows pointing outwards. A few of the fastest vessels were sometimes placed in the centre, ready to go to any point in the circle which was challenged by the enemy, and non-combatants could be protected in the same way. An example was adopted by the Corinthians at Chalcis in 429.[48]

A novel tactic was adopted by the Illyrians and was used during the First Illyrian War. In an encounter with the Achaeans off the Paxoi islands (229) they lashed their galleys together in groups of four and invited the enemy to ram them. They would then board the enemy craft in overwhelming numbers. With ten Achaean ships against them, they captured four quad-riremes and sank a quinquereme in this way before the rest of the enemy ships abandoned the fight and turned for home.[49] Thucydides has put on record the use of grappling irons by the Athenians during the Syracusan campaign. It was intended as a measure to counter the strengthening of prows by the Corinthians, preventing a rammer from getting away after the deed.[50] The Athenians, however, were not as enthusiastic as the Romans about fighting on deck. They relied for the most part on the usual naval tactics such as ramming with or without a preliminary *diekplous*, and it could be surmised that grappling might have been introduced primarily as a deterrent to attack. There appears to be no other mention of the use of grappling irons by the Athenians.

The Rhodians were the most accomplished seamen of their day, and it seems probable that the use of fire cauldrons as a defensive nautical weapon can be attributed to them. The device consisted quite simply of a cauldron containing flammable material suspended from two poles which projected outboard from the prow. It could be emptied onto any vessel that ventured too close. The tactic came into being in the War against Antiochus. Its first recorded use was at Panormus (190), the port of Ephesus, in defence against a treacherous attack by Polyxenidas on a

Rhodian fleet (p. 68). Unfortunately, only seven of the ships were equipped with cauldrons and they were the only ones that managed to escape. The device was used again later in the same year and on a larger scale at the battle off Myonnesus (C. Doğanbey, 190), in which many of the Roman ships were fitted with it. Eudamus in charge of twenty-two Rhodian ships engaged the enemy left wing; but the Romans with fifty-eight ships broke through the enemy centre where the enemy turned aside in terror of the cauldrons. In doing so they risked being rammed amidships. It is said that only two of the Roman ships were destroyed, in contrast to the enemy losses of forty-two captured or sunk (Appian says twenty-nine).[51]

Roman naval warfare was very different to the Greek tradition. Before the inception of the First Punic War in 264 all their battles without exception had been fought on Italian soil. They had not previously required a navy and they suddenly found themselves having to learn in a hurry how to build and sail ships. As they were adept at fighting on land and inept at naval tactics, they placed the whole emphasis on carrying marines and boarding enemy craft. In short, they adopted the old methods which the Greeks had abandoned at least two centuries previously. As an aid to boarding they developed an ingenious device called the *corvus* (raven), which is described by Polybius.[52] Basically it was a thirty-six-foot long boarding plank with rails on each side at knee height. A vertical pole in the prow passed through a large hole in the plank near its lower end, allowing the plank to be rotated and lowered onto an enemy deck by means of a pulley at the top of the pole. It was held fast to the victim by a large spike on the underside. When not in use the plank was carried upright against the pole. A marine walking the plank obtained security by resting his shield on the rail. It was put into use for the first time in the battle of Mylae (260, p. 169), when it took the over-confident Carthaginians completely off guard and gained a great victory for the Romans. After a further recorded appearance four years later off Ecnomus (256, p. 169) it appears to have been abandoned. In all probability it may have impaired the stability of the ships and rendered them liable to capsize in bad weather. Another Roman aid to boarding was developed much later by Octavian's brilliant admiral Agrippa and was introduced at the battle of Naulochus (36). It was a catapulted grab, which consisted of a reinforced pole with a claw at the end and with long ropes attaching it to the attacking ship. When it had grabbed a target, the ropes were hauled in. As both ships inevitably backed water, a tug-of-war ensued in which Octavian's heavier ships were likely to win.[53] In practice, however, this would seem to matter little. The diminishing distance between the ships was the operative factor.

In 56 Decimus Brutus, Caesar's admiral, equipped his fleet with long poles which carried a hook at the end, but this was devised for the sole purpose of cutting or pulling down the halyards of the ships of the Veneti in an engagement in the Gulf of Morbihan. The oak vessels of the Veneti were too heavily built to be rowed, and ramming was useless. As they were totally dependent on sail, Brutus had the idea of bringing down the sails to immobilise the craft for boarding. As it happened a sudden lull during the battle providentially becalmed the ships and did much of the Romans' work for them.[54]

Notes

1   Polybius, 5.79–86.
2   Xenophon, *Anabasis*, 1.8.
3   Polybius, 11.11–18.
4   Thucydides, 3.107–108.
5   Diodorus, 13.77–79.
6   Livy, 31.36.5–37.
7   Caesar, *Civil War*, 1.43–46.
8   Plutarch, *Pyrrhus*, 12.5–7.
9   Appian, *Mithridatic Wars*, 85.
10   Dionysius of Halicarnassus, *Roman Antiquities*, 7.6.2.
11   Plutarch, *Philopoemen*, 7.6–7.
12   Diodorus, 17.33.5; Curtius, 3.11.7–8.
13   Arrian, *Anabasis*, 3.14.2–3.
14   Plutarch, *Pelopidas*, 32.5–7.
15   Diodorus, 18.31.
16   Polybius, 11.18.4.
17   Livy, 7.9.6–11.1.
18   Appian, *Civil Wars*, 1.50.
19   Appian, *Spanish Wars*, 53.
20   Herodotus, 1.82.
21   (Caesar), *African War*, 14–17.
22   Caesar, *Civil War*, 3.85–99; Plutarch, *Caesar*, 42–45.
23   Florus, 1.11.2.
24   Plutarch, *Aemilius Paulus*, 20.1–2.
25   Livy, 8.9.
26   Livy, 10.28.12–29.1.
27   Livy, 24.14–16.
28   Herodotus, 5.105.
29   Livy, 35.27.1–9; Plutarch, *Philopoemen*, 14.4.
30   Livy, 2.16.8–9.
31   Livy, 4.31.6–33.
32   Thucydides, 3.97–98.
33   Livy, 34.5–36.6.
34   Caesar, *Civil War*, 2.37–42; Appian, *Civil Wars*, 2.45.
35   Herodotus, 7.189–191.
36   Herodotus, 8.7, 13.
37   Diodorus 16.21.
38   Arrian, *Anabasis*, 5.25ff.
39   Thucydides, 8.41–42.

40 Polybius, 3.83–4; Livy, 22.4–7.5.
41 Plutarch, *Themistocles*, 14.2.
42 Thucydides, 2.84.
43 Plutarch, *Marius*, 26.3.
44 Livy, 26.11.1–4.
45 Thucydides, 1.49.
46 Polybius, 16.4.14.
47 Polybius, 16.4.11–14.
48 Thucydides, 2.83–84.
49 Polybius, 2.9–10.
50 Thucydides, 7.62.
51 Livy, 37.30.
52 Polybius, 1.22.
53 Appian, *Civil War*, 5.118–121.
54 Caesar, *Gallic War*, 3.7–1.

Part Two

Tactics in Battle

Introduction

The term 'software' was used in the introduction to this work to cover the range of themes which have been discussed in the first part. Perhaps the largest of these topics concerns battle tactics which, however, have not yet been accorded even a chapter to itself. Various aspects of the subject have been included such as, for example, Hannibal's ambush of the Romans at the Trebia, Philip's feint withdrawal at Chaeronea, and the sections on turning movements in battle, diversions, and attacks in mid-manoeuvre among others. But these events when told in isolation do not give adequate weight to the topic of battle tactics as a whole. To give them their full due they need to be visualised and discussed in the context of the battles themselves. It is only in this way that they can be properly linked to the factors that brought them about and to their overall effect on the ultimate outcome of the combat. The purpose of the second part of this work is to rectify this deficiency. In addition, each battle is set out briefly in its historical background, which not infrequently contains other events which are relevant to the subject matter of this work.

When a reader is perusing an account of a battle, dramatic events usually stand out and are readily absorbed. More minor incidents are liable to make less impact and to be either overlooked or forgotten. The author himself is no exception to this frailty. On this account, a thematic summary is appended at the end of each battle as a check list and reminder. If an occasional incident is regrettably omitted, at least it serves to illustrate the point!

Mantinea (418)

Background

The first battle of Mantinea took place during the Peloponnesian War, in which truces and alliances were both made and broken. In 421 the Peace of Nicias was solemnised. Among other clauses the Athenians, with their allies, and the Spartans, with their allies, pledged that it was 'to be in force for fifty years without fraud or damage by land or sea'.[1] Two years later Argos invaded Epidaurus. As Epidaurus was an ally of Sparta, the Spartan army under King Agis II marched out against Argos to her defence. The contestants were on the point of starting to battle when the Argive commanders stepped forward and made proposals to Agis for a truce. This was granted, to the disgust of both armies, each of which felt that they had never had a better chance of beating the other.

Soon after this the Spartans received an urgent appeal for help from the Tegeates, who had been molested by the Mantineans. The Tegeates cunningly clinched the matter by saying that if help was not forthcoming, they would transfer their allegiance to Argos. This galvanised the Spartans into sending their whole force to Tegea and invading the territory of Mantinea. The Argives, who supported Mantinea, now took up a virtually impregnable position in the hills. This caused Agis to desist from hostilities against the Mantineans and to turn his attention back to the Argives, who had been Sparta's prime enemy of old. But he could not fight them where they were. He adopted a cunning ruse and began to divert the water courses from Tegea over Mantinean territory, flooding it and hoping that this would bring the enemy down to the plain.[2] The Argives did as much and descended to the plain, where they formed up in battle array with no enemy in sight. At that time the Spartans were returning from their aquatic operations when suddenly, and to their great astonishment, they found themselves confronted with a full army in battle order. As Thucydides says, they were more startled than they had ever been and they had to form up and deploy in record time.[3] Although King Agis and the Spartans were undoubtedly surprised by the confrontation, it seems that this was not a tactic planned by the Argives for that specific purpose. The Argive generals had led their army into the plain, where they camped with the intention of advancing on the enemy, who in fact was not there at the time. It was on the next day that the allies formed up in the order in which they meant to fight *if they made contact with the enemy* (my italics). It can be deduced that this was virtually a chance encounter which happened to occasion surprise, probably to both sides.

Battle of Mantinea

The first battle of Mantinea was the first set-piece battle between two hoplite armies to be recorded in detail. The sole source for the battle is Thucydides, who admits that he finds it impossible to give accurate numbers for either army.[4] In the case of the Spartans he tells us that the front rank consisted of 448 men across the whole line and that on average they were eight deep, but even after allowing for the exclusion of the 600 Sciritae, this results in a total which is generally considered to be far too low, especially as 'the Spartan army looked the bigger'. On the side of the Argives and their allies, he quotes 1,000 Athenians and their 300 cavalry and 1,000 'picked' Argives. This is little to go on, but the picked Argives were men who had been fully trained at the expense of the state, and the contingent of other Argives would undoubtedly have been many times larger. When the Mantineans and the various allies are included, the total is thought to have been at least 10,000. The respective deployments of the two armies are detailed by Thucydides and are shown in the accompanying battle plan.

When the two armies first set eyes on each other, the Argives and their allies were already in battle order; the Spartans, on the other hand, were taken completely off guard. It might be thought that under these conditions the allies, advancing as quickly as possible, could have caught the Spartans in disorder and inflicted an immediate defeat. That this did not happen reflects on the high standard of Spartan organisation and training. As Thucydides says, 'they had only the shortest possible time for getting ready', but each man knew his place and fell in promptly. As the two armies approached each other, both armies experienced the usual shift to the right as each man sought the protection afforded to his unprotected right side by his neighbour's shield.[5] As a result, the Mantineans on the allied right wing extended a considerable distance beyond the Sciritae, while the Spartans and Tegeates overlapped the Athenians by an even greater margin. Agis, however, thought that the Mantineans extended too far beyond his left wing for his liking, and that there was a considerable risk that his wing would be encircled. To counteract the threat he ordered his entire left wing (the Sciritae and the contingent next to them) to move further to the left and equalise the lines. This left a gap in the Spartan line between left wing and centre. Agis then ordered two polemarchs on the right wing to move their

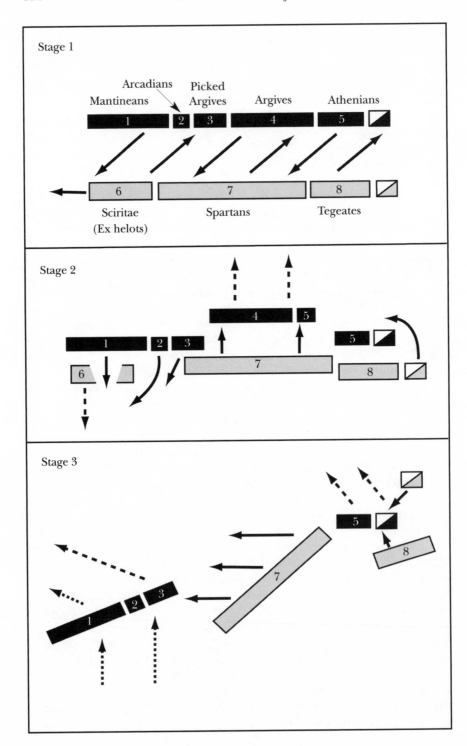

men across to the left wing to fill the gap. In his estimation this manoeuvre would still leave him with a numerical superiority on his right. By then, however, both armies were getting on the move, and the polemarchs refused to obey the order at such short notice. Their decision would probably have been a correct one if they had been part of a poorly trained citizen army. But this was a Spartan army and one of the most highly trained professional armies in Greece in which the commander was fully capable of assessing risks and taking decisions. The polemarchs were guilty of disobedience and were later charged with cowardice and banished from Sparta.[6]

Returning to the moment in question, Agis responded to the polemarchs' refusal to move by ordering the left wing to move back to its original position and rejoin the main body in order to plug the gap. However, the enemy got in first. The Mantineans charged the Sciritae opposite them and broken through them while they were in mid-manoeuvre. The rest of the allied right wing, the Arcadians and picked Argives, then swept into the gap and began to encircle the enemy wing. Many of the enemy were killed and the rest were driven back off the field as far as their baggage wagons. Matters were looking bleak for the Spartans until Agis turned the scales with a brilliant recoup. He charged the main body of the Argives and put them to flight and then turned his attention to the Athenians on the enemy left wing. Here the Tegeates already outflanked the enemy wing and the Spartans and Tegeates together started to encircle them. The Athenians would have been totally destroyed if Agis had not at this point decided to turn to the relief of his beleaguered left wing. The Mantineans and their allies had been engaged in chasing the Sciritae off the field when, seeing Agis charging toward them, they stopped the pursuit and turned to flight. In the process they were attacked by the Spartans on their unprotected right flank and many of the Mantineans were killed. This interlude had taken the pressure off the Athenians, who then had time to escape. The losses on the Argive and allied side amounted to 1,100 in total; those among the Spartans and their allies are said to have been about 300 killed, but Thucydides acknowledges uncertainty in this figure.

Thematic Summary

1   Agis' ruse of diverting the water courses.[2] Unlike all the ruses described in earlier chapters, this one this did not involve any deception or surprise. The sole object was to lure the enemy down to the plain.
2   The chance encounter between the two armies, which caused maximal surprise among the Spartans.[3]
3   The natural shift of the phalanxes to the right as they advanced, resulting in overlapping of the enemy left wing in each case.[5]
4   The disobedience of the two polemarchs and its consequences.[6]

5   The attack of the Argive right wing through the gap in the Spartan line.
6   The outflanking of the Athenians on the left wing by the overlapping
Spartan wing.
7   Agis' attack on the unprotected shieldless flank of the enemy as they
abandoned their pursuit and fled.

Notes

1   Thucydides, 5.18.
2   Thucydides, 5.64–65.
3   Thucydides, 5.66.
4   Thucydides, 5.67–74.
5   Thucydides, 5.71.
6   Thucydides, 5.72.

The Nemea (394)

Background

In 405 the Athenian disaster at Aegospotami cost Athens the position of
leader among the Greek states. The title of hegemon passed to Sparta in
what proved to be a change for the worse. Sparta's rule was autocratic, harsh
and high-handed and was guaranteed to arouse hostility among the states.
They were particularly aggrieved by Sparta's avarice as manifested in her
failure to reward any of the states which had helped her during the Peloponnesian war. Many of them had suffered more and striven harder on her
behalf than Sparta herself. It was not unnatural that the states banded
together to form a confederacy against her. The first break came with Persia
after Sparta had supported Cyrus in his rebellion in 401 to oust his brother
Artaxerxes from the throne. Sparta had supplied Cyrus with troops, which
was regarded in Persia as an act of war against the Great King. As a result it
suited Persia to stir up trouble against Sparta in the form of bribes to the
other Greek states. Sparta herself foolishly started the ball rolling when on
some minor pretext she invaded Boeotia, whereupon Thebes buried the old
hatchet against Athens and turned to her for help. In the ensuing hostilities
Sparta's ablest general, Lysander, was killed at the siege of Haliartus in 395
and there was no man of his ability to replace him. This great blow for
Sparta encouraged four of the larger states, Thebes, Athens, Corinth and
Argos, to form a confederacy against her. They came to blows in the
following year (394) at the battle of Corinth. It took place west of Corinth
and to the east of the Nemea river from which it derives its name and is now
generally referred to simply as 'the Nemea'.

Battle of the Nemea

There is only one, inadequate and perfunctory, account of the battle in
Xenophon's *Hellenica*.[1] In mitigation, it has to be said that Xenophon was
writing his memoirs and not a historical treatise. Diodorus provides only a

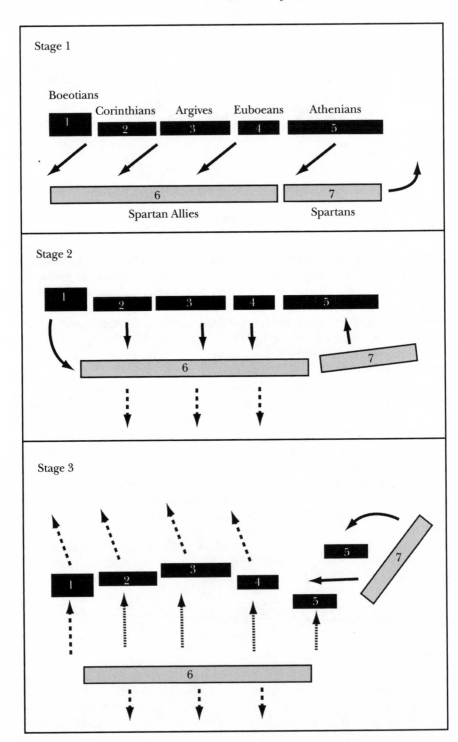

Stage 1

Boeotians

Corinthians   Argives   Euboeans   Athenians

| 1 | 2 | 3 | 4 | 5 |

| 6 | 7 |

Spartan Allies   Spartans

Stage 2

| 1 | 2 | 3 | 4 | 5 |

| 6 | 7 |

Stage 3

| 1 | 2 | 3 | 4 | 5 | 7 |

| 5 |

| 6 |

single paragraph but he does give a few useful figures.[2]

The confederate army consisted of 24,000 infantry with contingents from Athens, Argos, Boeotia, Corinth and Euboea, and 1,550 cavalry. There were also some light troops mainly from Corinth. It was opposed by the Spartans and their allies, who are listed by Xenophon to a total of 13,500. However, Diodorus gives a more realistic total of 23,000 infantry and at least 500 cavalry. The respective deployments of the two armies are shown in the accompanying battle plan. This also shows that the Boeotians on the confederate right wing were drawn up in an unusual depth. Xenophon does not state the number in each file but, as the Theban files at Delium (424) were twenty-five deep, it was probably similar.

In the engagement the confederates were the first to advance with the Boeotians in the lead. As they did so, they *shifted to the right* and the rest of the line followed suit until, according to Xenophon, the Athenians on the left wing hesitated, aware of the risk that they might be encircled. But the alternative offered the even greater danger of creating a gap in the line, and this thought led them to keep in contact as the lesser evil. During these happenings the Spartans were prevented by a lot of natural cover in the area from seeing what was going on. As a result they were not immediately aware that the enemy had started to advance. When they realised this, they had to draw up their line in a hurry. Xenophon tells us that an order was then passed down the line to the men to keep in contact with those who were leading and who were, in fact, the Spartans themselves. It might be thought that in a well-trained Spartan army such an order would have been unnecessary unless there was something special afoot. In the event the line is said to have *inclined to the right* and extended so far beyond the enemy's wing that only six of the Athenian tribes were covered by the Spartans. The rest of the Spartans were unopposed. These italicised shifts or movements to the right are discussed at the end.

When the armies had approached each other the Boeotians on the confederate right outflanked the enemy line. They wheeled to the left and attacked the Spartan allies at the end of the line in the flank and routed them. The rest of the confederate line, including those Athenians who were opposed to the Spartan allies, attacked their opposite numbers with similar results. All the defeated Spartan allies then took to flight and were pursued by the victorious confederates. At the same time the Spartans who were overlapping the enemy left wing wheeled to the left and attacked the other six tribes of Athenians (the ones who had been opposing them) in the flank, killing many of them and putting the rest to flight. By this time, the confederates who had been chasing the Spartan allies had given up the chase and were returning to the field. The Spartans accordingly marched on down the line attacking them as they returned, presenting the Spartans with an ideal opportunity for taking them on their exposed and unprotected side. In the process the Spartans missed the Athenians who had opposed the

Spartan allies because they were lagging behind the others and were still at a distance, but they caught the Argives, who had just returned, and many of whom were slain. Then, proceeding on their way, they attacked the Corinthians, followed by some of the Thebans, many of whom were also killed. Diodorus alone quotes the losses. He gives the figures as 2,800 of the confederates as opposed to 1,100 on the Spartan side.

What was the nature of the initial shifts or movements to the right on both sides as they advanced? Although there are apparent similarities between the battles of Mantinea (418) and the Nemea in this respect, Anderson emphasises a difference which may have a bearing on this point. At Mantinea the two armies confronted each other unexpectedly and their deployments were made in haste. When they advanced both sides showed the usual almost automatic shift to the right, as explained by Thucydides.[3] At the Nemea the situation was different. The two armies had been encamped opposite each other for some time and had plenty of time to formulate their plans. They might have learned a lesson from Mantinea and decided that any move they made to the right would be deliberate and calculated.[4] In the case of the Spartans, their movement to the right was too large to suggest a spontaneous drift. Moreover, it was accompanied by a definite order to the men to keep in contact with those who were leading.[5] This indicates that the movement was a planned manoeuvre in which the men probably turned to the right into column and marched to the right. The position with regard to the confederates is less clear. Xenophon uses the same words (variously translated) to describe the movements to the right of both armies. However, there is no unambiguous statement as to whether the resulting outflanking of the enemy wing was intentional or merely a consequence of the move. Any confirmatory evidence that an advance to the right was a deliberate manoeuvre for this purpose has to be found in other happenings, as already seen in the case of the Spartans. In the case of the confederates, some evidence is to be found in the behaviour of the Athenians when they halted, aware that they might be outflanked by the Spartans if they continued moving to their right. They were at least aware of the situation and the risk involved, which suggests that the Boeotian movement was not just a spontaneous and almost unconscious drift. Anderson cites Xenophon's view that the Boeotians deliberately advanced obliquely to the right, as their countryman Epaminondas may have done (in opposite sense) at Leuctra twenty years later. This is discussed in connection with that event below (p. 140), in which Epaminondas almost certainly adopted an oblique echelon formation with the object of refusing his other wing. This did not apply to the Boeotians at the Nemea, but Epaminondas may also have advanced obliquely to the enemy line. If he did so, it is suggested only in Plutarch's account – not Xenophon's.

Thematic Content

1   The initial shift to the right by the Spartans was almost certainly a deliberate march and not just a spontaneous and unregulated drift The case for the confederates is more debatable, but there is some evidence to suggest that their move to the right was also deliberate.

2   The extended right wings of both armies successfully outflanked the opposing wings.

3   An attack by the Spartans took the enemy on their unprotected shieldless side when they were returning from the pursuit.

Notes

1   Xenophon, *Hellenica*, 4.2.14–23.
2   Diodorus, 14.83.1–2.
3   Thucydides, 5.71.
4   J. K. Anderson, *Military Theory and Practice in the Age of Xenophon*, Berkeley, University of California Press, 1970, pp. 141–2.
5   Xenophon, *Hellenica*, 4.2.19.

Leuctra (371)

Background

The great Theban general Epaminondas was the first commander in the military history of Greece to apply battle tactics systematically and to refine them to a previously unknown degree of excellence. His great victory over a numerically superior Spartan army at Leuctra was the first occasion on which the Spartans had been defeated by a smaller force in a major conflict. It wrested from Sparta her hegemony (leadership) over the other states.

The struggle for hegemony among the independent states of Greece had been a feature for over a century. Previous to that Argos and Sparta had been locked for two centuries in a struggle for leadership within the Peloponnese. The battle of Sepeia (*c*.494) finally put Sparta at the top in that limited sphere. Xerxes' invasion of Greece was a larger affair, as a result of which Athens became the acknowledged leader within the states as a whole. The subsequent development of her empire confirmed her supremacy until the final encounter in the Peloponnesian War at Aegospotami (405). But the real turning point had come with the Athenians' disastrous Syracusan expedition, in which after two years their expeditionary force was totally destroyed. The Athenians still managed to make some recovery and win a few naval battles, notably at Cyzicus (410) after which the Spartans made peace overtures to Athens. Mistakenly they were rejected. Five years later the Athenians lost their whole fleet bar eight ships to the Spartan commander Lysander without even lifting a finger. Refusing to submit, Athens endured a winter of starvation which forced her to surrender. Lysander installed a garrison in the Acropolis and the hegemony passed to Sparta.

As the battle of Leuctra took place only twenty-three years after the Nemea, much of what has been said about the background to that battle is again applicable. In the words of Green: 'Sparta emerges from the next three decades as perhaps the most inept state ever to hold a leading position in Greece.'[1] She was autocratic, demanding, and brutal, and her representatives abroad were corrupt and tyrannical. In the later stages of the war she had obtained her position with the help of Persian gold but the relationship was not to last. When Cyrus attempted to replace his brother as the Great King in 401, Sparta backed him and supplied him with troops in an act of war against Persia. This led to open hostilities in which Agesilaus of Sparta conducted a campaign in Asia (396–5) with the avowed intention of liberating tLe Asiatic Greeks from Persian domination. During this period Athens was steadily working away at restoring her former naval dominance, with Persian help, and she formed a second naval confederacy. Thebes, also, united the Boeotian cities in a federation. These events led to a treaty between Athens, Sparta, and Thebes, which was drafted in 371 (called the Peace of Callias). It reaffirmed the autonomy of every Hellenic city, none of which could be compelled to act as a member of a league. In consequence, all parties were to recall their garrisons from foreign towns. Athens and Sparta signed, thereby abrogating their empires, but when Thebes insisted on signing on behalf of all Boeotian cities, the treaty collapsed. In the light of Sparta's hatred of Thebes, a showdown between them was inevitable and, in contravention of the Peace of Callias, King Cleombrotus of Sparta invaded Boeotia. His objective was Thebes but he was foiled by Epaminondas, who blocked the main route with an army. Cleombrotus turned southwards to bypass the block by a difficult route. When he reached the heights overlooking Leuctra on its southern aspect, he found that his way was again barred by the Theban army, which was already encamped on the hills to the north of the valley. The two armies descended to the small plain between them and confronted each other. It had been chosen by Epaminondas as a place where the Spartan superiority in numbers would be of little advantage to them.

Battle of Leuctra

There is no complete account of the battle. Plutarch gives the best account from the Theban angle.[2] Xenophon gives some useful information but his account has many omissions and does not even mention Epaminondas or Pelopidas.[3] Diodorus, also, makes no mention of Pelopidas and the Sacred Band.[4]

Plutarch relates that the Spartan army consisted of 10,000 infantry and 1,000 horse,[5] although the latter were in a wretched condition.[6] It is known that the Spartans themselves comprised four *morae*, from which it has been calculated that the Spartan strength may have been little over 2,000 men.[7] As the Spartan allies have been itemised to a total of 8,000,[8] these figures are in agreement with Plutarch's grand total. They also show that the Spartans themselves, comprising the right wing, only amounted to one fifth of the army's infantry. Against them Epaminondas had not more than 6,000 men in all, according to Diodorus,[9] but their cavalry were in good fettle. Epaminondas was faced with the problem of defeating a force of

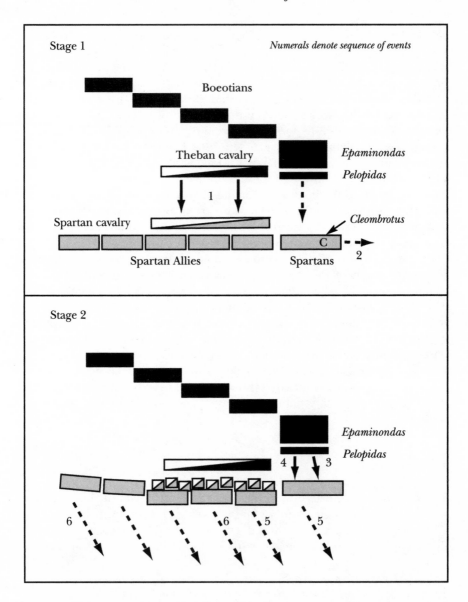

considerable numerical superiority. His solution was unique at the time, representing a complete break with all previous practice and tradition. As the Spartan command centre was invariably on their right, Epaminondas' massed his phalanx on the left opposite the Spartan phalanx, which was probably twelve deep. The Theban phalanx, on the other hand, was unusually deep with at least fifty men per file.[10] The Sacred Band of 300 men were probably stationed in the front of the phalanx. (Four years previously at Tegyra this small body of men had gained the distinction of defeating a larger Spartan force for the first time).[11] Epaminondas' allies, who were less dependable, were deployed in echelon on the right of his phalanx and they were instructed to refuse battle. Their task was to fix and pin down the Spartan allies, who occupied the centre and left of their line, preventing them from going to the assistance of the Spartan phalanx. The Theban line was therefore at an oblique angle to the enemy's formation and presented a narrow but dense front on the left. Contrary to custom, the Spartans stationed their cavalry as a screen in front of their centre, and the Theban cavalry opposed them. This was a departure from the usual practice at that time in which the cavalry were generally placed on the wings.

The action was begun by the cavalry and the Thebans rapidly gained the ascendancy, as might have been expected from the respective conditions of the horses. The Spartan cavalry were a poor lot and were easily forced back onto their own lines, which they disrupted. This effectively prevented the Spartan allies from giving any assistance to Cleombrotus and his wing in the events that followed. While the cavalry action was in progress Cleombrotus noticed the impending threat to his right wing from the Theban phalanx. According to Plutarch, it was advancing obliquely and was threatening to draw his right wing away from the rest of his line. Cleombrotus decided to extend his wing further to the right with the object of outflanking the enemy phalanx by means of his superior numbers. The manoeuvre had started to disorganise his own line when, at the crucial moment, he was caught in mid-manoeuvre by a lightning charge at the double by Pelopidas with his Sacred Band. (Plutarch is the sole source for this manoeuvre).[12] In the fracas Cleombrotus was killed amid a pile of corpses, which must have further disrupted the Spartans.[13] Nevertheless, they managed to recover his body before the next onslaught, which was led by Epaminondas. The action of the Sacred Band had paved the way for him and he had been slowly advancing his massive phalanx. He now crashed the full weight of its fifty-deep formation into the mêlée. When half of the Spartans had been killed, the rest broke and fled to their camp, followed by the allied contingents who had been mere spectators. This put an end to a contest which had been fought entirely on the Theban left. Xenophon says that about 1,000 Spartans were killed, including 400 of the 700 Spartiates. Diodorus gives a larger figure of more than 4,000 Spartans against Boeotian losses of about 300.

Two topics deserve further mention. The first is the Spartan line-up which, according to Diodorus, attacked both of the enemy wings with its line in crescent formation. Cawkwell finds this unusual feature 'baffling', and he points to the absence of even a hint of anything unusual in the other sources.[14] The wording, however, suggests that if Diodorus is correct and the wings did advance to attack, the line would have bowed because the centre was prevented from advancing by the cavalry in front. On the Spartan right an early advance by Cleombrotus after the cavalry had engaged is also mentioned by Xenophon.[15] Any resulting tendency of the Spartan line to adopt a crescent shape would have been further enhanced when the Spartan cavalry were driven back onto their centre and forced it back.

The second point for discussion concerns the meaning of an 'oblique advance', which is ambiguous and could mean two different things. At Leuctra Epaminondas refused his weaker right wing by placing the contingents in echelon so that the whole line was oblique to the enemy line. In this instance, the term 'oblique advance' is obviously appropriate, as Cawkwell says.[14] At the same time, however, there seems to be no reason why the phalanx, or indeed the whole oblique formation, could not have advanced to the left by marching down a line which was oblique to the enemy line until it drew close to it, and then wheeling to confront the enemy head on. (To have attacked obliquely while still on a diagonal line of march would have exposed the shieldless side of the phalanx to the enemy). This is an alternative meaning to the term 'oblique advance' but the two manoeuvres could coexist. The words of Plutarch indicate that they did so at Leuctra.[16]

As a result of the Theban victory at Leuctra, the prestigious hegemony passed to Thebes, but only for ten years. During that period it had depended on one man, Epaminondas, who was killed in combat at Mantinea in 362. In that battle his tactics were similar to those at Leuctra, but he added two other tactics which are worth mentioning in the present connection. When he advanced onto the field, he did not take up a position opposite the enemy but led his men to the foot of the mountains as if he had no intention of fighting that day, thereby catching the enemy off guard. To this piece of dissimulation he added a defensive manoeuvre by posting a body of foot and horse on some high ground on his right to prevent a flank attack by the enemy's left wing on his phalanx.[17] With his death the Thebans lost the greatest tactician of the age.

Thematic Summary

1   The tactics of Epaminondas were so novel that the Spartans were taken off guard and were unprepared.
2   Epaminondas was the first Greek commander to place emphasis on heavy concentration of force at one point, in this case about one fifth of the enemy army, but it included their command post. The density of the Theban phalanx was pushed to the recorded limit of fifty men, giving it a narrow but deep front.[10]
3   As a result of the great depth of the phalanx many of the men were not committed at the start of the battle. They were a convenient reserve force.[14]
4   Contrary to custom, the cavalry were situated in front of the centre, where the superior Theban force drove the enemy horse back onto their own lines, disrupting them.[3] This prevented them from going to the

assistance of their right wing.

5   Epaminondas' oblique formation meant that his right wing with his less reliable troops was refused and did not engage.[4] Its job was to 'fix' the opposing Spartan allies, preventing them from going to the assistance of the Spartans.

6   Epaminondas' oblique advance tended to draw the Spartan right wing away from the centre and left.

7   Cleombrotus started to extend his right wing further to the right to outflank the Theban phalanx.

8   The charge of the Sacred Band caught Cleombrotus in mid-manoeuvre, further disrupting the enemy prior to the main attack by the phalanx.[2]

9   Epaminondas' attack on the disrupted enemy right wing was utterly decisive.

Notes

1   P. Green, *A Concise History of Ancient Greece*, London, BCA, 1974, p. 149.
2   Plutarch, *Pelopidas*, 23.
3   Xenophon, *Hellenica*, 6.4.8–15.
4   Diodorus, 15.53–56.
5   Plutarch, *Pelopidas*, 20.1.
6   Xenophon, *Hellenica*, 6.4.10–11.
7   N. G. L. Hammond, *A History of Greece to 322 BC*, 2nd. edn, Oxford, Oxford University Press, 1967, Appendix 6.
8   J. Warry, *Warfare in the Classical World*, London, Salamander Books, 1980, p. 60.
9   Diodorus, 15.52.2.
10   Xenophon, *Hellenica*, 6.4.12.
11   Plutarch, *Pelopidas*, 17.1–5.
12   Plutarch, *Pelopidas*, 23.2.
13   Diodorus, 15.55.5.
14   Diodorus, 15.55.3; G. L. Cawkwell, *Classical Quarterly*, 22, 1972, pp. 261–2.
15   Xenophon, *Hellenica*, 6.4, 13.
16   Plutarch, *Pelopidas*, 23.1, 4).
17   Xenophon, *Hellenica*, 7.5.21–22, 24.

Chaeronea (338)

Background

Philip II of Macedon, the victor at Chaeronea, was not only a great soldier but also a statesman and diplomat of no mean calibre. His first claim to fame was the reorganisation of the haphazard Macedonian soldiery into the most efficient military system in the known world at that time. This formed the basis for his two prime aims: to gain supremacy over the Greek states, which he achieved, and to subdue the Persian empire, which he did not live to achieve and which was subsequently undertaken by his son, Alexander. In his youth he had spent around three years as a hostage in Thebes where he became well acquainted with Epaminondas and Pelopidas, from whom he learnt much. He was a great admirer of Athenian culture.

On his accession, Philip's first priority was the submission of the neighbouring hostile tribes so that he could devote himself to his plan without having constantly to look over his shoulder. He then began to interfere in Greek politics, in which he came up against an arch-enemy in the person of Demosthenes. It was a turbulent period for Greece, in which the city-states were divided and the politicians hurled abuse at each other. Philip was adept at playing one side off against another, and he seemed to have the knack of getting himself invited to do things which were in his own best interest. In 346, for instance, he accepted an appeal from the Amphictionic Council to lead a campaign against the dissident Phocians. In recognition of his success, the Phocians' voting rights in the Council were transferred to him and, in addition, he was invited to preside over the Pythian Games. He was a great champion of Thessaly where, in 344, he expelled some tyrants and then proceeded to reorganise the administrative systems. For these acts he was rewarded by the Thessalians with the appointment of archon of their League for life. Better still, the post carried with it the use of their cavalry, the finest in Greece.

The affair which ultimately ended in the battle of Chaeronea took place in 339. Delegates from Locris proposed to the Amphictionic Council that Athens should be fined for the improper re-dedication of certain spoils.

Athens was anxious to evade the issue, which could involve the declaration of a Sacred War against her. When the Athenian orator Aeschines was asked to reply, he countered the charge by accusing the Locrians of Amphissa of cultivating land sacred to Apollo. The Council then declared a Sacred War against Locris. When Thebes and Athens failed to support it, Philip was invited to take command of the Amphictionic forces. He accepted with alacrity, having possibly engineered the invitation himself. But instead of marching against Amphissa, he proceeded to occupy the fortress of Elatea, which controlled access to Boeotia. A showdown was clearly in the offing. Demosthenes managed to achieve the near-impossible, namely a military alliance between Athens and Thebes, and a combined force proceeded to hold the passes. When Philip's next move threatened their flank, they withdrew to the plain of Chaeronea where they took up a strong defensive line. In August or September Philip moved southward through the pass of Parapotamii between Elatea and Chaeronea and entered the plain of Chaeronea to confront the enemy.

Battle of Chaeronea

Less is known from the ancient chronicles about the battle of Chaeronea in 338 BC than almost any other battle of comparable significance. That it changed the face of the known world and gave power over Greece to Philip II of Macedon would scarcely be surmised from the few lines of Diodorus and a brief entry in Polyaenus' *Stratagems*. The Macedonian force is reported by the former to have consisted of at least 2,000 cavalry and 30,000 infantry.[1] The strength of the allies is unknown. Justin puts them at 'far superior' in numbers to the Macedonians,[2] but this is in stark contrast to Diodorus who gives Philip the numerical advantage.[1] Modern estimates cite a backbone of 12,000 Theban hoplites and 10,000 Athenians but there were also contingents from Achaea, Corinth, Megara, Phocis, and other states with a stiffening of 5,000 mercenaries, totalling around 35,000. The phalanx probably comprised about 30,000. The Athenians were commanded by three generals, Chares, Lysicles and Stratocles. Concerning the battle itself we are almost entirely dependent upon reconstructions, the most outstanding of which is by Hammond.[3] It is based on archaeological and topographical evidence as well as military considerations, and it brings a lot of loose ends together. Important determinants were the identification of (a) the Acropolis of Chaeronea, (b) the mound on which the Sacred Band took its stand and (c) the three streams which entered the plain from the south. Readers are referred to Hammond's account for the evidence and the reasoning involved.

The two armies confronted each other in the plain which is bounded by the foothills below the Acropolis of Chaeronea on the west and the river

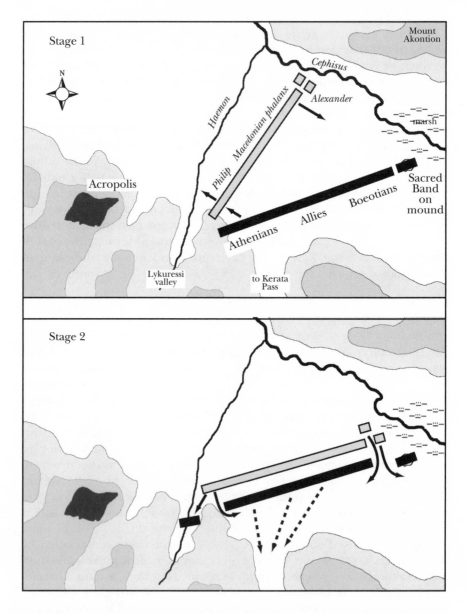

Cephissus to the north east. They deployed at dawn. The Greeks had already occupied their position before Philip arrived. The Athenians were on the left, and next were their allies and mercenaries. The Thebans were on the right with the Sacred Band beyond them. This body comprised 150 pairs of lovers who had never before been defeated in battle. They had taken their stand on a mound near the Cephissus river with marshland between river and mound, which provided security on their right flank. The mound has been excavated and identified beyond reasonable doubt. Hammond estimates that if the Greek line was eight deep with a spacing of one metre it would have been three kilometres in length. The left wing would then have rested on a spur just east of the Lykuressi valley. Light-armed troops (not shown in the battle plan) were stationed in the gap between this point and the foothills below the Acropolis. It was a strong position with easy access to a line of retreat to the Kerata Pass, if such should be needed. Opposing the allies, Philip advanced his line obliquely in relation to the allied line with his right wing of picked troops leading and under his command. Still further to the right and beyond the wing he stationed a body of light-armed troops (also omitted from the plan) in the gap between the wing and the citadel. On his extreme left near the Cephissus he placed the heavy cavalry under his son Alexander, then eighteen years old. Between these two extremes was the general phalanx. The length of the phalanx has been estimated at nearly two-and-a-half kilometres, assuming a depth of ten men which has been recorded as the norm in the early Macedonian phalanx. Although Philip's oblique advance is not mentioned in the chronicles, it becomes obvious from the subsequent events.

The action started with a deft move by Philip, which effectively determined the future course of the battle. It is recorded by Polyaenus.[4] When Philip's right wing had made contact with the Athenian wing, it started to fall back gradually and in close formation but still maintaining contact with the centre. The withdrawal gave the Athenians the impression that they were winning, and they attacked with over-confidence and in a somewhat disorderly state, while Stratocles urged them to keep pressing the enemy back to Macedonia. The Macedonian withdrawal, however, was a feint. Philip was heading for some high ground which would provide a springboard for a counter-attack. Most commentators have assumed this to be the foothills but this assumption raises a number of problems. Hammond is convinced that the high ground was provided by the banks of the river Haemon, which had been built up to prevent the flooding of the surrounding land for which there is some evidence. When his men had attained the advantage of the higher position afforded by the banks, they launched a counter-attack against the Athenians. Plutarch, a native of Chaeronea, identifies the Haemon with the stream that was called the Thermodon and conjectures that it derived the name Haemon from the blood which turned its waters red after the battle.[5]

If the Haemon is accepted as the limit of Philip's withdrawal, several other inferences follow automatically. In the first place, Philip must have retreated not only backwards but also to his right and this would have drawn the Athenians to their left as they advanced to maintain contact with the enemy. This in turn would have extended and weakened their line, which would have created the danger of a gap opening somewhere along it. There is no mention of the Athenians surging through such a gap, and it seems clear that they retained a solid front. At the other end of the Greek line we know that the Sacred Band refused to move but stood resolutely on their mound, on which they fought to the last man.[6] If, as seems likely, the Thebans maintained contact with the Athenians by inclining to their left as they advanced, the gap would have developed between the right flank of the Theban infantry and the Sacred Band. It was clearly Philip's intention to create such a gap in the line through which Alexander and the cavalry could surge. Moreover, it was necessary that the gap should be created by his own withdrawal before he himself counter-attacked the Athenian left wing and drove it back.

While Philip was withdrawing to the Haemon, the Macedonian left wing and centre was advancing steadily until it was close to the enemy line. When the expected gap developed, Alexander and his cavalry surged into it and broke the line. He himself led the cavalry which surrounded the Sacred Band and annihilated it.[7] The way was then clear for the cavalry to attack the Theban phalanx in the flank and rear and roll up the line from the east end. The Greeks were routed and fled, many of them managing to escape to the Kerata Pass. Meanwhile, Philip had launched his counter-attack on the Athenians on the left wing. They were driven back, but for them escape to the Kerata Pass was no longer possible. Having been drawn westward as far as the Haemon, they were driven back into the Lykuressi valley, through which the Haemon flowed and which was a cul-de-sac where many were killed or captured. Philip was then in a position to roll up the enemy line from the west end. There were many more fugitives (including Demosthenes) but they were able to escape over the Kerata Pass. Diodorus says that 1,000 Athenians were killed and 2,000 captured,[8] most of them probably in the Lykuressi valley. There were also heavy losses among the Boeotians, but no other figures have been given.

After his victory Philip wanted to appear in a favourable light and he did not pursue the defeated. He was harsh in his treatment of the Thebans, against whom he bore a grudge; toward the Athenians he was lenient, knowing that he would need their help, and particularly their navy, in his designs against Persia.

When the mound upon which the Sacred Band fought to the last man was excavated it was found to be a *polyandrion* (communal grave). Originally thought to be the resting place of the Sacred Band of 300 it was found to contain only 254 warriors. It is now thought that these were Macedonians who were killed in that area.

The Tactical Mechanism of Philip's Withdrawal

Philip's initial withdrawal to the Haemon requires further consideration. There are two ways in which it could have been effected. In the first, Philip's right wing would have marched slowly backwards with its front and spearpoints facing the enemy. The second method would have involved a countermarch, a manoeuvre whereby the phalanx was inverted so that it faced in the direction from which it had come, the leaders being at the new front (see Glossary of Tactical Definitions). The phalanx would then have marched forwards away from the enemy with its shields swung round to protect the mens' backs. There were three types of countermarch which differed considerably in detail. The Macedonian countermarch is a manoeuvre which appears to be a retreat and this would encourage the enemy.[9]

Philip's withdrawal is told only by Polyaenus very briefly, but two key words have been variously interpreted. They have given rise to divergent opinions regarding the mechanism which was adopted. One of these words is *hoplon*, which usually refers to the hoplite's specific type of shield and is not applicable in the present context. However, in the plural it can denote weapons, arms and armour, indicating that the Macedonian phalanx could have marched backwards protected in front by its spears pointing at the enemy. The other operative word is *anastrephein* which means to turn back or retire or, specifically of soldiers, to face about or to be reversed or inverted or to rally. These various meanings would seem to cover both of the mechanisms which are under discussion here. It is apparent that the words of Polyaenus provide no indisputable answer to the problem. If they did, there would be no case for discussion and no divergent opinions! There are, however, one or two other points which are worth mentioning. In the first place, Polyaenus says that the phalanx retired slowly step by step. This inherently favours a backward march providing the distance was not too great. Hammond has estimated that it was about 150 metres and would take about half an hour. On the other hand, any good enemy commander would realise that a backwards march would not persist indefinitely and he would question its ulterior purpose and suspect a trap. It so happened that none of the three Athenian generals could be classed as great, and Philip probably knew this and might have gambled accordingly. In favour of the counter-march theory, it is obvious that seeing the enemy turning their backs and marching away would do far more to stimulate the Athenians' elation and feeling that they were winning than facing a hedge of spears. Polyaenus' statement that the Macedonians marched step by step certainly suggests a backwards march but it could also be applied to a slow countermarch. The manoeuvre itself would take some time. The time involved by either method was the really important factor in Philip's thinking. It had to be sufficient to allow the Greek line to close up to the left and create the vital gap further down the line.

Hammond and his adherents favour a backwards march by Philip's wing. On the other side of the coin, General Fuller clearly envisaged a counter-march when he wrote apropos Chaeronea that 'with *hoplites* few things could be more difficult than to retire in face of an advancing enemy, turn about and launch an attack' (the italics are mine).[10] Fuller, writing in 1958, never mentions a backwards march, which Hammond had proposed twenty years earlier. The final verdict remains open to debate.

Thematic Appraisal

1   Philip's feint withdrawal was the key tactic from which stemmed virtually all the subsequent planned manoeuvres:[4]

2   It lured on the Athenian left wing to the front *and left*, thereby extending and weakening the whole line.

3   This meant that a gap was created somewhere along the line, probably between the centre and the Sacred Band on the extreme right.

4   Through this gap Alexander and the cavalry charged, making the first break in the line.

5   Alexander surrounded the Sacred Band, who had refused to move and were annihilated.[6]

6   Meanwhile Philip counter-attacked the Athenian left wing and routed it.

7   The rest of the Athenian line was then rolled up from both ends.

Notes

1   Diodorus, 16.85.5.
2   Justin, 9.3.9.
3   Hammond, *Klio*, 31, 1938, pp. 186–7, 201–18.
4   Polyaenus, 4.2.2, 7.
5   Plutarch, *Demosthenes*, 19.
6   Plutarch, *Pelopidas*, 18.5.
7   Plutarch, *Alexander*, 9.2.
8   Diodorus, 16.86.5.
9   Asclepiodotus, 10.13.
10 J. F. C. Fuller, *The Generalship of Alexander the Great*, Ware, Wordsworth, 1998, p. 35, note 1.

The Hydaspes (326)

Background

Alexander's complex turning of the Hydaspes (the river Jhelum) provided the immediate background to the battle. It was the largest and most involved manoeuvre of its kind in the classical era. The following account of this and the battle is based on Arrian's *Anabasis*, the most complete and most universally accepted account.[1] Other versions mentioned below are those of Curtius Rufus,[2] Diodorus,[3] and Plutarch,[4] although Diodorus does not describe the river crossing. When Alexander arrived on the west bank of the river, he was confronted on the opposite bank by Porus, King of the Pauravas, with all his forces and many of his numerous elephants. It was obvious to Alexander that a direct crossing of the river was out of the question and that he would have to resort to guile. He had previously been told about the reception that awaited him and had sent men back to the river Indus to collect the boats which he had used in the crossing of that river and to bring them to the Hydaspes. This involved cutting them into two or three sections and transporting them in carts for subsequent reassembly. Meanwhile, Alexander encouraged his men to move around in groups, making skin floats, searching for possible crossing places, and generally appearing to be fully occupied. Porus, intent on shadowing them and observing all their activities, was kept perpetually on the move without any respite. At night Alexander kept moving his mounted troops up and down the bank and making as much noise as possible until Porus realised that he was being bluffed and was lulled into a false sense of security, as Alexander had intended. Porus thought that Alexander would probably wait several months until the rainy season had ended before attacking. Alexander, on the other hand, was keen to strike as soon as possible. It had reached his ears that Abisares, the ruler of Kashmir, had expressed his intention of joining Porus, and Alexander naturally wanted to move before that could happen.

The place which Alexander had earmarked for a crossing was said by Arrian to be at a bend about eighteen miles (twenty-nine kilometres) upstream, where a wooded promontory projected into the river opposite an equally wooded island. In modern times, searches for these features have resulted in several theories regarding Alexander's route. These have been reviewed by Fuller, who in a critical assessment accepts the convincing conclusions of Sir Aurel Stein that Alexander camped at modern Haranpar and crossed the Hydaspes seventeen and a half miles upstream at Jalalpur.[5] At this point there is a well-marked headland, which could correspond with Arrian's promontory, and a large island in the Jhelum. The theory embraces all the described features with one exception, namely that the river takes only a slight bend at that point, not a sharp one. To explain this discrepancy Fuller suggests that Ptolemy might have relied on a distant impression without actually examining the far side of the headland. It was at the headland, under the trees, that Alexander collected the skin floats, which were then filled with hay, and the boats which had been reconstructed. On his visits to the site he was careful to maintain secrecy from prying eyes by making a detour away from the shore. To add to the deceptions, Curtius relates that a royal tent with all its trappings was erected near the base camp with a permanent guard and an officer dressed to impersonate the King.[6] When the real Alexander set out to effect the crossing, he left Craterus in the base camp with a sufficient force to deceive Porus. To get a large enough force across the river Alexander planned to supplement the main crossing with subsidiary crossings. These would be effected by groups of men who had been concealing themselves at selected fords between the base camp and the main crossing. They were to cross after Alexander had cleared the opposite bank of enemy. Craterus was given instructions not to attempt a crossing himself unless or until Porus moved away from his usual station on the opposite bank.

It was the summer solstice, a rainy season, and during the night of the crossing there was a violent storm which helped to conceal the noise created by the all the preparations and the embarkation. The rain stopped just before dawn as the troops were being embarked. They numbered about 6,000 infantry and 5,000 cavalry. They crossed and disembarked on what they assumed to be the mainland, only to find that it was another – and larger – island, which was separated from the mainland by a narrow but heavily swollen branch of the river. With a sense of enormous relief they eventually found a ford and managed with difficulty to wade across in water which was up to their armpits and the horses' necks. As soon as they left the island they were sighted by enemy patrols who galloped off to report. For a second time Alexander marshalled his men and led off himself with the horse. There are conflicting accounts of the subsequent events but Arrian accepts the account of Ptolemy, son of Lagus. The latter says that it was Porus' son who appeared with 2,000 horse and 120 chariots. (The various reports range from 1,000 to 4,000 cavalry and 60 to 120 chariots). When Alexander heard about the size of the force, he charged at once and broke the Indian cavalry, killing 400 of them including Porus' son. The chariots got stuck in the mud caused by the rains and proved useless. When these events were reported to Porus, he found himself in a dilemma. The troops under Craterus in the base camp had taken advantage of the diversion and were to be seen beginning to cross the river. Which party should he attack? He made a quick decision to fight it out with the King of Macedon himself. Leaving only a few elephants and men to deter Craterus from landing, he marched with the rest of his force of 30,000 infantry, 4,000 cavalry, 300 chariots and 200 elephants to confront the enemy. Selecting a place with a sandy surface, free of mud, he drew up his men and awaited their arrival.

Battle of the Hydaspes

When allowance is made for previous losses, it is calculated that Porus had with him 30,000 infantry, 3,600 cavalry, 180 chariots and 200 elephants. In the van he placed his elephants about a hundred feet (thirty metres) apart to cover the whole line. The various infantry units formed the second line, which was also arranged so as to fill in the gaps between the elephants. In addition, there were also some infantrymen on both wings, outflanking the elephant line, and finally cavalry on both wings with chariots in front of them.

After Alexander's infantry had caught up with him following his cavalry attack on Porus' son, he allowed them to recuperate. When the strengths of the various units are added up, it is seen that his total numbers were around 23,000 infantry and 8,500 Cavalry. In other words he was weak in foot soldiers by comparison with Porus but had more than double the number of cavalry. When he looked at the enemy's array of elephants, he realised that a frontal attack was out of the question. He decided to rely on his superiority in cavalry and to move the larger part of his cavalry toward the enemy left wing with a view to making a mass attack in that sector. Next, he sent Coenus and Demetrius with their cavalry across to their left with instructions to watch the enemy cavalry on Porus' right and to follow them as soon as they moved across to their left to join the other cavalry. Clearly he would only be in a position to do this if he had remained unseen in the meantime. This posed no problem as there were various undulations around the periphery of the field.

As soon as the opposing armies were within range, Alexander sent his mounted archers against the enemy left wing in the hope of disrupting it. This was followed up immediately by a charge of the Companions led by Alexander himself, intent on catching the enemy while they were still disordered. In the process nearly all the chariots were put out of action by the cavalry.[3] At this point Porus decided to pool all his cavalry by withdrawing the horse from 'other sections' (i.e. his right wing). Fuller,[7]

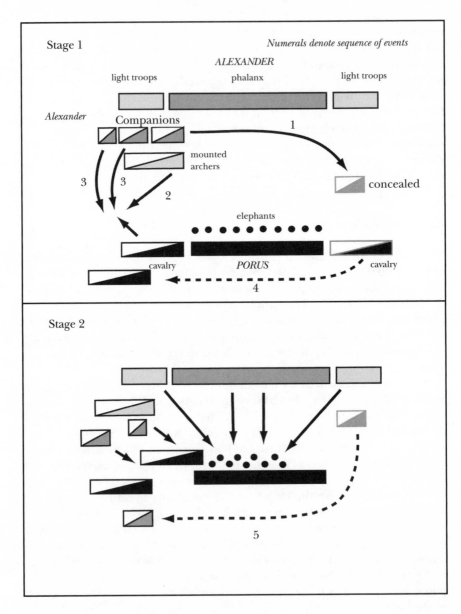

followed by Green,[8] holds that this action by Porus was engineered by Alexander, who had deliberately attacked with a bare sufficiency of horse. The idea was to encourage Porus to think that, if reinforced, he could win the next round. However, when Coenus observed the Indian cavalry on the enemy right wing moving to the left behind the lines, he and Demetrius with their men emerged from cover and followed the Indians, as instructed. It was not long before they appeared behind the enemy who had joined the left flank.[9] This forced the enemy to divide his force and face both ways, a part still opposing Alexander while the rest turned to face Coenus. Another opportunity now presented itself to Alexander, who pressed his attack while the enemy were wheeling about. In confusion the Indian cavalry fell back for protection upon their elephants, who were being driven forward to oppose the Macedonian cavalry. The Macedonian phalanx now advanced along the whole line, preceded by the light armed troops. Volleys of javelins were aimed at the mahouts and their beasts, which went wild and plunged into the infantry of both sides, inflicting considerable damage and death. The Indian cavalry, caught up in the middle of the struggle, managed to rally and attack their Macedonian counterparts, but once again they were fought off and were pushed back onto the elephants. The Macedonian cavalry then combined together into a single group which successively charged one sector then another, inflicting heavy losses on the enemy and driving the elephants back further until they were completely boxed in. As they blundered about in the confined space, they trampled to death both friend and foe alike. It was the Indians who suffered most, jammed in with the elephants and with no space to move. The Macedonians fared less badly at this juncture as they were nearer the fringe. In due course, the elephants became tired and were content to back away with nothing more than trumpetings. To Alexander this was the signal to bring the confrontation to an end. He surrounded the whole mass and then ordered his infantry to lock shields and advance. Most of the surviving Indian cavalry were cut down, as also were many of the infantry. The survivors who managed to find a gap were pursued by Craterus and his men, who had crossed the river when they saw that the way was clear, and were all fresh for the chase.

Porus fought courageously to the bitter end. If any of his men were still resisting, his splendid figure was to be found in the thick of the action until he was wounded in the shoulder, after which he was forced to withdraw. It was the only part of his body which was not protected by his tough corselet. Alexander, anxious to meet him face to face, rode up to him and asked if he wanted anything. Porus replied that he wished nothing more than to be treated as a king. Alexander was so impressed by his courage and dignity that he not only restored his kingdom to him but more than doubled the extent of his realm. From that day Porus remained a loyal friend for the rest of his life.

Arrian puts the casualties at 20,000 Indian infantry killed, but he does not distinguish between the killed and the captured. Diodorus gives much the same total of 21,000 but says that 9,000 of them were captured. For the Indian cavalry Arrian puts the losses at 3,000, virtually the whole force. On the Roman side, Arrian lists the slain as eighty infantry, ten mounted archers, and 220 cavalry of whom twenty were Companions. His figure of eighty losses among the Roman infantry seems remarkably small in view of the carnage; Diodorus puts them more realistically at 700.

Thematic Summary

1   The most notable event in the present connection was Alexander's crossing of the Hydaspes in the face of his enemy on the opposite bank. The complex preparations were accomplished with the aid of numerous feints and other deceptions. Porus was kept continually on the move until he decided it was all bluff and relaxed his vigilance. On every visit to the site of the crossing (about eighteen miles from his base) Alexander made a detour inland to maintain secrecy. It is even reported that a look-alike of Alexander held sway in a mock royal tent near the base.

2   Chance lent a helping hand in the form of a storm on the night of the actual crossing. It drowned the various tell-tale noises.

3   The chariots sent to oppose Alexander on the far bank got stuck in the mud and were useless.

4   In the battle, the enemy's numerous elephants prevented a frontal attack. Alexander responded by launching a mass attack against his left flank. He surmised correctly that Porus would be forced to move his cavalry on the right wing across to the left. With foresight Alexander had planted cavalry opposite them but out of sight. Their job was to break cover and follow the Indian cavalry, which forced the latter to divide their force and face both ways.

5   Alexander sent his phalanx to attack the elephants, which were forced back against their own side. They boxed in the Indian cavalry and infantry many of whom were trampled to death in the confined space.

6   Craterus and his force in the base camp crossed the river when the way was clear and, being fresh, conducted a vigorous chase of those who had escaped.

Notes

1   Arrian, *Anabasis*, 5.8.4.–15.2 (background); 8.15.3–19.3 (battle).
2   Curtius, 8.13.5–14.
3   Diodorus, 17.87–89.3.
4   Plutarch, *Alexander*, 60, 62.1.
5   J. F. C. Fuller, *The Generalship of Alexander the Great*, Ware, Wordsworth, 1998, pp. 181–5.
6   Curtius, 8.13.20–21.
7   Fuller, op. cit. pp. 196–7.
8   P. Green, *Alexander of Macedon, 356–323 BC*, Berkeley, University of California Press, 1991, chapter 9, p. 397.
9   Arrian's account of the movements of Coenus and Demetrius are ambiguous and lacking. This has given rise to a wide variety of interpretations, e.g. 1, that Coenus moved across behind the lines as described here, 2, that he moved in front of the lines, and 3, that he moved across to the Hydaspes on the extreme right. The reader is referred to Fuller (op. cit., p. 195 note 2) for a critical review of these and other interpretations.

Paraetacene (317)

When Alexander the Great died at Babylon in 323 he left no successor, only a corps of generals and an ominous situation. Tradition holds that when asked on his death bed who he would like to succeed him, he replied 'the strongest'. This proved to be a recipe for almost perpetual trials of strength as long as two of the aspirants remained alive to fight it out. Although various parts of the Empire were assigned to various Successors (the Diadochi), power lusts reigned and the most bitter in-fighting was virtually assured. The one who was best qualified to reunite the empire and to emerge through the murk of political intrigue and diplomatic warfare as the ultimate successor was Antigonus Monophthalmos. He was one of the oldest and most able of Alexander's generals, possessing colossal energy and drive. After Alexander's death, he was allotted a large part of Asia Minor and, of greater importance, a considerable portion of Alexander's army. His most dangerous opponent and rival was Eumenes, who had accompanied Alexander on his anabasis as chief of the royal secretariat. Alexander, impressed by Eumenes' potential military abilities, gave him one of the most prestigious posts in the army as hipparch of the crack Companion cavalry. A few years after Alexander's death Eumenes obtained the command of the Argyraspides (Silver Shields), veterans of Alexander's campaign, who were with Eumenes during his war against Antigonus.

Antigonus, recognising in Eumenes his most formidable opponent, put all his energies into destroying him. He followed his rival through Phoenicia into the interior and then through Babylonia to Susa. There, Eumenes managed with difficulty to acquire the allegiance of a body of Macedonian troops who were on the point of being disbanded. These reinforcements brought his numbers up to an approximate parity with those of his enemy and they also gave him a considerable superiority in elephants. It was near Susa that Antigonus caught up with Eumenes. When Eumenes heard of his rival's approach, he marched to the river Pasitigris (Karun) and encamped on the left (east) bank. This river flowed from the mountains down into the Tigris. Running west of it and parallel with it there flowed a tributary, the

Coprates (Dez), to which Antigonus advanced from Susa in the west. These two rivers, therefore, flowed between the two armies, and between the rivers was a stretch of 'no-mans land'. When Antigonus started to get his men across the Coprates onto this land, Eumenes crossed the Pasitigris with a part of his force and caught the enemy completely off guard. They fled to their boats, which became so overladen that they sank under the weight of escaping humanity. Those who tried to swim were carried away and drowned.[1] This engagement on the river Coprates, which took place in July, 317, was a preliminary to two much larger confrontations, the battles of Paraetacene later in the summer of 317 and Gabiene in the following winter early in 316. These battles are good examples of Hellenistic warfare on a grand scale. Diodorus is the primary source for both of them.[2]

In the period before the first battle there was a saga of machinations, disinformation and dissimulation, as each tried to outgeneral the other. These events – and the battles – are well documented by Diodorus at his best. They have been told in the first part of this work but are repeated here for the sake of continuity and in view of their illuminating insight into some aspects of the art of warfare in that age. After Eumenes' victory over Antigonus at the river Coprates Antigonus retired to Media to lick his wounds; Eumenes moved to Persepolis. While he was there, Eumenes heard that his enemy had broken camp and was moving against him. When they were one day's march apart, both men prepared for the fray. But deserters from Antigonus' army came to Eumenes to tell him that his adversary intended to break camp that night. Eumenes was certain that his rival would make for Gabiene, which was unplundered and could supply ample provisions, and it gave him the idea that he would do better to move there himself – and to get there first. Accordingly he, in his turn, sent 'deserters' to tell Antigonus that he would fight that night, while he had every intention of decamping immediately.[3] On the strength of this disinformation Antigonus decided to stay and fight, but there was no enemy. Eumenes had decamped and had gained a head start on him. It was obvious to Antigonus that he and his army would be unable to catch up with his rival and so he resorted to another ruse. He left his army to follow at leisure while he himself took the cavalry and pursued Eumenes at top speed. He caught up with his adversary in the district of Paraetacene, a rugged and mountainous region to the north and east of Susa which is incorporated in the modern Zagros Mountains. When Antigonus saw Eumenes descending on to a plain, he showed himself on the high ground, giving Eumenes the impression that he had his whole army with him.[4] Eumenes immediately started preparing for battle, while Antigonus earned a brief respite to bring up his army and rest the men.

Battle of Paraetacene (*317, summer*)

When Antigonus descended from the heights into the plain, he marched down in battle order. The two armies immediately confronted each other. Eumenes had already deployed his men as soon as he caught sight of his rival on the ridge. Antigonus is recorded as having more than 28,000 heavy infantry, 8,500 horsemen, and 65 elephants; Eumenes boasted a total of 35,000 foot soldiers, 6,100 horsemen, and 114 elephants. But Diodorus also details the composition of each army unit by unit. When the figures for Eumenes' infantry are totalled, they amounted to only 17,000, which was the composition of his phalanx. It seems that this figure did not include his light armed troops which could have amounted to 18,000. The total figure of 35,000 is not open to doubt. Eumenes is said to have fielded nearly 37,000 infantry in the second battle (Gabiene) after an interval in which there is no record of any major recruitment.

In his deployment, Eumenes placed his left wing in contact with the rising ground at the base of the hill. The wing consisted of 3,300 cavalry with an advance guard of a hundred picked mounted archers on the extreme left. In front of the whole wing he drew up forty-five elephants in a curved convex line with bowmen and slingers in the intervening spaces. Next, in the centre, he placed his phalanx, putting his crack troops, 3,000 Silver Shields who had fought with Alexander the Great and a similar number of hypaspists, at the right end of the line with forty elephants in front of the whole. The right wing consisted of cavalry to a total of 2,900. His own squadron was on the extreme right with an advance guard of two troops of fifty mounted men and, finally, 300 of his swiftest cavalry at an angle behind him. In front of the wing he drew up forty elephants (which, when totalled, slightly exceed the reported figure of 114 beasts).

Antigonus, noticing from the heights that Eumenes had strengthened his right wing, proceeded to oppose him with the lightest of his cavalry, 1,000 of his Median and Parthian mounted archers and lancers. They were well-trained in wheeling tactics and were told to avoid a frontal action but to take it in turn to advance to attack, then wheel and retreat, continually threatening the enemy. On this wing Antigonus also stationed Tarentines (mounted javelin men) and various cavalry units and lancers to a total of 6,900 men. The whole wing was under the command of Pithon. The phalanx in the centre was composed of 12,000 mercenaries and mixed infantry on the left, then more than 8,000 mixed troops in Macedonian equipment, and finally 8,000 Macedonians on the right. Next to them were 2,000 mixed cavalry, then 1,000 Companions under his son Demetrius, and finally at the outer end a squadron of 300 cavalry with Antigonus himself. Four hundred horsemen formed an advance guard for the wing, bringing the grand total of cavalry up to 10,600 (originally recorded as 8,500). In front of the right wing Antigonus drew up his thirty strongest elephants in a

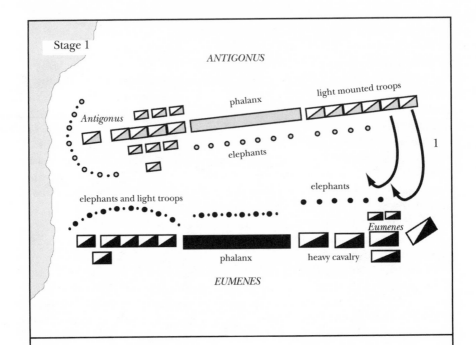

Tinted areas represent hills

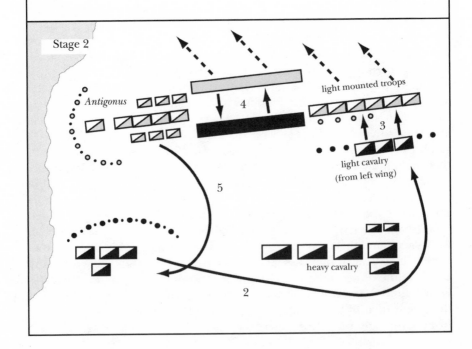

curved line protecting the flank with light armed men in the intervals. Most of the others were placed in front of the phalanx but there were a few in advance of the left wing.

The action was started by Pithon's light cavalry on Antigonus' left wing. They darted out repeatedly, the various squadrons taking it in turn to harass Eumenes' right wing in the flanks with their arrows and inflict wounds at no cost to themselves. When Eumenes saw that his flank was hard pressed and unable to defend itself, he sent for his own light cavalry from his left wing and led them with some light infantry in a flank attack against Pithon's men. The elephants followed the attackers with the result that Pithon's troops were routed and fled to the foothills. While this was going on, the phalanxes had engaged. In this quarter Eumenes' men eventually triumphed, largely owing to the bravery and skill of the renowned Silver Shields and in spite of their advanced ages ranging from sixty to over seventy years. At this point, with everything seemingly against him, Antigonus effected a brilliant counterstroke. He noticed that the advance of Eumenes' phalanx in pursuit of his own had detached it from his left wing and created a gap in the enemy's line. With a detachment of cavalry he charged through the gap and struck the enemy wing in the flank. The attack was so unexpected that the wing was put to flight and many were killed.[5] Taking some light cavalry, Antigonus then rallied his fugitives and reformed them along the foothills. By then darkness was falling and, under a full moon, both generals set about redeploying their troops in battle order. But as midnight approached both armies were so exhausted and hungry that, by almost mutual consent, they abandoned any idea of further hostilities and withdrew to their camps. Eumenes was set on marching back to the field and disposing of the bodies, thereby claiming a victory, but his men refused to obey. Antigonus, on the other hand, forced his men to make camp close to the bodies, which gave him control of their burial and a claim to the victory. In terms of casualties he was the loser with 3,700 foot killed and 4,000 men wounded in contrast to Eumenes' figures of 540 and 1,000 respectively.

After this indecisive conflict the two armies separated to find winter quarters. They resumed hostilities early in the following year when they came to blows again in the battle of Gabiene (next battle).

Thematic Summary

1   Deserters told Eumenes that Antigonus intended to break camp and move to a more fertile area. This was the truth.
2   Disinformation: Eumenes sent 'deserters' to Antigonus to say that he would fight where he was, while in fact he intended to move.[3] As a result, Antigonus changed his mind but found that his rival had departed, gaining a head start.

3   Dissimulation: Antigonus chased Eumenes at top speed, leaving his army to follow. When he saw Eumenes descending onto a plain, Antigonus showed himself on the heights, giving the impression that he had his army with him.[4] The battle took place a couple of days later.

4   Antigonus opposed Eumenes on his right wing with cavalry expert at wheeling and hit-and-run tactics. They inflicted damage with their arrows but sustained none themselves.

5   To counteract the above, Eumenes brought his light cavalry from his left wing to the right wing.

6   When Eumenes advanced his phalanx, it became detached from his left wing. Antigonus launched an unexpected charge through the gap and outflanked the wing.[5] This equalised the score and turned a potential defeat into an indecisive outcome. Both sides were too weary to continue.

Notes

1   Diodorus, 19.25–26 (background); 27–31 (battle).
2   Diodorus, 19.17–18.
3   Diodorus, 19.26.3.
4   Diodorus, 19.26.7–8.
5   Diodorus, 19.30.9.

Gabiene (316)

After the battle of Paraetacene Antigonus wintered in Media, while Eumenes moved south-eastwards into the lusher land in the district of Gabiene. The sources are Diodorus and Plutarch's life of Eumenes.[1] Here his troops were scattered around in their winter quarters as much as six days' march apart. As Antigonus' army was inferior in numbers to his rival's, the idea occurred to him to make a winter march to Gabiene and to take the other by surprise while his army was scattered. There were two routes to Gabiene. One was easy but would involve a twenty-five-days' march through inhabited country in which Antigonus would be readily observed. The other route was over a waterless desert, a march of only nine days. Antigonus opted for the latter course. He gave permission to his men to build camp fires by day, but they must extinguish them completely at night so that they would not be seen from the heights surrounding the plain. After a few days the men became so cold at night that they ignored the order, and their fires were duly seen and reported to Eumenes.[2] It was his turn to adopt a ruse which would delay his enemy for a few days and give himself time to assemble his army from their quarters. He took some of his men, each one carrying a jar containing combustible material, and chose a place on the high ground facing the desert. He ordered the men to light the fires at distances of about thirty feet (ten metres) apart during the first watch, to dim then in the second watch and thereafter to leave only a few burning.[3] The ruse succeeded. Some shepherds saw the 'camp' in the hills and hurried to tell Antigonus, who abandoned his advance and turned into unplundered country to give his troops a break. A few days later the two armies encamped at a distance apart of about forty stades (about four-and-a-half miles) and prepared to fight the second round. The battle took place in the province of Gabiene, somewhere near the site of the old Royal city of Gabae (Esfahan).

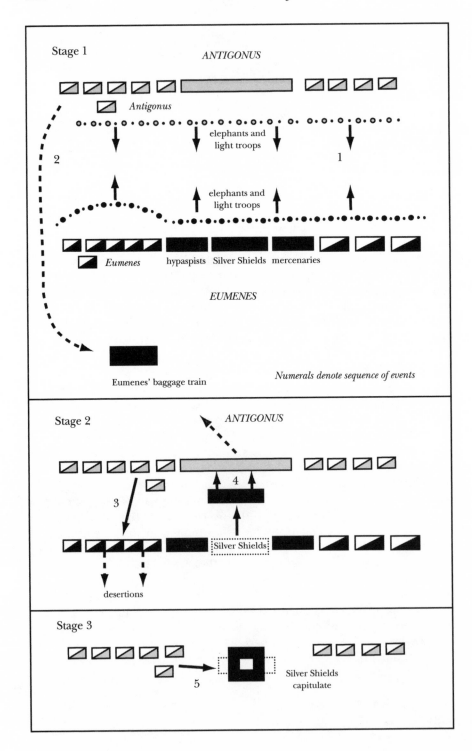

Stage 1

ANTIGONUS

Antigonus

2

elephants and
light troops

1

elephants and
light troops

Eumenes   hypaspists Silver Shields mercenaries

EUMENES

Eumenes' baggage train

Numerals denote sequence of events

Stage 2

ANTIGONUS

3

4

Silver Shields

desertions

Stage 3

5

Silver Shields
capitulate

Battle of Gabiene *(317–316, winter)*

Diodorus puts the total number of Antigonus' army at 22,000 foot, 9,000 horse including some recent enlistments, and 65 elephants. Eumenes had 36,700 foot, 6,000 horse and 114 elephants. In his deployment Antigonus placed cavalry on both wings, giving the command on the left to Pithon. The right wing was commanded by his son Demetrius with whom he himself intended to fight. The phalanx was in the centre and the elephants were extended across the whole front, interspersed with light armed troops.

When Eumenes heard that his rival had taken his place on the right with his best cavalry, he placed his best troops on the left. These included most of the satraps, each with the pick of his cavalry, and he himself intended to fight with them. In front of this wing he drew up his sixty best elephants in an arc with light troops between them. The phalanx was in the centre with the hypaspists next to the left wing, then the Silver Shields and finally the mercenaries and the mixed infantry with Macedonian equipment. On the right wing he placed his weaker cavalry and elephants with instructions to 'refuse' battle.

The action began with the elephants. The surface of the plain was dry and salty and without any cultivation whatever. In consequence the elephants, followed by the cavalry, stirred up such a cloud of dust that it became impossible to see what was happening. Antigonus decided to take advantage of these conditions and he sent some light cavalry against the enemy's baggage train, which was nearly half a mile in the rear. The detachment had no difficulty in riding around the enemy's flank without being detected and taking possession of the train, which was almost undefended.[4] It was packed with a horde of non-combatant humanity, including the wives and families, concubines and slaves of many of the fighting men, to say nothing of gold, silver and accumulated loot. A haul such as this provides the captor with an immense psychological advantage over his opponent, as was soon to become apparent. In the meantime Antigonus himself at the head of a large number of cavalry attacked the opposing horse and struck such panic into the satrap of Persia that he retired from the scene with his own cavalry, drawing away 1,500 others into the bargain. Eumenes, with only a few remaining troopers on his extreme left, forced his way toward Antigonus and engaged him fiercely but was defeated by the enemy's superior numbers. He adopted the only course open to him by riding around to his right wing and assuming command of the troops who had initially been ordered to refuse battle. This left his phalanx unprotected on its left flank. In spite of this, the 3,000 Silver Shields charged their opponents to such good effect that they slew over 5,000 of them and routed the rest without the loss of a single man. By this time the news that Eumenes' baggage train had been captured had become common knowledge among his men. When Eumenes tried to rally his cavalry, they refused to listen but withdrew from the field to 'a certain river' (unnamed). To make matters worse, Antigonus sent Pithon with some cavalry to attack the unprotected Silver Shields, who formed themselves into a protective square and likewise withdrew to the river. There Eumenes joined them and tried to encourage them to fight on, but the Macedonians, with thoughts only for their captured wives and families, refused to heed any exhortations. Instead, they entered into negotiations with Antigonus, as a result of which they seized their leader and handed him over.[5] In exchange, the baggage was handed over to them and they agreed to enrol in Antigonus' army. Antigonus pondered on the fate of Eumenes. They had formerly been friends and Antigonus would have welcomed him as an ally, but he felt he could not trust the other and decided to have him killed. The fate of Antigenes, the commander of the Silver Shields, was the worst barbarity. He was put in a pit and burnt alive.

In his biography of Eumenes, Plutarch records that most of his generals were actually plotting against him before the battle. They had agreed unanimously to make use of his expertise during the battle and then to dispose of him immediately after it.[6]

The removal of Eumenes from the scene left Antigonus free to pursue his ambition of reuniting Alexander's empire under his control. His aims were ultimately thwarted by his death at Ipsus (next battle).

Thematic Summary

1   Antigonus took a short cut to take Eumenes by surprise while he was in winter quarters.
2   The ruse was revealed to Eumenes by camp fires lit by his men in disobedience of his orders.[2]
3   Eumenes gained time by lighting burners to simulate a camp on high ground facing his rival, causing Antigonus to abandon his advance.[3]
4   In battle, the elephants raised such a dust storm that Antigonus was able to send troops unnoticed to capture Eumenes' baggage train.[4]
5   The loss of their baggage train caused a revolt among Eumenes' men, who handed him over to the enemy in exchange for the baggage.[5] Eumenes was executed by his rival.

Notes

1   Diodorus, 19.37–39 (background); 39.6–44.3 (battle); Plutarch, *Eumenes*, 15 ff.
2   Diodorus, 19.37.1–2.
3   Diodorus, 19.38.3.
4   Diodorus, 19.42.1–3.
5   Diodorus, 19.43.8–9.
6   Plutarch, *Eumenes*, 16.1–2.

Ipsus (301)

Antigonus' victory over Eumenes at Gabiene in 316 gave him control over an enormous tract of land ranging from the Hindu Kush to the Aegean. He also benefited from the appropriation of Alexander's imperial treasure, which had remained untouched until that time. Nor did his success reduce his ambitions which now became patently clear. In 306 his assumption of the title of 'King' for himself and for his son Demetrius reinforced his ultimate intention of uniting the empire of Alexander the Great under himself as sole ruler. Not surprisingly, the other generals were alarmed at these developments and they formed a coalition demanding a redistribution of the imperial monies and a reallocation of the territories. With this ultimatum they in effect declared a war, which, after many convolutions, was finally resolved at the battle of Ipsus in 301. Pitted against Antigonus and his son Demetrius Poliorcetes were Cassander, Ptolemy, Seleucus and Lysimachus, but only the last two were actively engaged in the final dénouement at Ipsus.

Seleucus I (Nicator) had fought with Alexander in the Companion cavalry and he later commanded the crack heavy infantry formation, the Hypaspists. He became governor of Babylon, from which he extended his authority over the eastern provinces. After campaigning in India, he came to terms with the Indian ruler, Chandragupta, and in return was given a corps of elephants, allegedly 500 of them. They were to play a significant part at Ipsus. His ally, Lysimachus, a former member of Alexander's Companion cavalry, became governor of Thrace after Alexander's death. After Antigonus' victory at Gabiene, Lysimachus joined the coalition against Antigonus, but he was so busy attending to his own territory that he was little more than a sleeping partner until 302, the year before Ipsus. In that year, and with Cassander's help, he suddenly crossed the Hellespont and overran western Asia Minor, taking the cities by surprise. At that time Antigonus was engaged in inaugurating his new capital of Antigoneia in northern Syria. He hurriedly summoned his son back from Greece and hastened with his forces to Asia Minor.

Originally Antigonus and his son, Demetrius, had adopted a sensible approach in trying to pick off their rivals one by one. In 307 Demetrius swooped across the Aegean, entered the Piraeus and surprised the garrison, gaining control of Athens. The inhabitants greeted him rapturously and addressed both father and son as 'kings'. In the following year Demetrius made a determined and brilliant attack on the Egyptian fleet at Salamis in Cyprus, from which Ptolemy limped away with only eight ships. In the same year, Antigonus proceeded to march into Egypt with a large force of 88,000 men, supported by the fleet under Demetrius. But they failed to reckon with nature's elements, which turned the expedition into a disaster. This ' victory' for Ptolemy, induced him to give himself regal status and to persuade his allies in the coalition to style themselves as 'kings', in effect proclaiming that 'there shall be no single emperor'. In the next Antigonid move, Demetrius went to Rhodes with a combined force to forge an alliance, but he carried his demands too far. The Rhodians decided to allow themselves to be invested and they withstood the siege for a whole year in spite of all Demetrius' state-of-the-art machinery. He returned to Greece, where he scored successes which alarmed Cassander and drove him to make an urgent appeal to his allies. In response, the four members of the coalition agreed to combine in an all-out effort against the common foe. It was at this time that Lysimachus, with Cassander's material assistance, made his timely surprise dash to Asia Minor. Antigonus reacted by summoning his son in Greece to join him and hastening with his forces to meet Lysimachus. The latter, however, did not feel sufficiently confident to confront his rival in open battle, but he did manage to keep him 'on hold' for the rest of the season in a 'catch-me-if-you-can' type of campaign. Early in 301 Ptolemy advanced to meet up with Lysimachus, but he was deterred by a false rumour that Antigonus had already defeated the other members of the coalition, and so he withdrew. The situation was saved by Seleucus who, marching from India, effected a junction with Lysimachus. This enabled them to bring Antigonus and Demetrius to battle near the village of Ipsus in Phrygia in what has been called 'the battle of the dynasts'.

Battle of Ipsus

There is less extant information about the battle of Ipsus than any other known major battle in the Hellenistic world. Diodorus' account breaks off on the eve of the encounter itself, which is mentioned in only two fragmentary snippets.[1] Appian tells us only that Antigonus commanded and fought in person, even though he was more than eighty years old, and that he was killed in the battle.[2] The remaining extant account is by Plutarch, who fortunately provides sufficient information on the key points in the encounter to give us the gist and the outcome.[3] The site of Ipsus remains uncertain or at any rate remained uncertain until very recently, when it was suggested that the battle took place near the tiny village of Sipsin in

Phrygia,[4] which is not shown on any of the usual large scale tourist maps. The quoted coordinates (decimally 38.85 N and 30.53 E) place it within about five miles of modern Afyon, which lies at the junction of major routes from Ancyra, Sardis and from the Hellespont via Dorylaeum. Even if the site has not been confirmed archaeologically or otherwise, this location is suggestive as these are the routes most likely to have been used by the converging armies of Antigonus and Demetrius, on the one hand, and Seleucus with Lysimachus on the other. Seleucus is known to have approached from the east via Ancyra, after which he met up with Lysimachus. During the preceding winter Antigonus had been trying to get to grips with Lysimachus in the region of Dorylaeum (Eskişehir) north of Afyon, and Demetrius' operations seem to have been in Asia Minor somewhere between Sardis and the Hellespont.

Antigonus and Demetrius took the field with a total of more than 70,000 infantry, 10,000 horse and 75 elephants. They also had with them the seventeen-year-old Pyrrhus of Epirus. On the other side, Seleucus and Lysimachus had 64,000 infantry, 10,500 horse including Seleucus' mounted archers, and allegedly 400 elephants (Diodorus says 480) and 120 chariots. The elephants, given to Seleucus by Chandragupta, were said originally to be 500 in number but this figure is regarded by some as traditional. The figure of 400 or more in an army would present a major logistic problem and is almost certainly exaggerated. Tarn suggests that around 150 is more credible, and comparable to the number of beasts reported in other large battles in the Hellenistic era.[5]

After the armies had engaged, Demetrius with the pick of the Antigonid cavalry clashed with the opposing cavalry under Antiochus, the son of Seleucus. He fought furiously, routing the enemy and chasing them off the field. Plutarch refers to this as an extended pursuit carried out with excessive eagerness, a blunder which Demetrius was soon to regret. It is possible, however, that he may simply have got caught up in the mêlée and had been unable to extricate himself, as can happen in a cavalry dash. Whatever the truth, what did happen behind him was that Seleucus seized his chance and redeployed his elephants so as to block Demetrius' return to his phalanx, which in consequence remained unprotected. Seleucus refrained from attacking this inviting target but kept riding around it to keep the enemy in a state of fear while he called on the men to desert to him. This, in fact, is what happened. A large body of them did detach themselves and went over to his side. Those that remained loyal and held their ground were then attacked and routed. Antigonus stood his ground to the last, hoping against hope that his son would return to his rescue. In the end he succumbed to a shower of javelins, whereupon his entourage abandoned his body with the exception of one faithful follower.

This account embodies everything that is reported in the ancient chronicles apart from one fragmentary statement by Diodorus, which tells us only that the elephants of both sides fought equally in courage and strength.[6] The sum of our knowledge leaves many unanswered questions. For an essential start, what were the deployments of the two armies? And what became of the rest of the cavalry on both sides? If Seleucus' cavalry had already routed Antigonus' remaining horse, he seems to have used his horse to encircle the opposing phalanx. Or did he employ elephants for the purpose? Unless or until further information comes to light, the whole field is open to pure speculation.

Demetrius fled the field with only 5,000 foot and 4,000 horse, reaching Ephesus after an 'unbroken flight'[3] From there he sailed to Greece to find that the Athenian ardour for him had evaporated and he was unwelcome. They did, however, allow him to remove the ships which he had left there. Two years later his fortunes took a turn for the better when his old opponent Seleucus asked for the hand of his daughter, Stratonice, in marriage.

The battle of Ipsus effectively solved the question of a sole successor for Alexander the Great in a reunited empire. There was not to be one, certainly not from among Alexander's immediate successors. Antigonus, the most probable contender, had anyway passed his eightieth year and could never have mustered the energy or survived for long. Of the surviving successors, Seleucus was the only possible candidate, and he continued to fantasise and nourish the hope for a further twenty years. In 281 BC he brought Lysimachus, his former partner at Ipsus and the only other surviving member, to battle at Corupedium (almost certainly the Plains of Cyrus near Sardis). Lysimachus was killed but the victory did Seleucus little good. He himself was assassinated by Ptolemy Ceraunus within the year.

Thematic Content

1   The extended pursuit of the enemy cavalry by Demetrius.
2   Demetrius' return to the field was blocked by elephants, to the proximity of which horses have a strong aversion.
3   Seleucus refrained from attacking the enemy's phalanx, which was not protected by Demetrius' cavalry, but rode around it encouraging the men to desert.

Notes

1   Diodorus, 20.113; 21.1.2.
2   Appian, *Syrian Wars*, 55.
3   Plutarch, *Demetrius*, 28.3–30.1.
4   Google: Sipsin, Turkey Page, 19/04/2003.
5   W. W. Tarn, Two notes on Seleucid history, *Journal of the Hellenic Society*, 60, 1940, pp. 84–94.
6   Diodorus, 21.1.2.

Mylae (260)
&
Ecnomus (256)

T he naval battles off Mylae and Ecnomus Promontory are considered
together here as counterfoils because from the tactical point of view
they were fundamentally different. Apart from the fact that Mylae
was the Romans' first real test at sea and a resounding victory, it has only two
features of interest to commend it – the initial state of mind of the
Carthaginians and the Romans' mechanical ingenuity. In contrast, the battle
off Ecnomus was replete with tactics which were similar to military
equivalents. No other ancient naval battle can boast a battle plan which
could almost be mistaken for a military set piece battle.

Background

During the first two centuries of the Republic, Rome was utterly
preoccupied in gaining the mastery of Italy through an interminable series
of struggles against the surrounding tribes and invading Gauls. By the end
of the year 272 she had finally achieved her object and had gained control
over the whole of peninsular Italy. The subsequent respite was short-lived. In
264 an affair at Messana which involved both the Romans and the
Carthaginians triggered Rome's first major encounter with an overseas
power. This was the First Punic War, in which the winning prize was Sicily.
Rome's previous wars had taken place entirely on Italian soil. Apart from a
few cruisers to guard her coastline, she had had no need of a navy. But now,
confronting a powerful seafaring nation for the control of an island, Rome
realised that she had no alternative but to become a naval power. She set
about it with a will in true Roman fashion. At the very start of the war when
the Romans were transporting their army to Sicily in borrowed boats, a
Punic quinquereme ran aground and fell conveniently into the hands of the
Romans. They used it as a model and built a fleet of a hundred quinqueremes (and twenty triremes) to match the Carthaginians' complement in
type and numbers. The quinquereme was the standard warship on both
sides during the First Punic War. It had three tiers of oars totalling 160,

which were rowed by a total of 270 seamen, and a crew of thirty. In time of war each ship also carried up to 120 marines. Building a fleet was half the battle; training the crews was the other half.

Rome's fleet was first put to a proper test at a battle off Mylae (Milazzo) in 260. When the Romans heard that the enemy were congregating in that area and ravaging the land, they took the initiative. The battle is famed not only as Rome's first naval fight but also her first victory at sea, thanks to an invention called the *corvus* ('raven') with which their ships were equipped. The Romans were fully aware that they were novices at sea and that their ships were inferior in speed and manoeuvrability to the Carthaginian vessels. To overcome this deficit they devised the *corvus* for the purpose of turning a naval attack into something more akin to a fight on land, at which they were adept. It consisted of a wooden gangway with a width of 1.2 metres (four feet) and a length of eleven metres (thirty-six feet). This had an oval hole near one end through which passed a stout vertical pole that was fixed to the deck on the prow to form a type of universal joint. The plank could be raised and lowered by means of a rope and a pulley at the top of the pole. It was normally carried in the upright position but in action it could be swivelled through a wide arc and lowered onto an enemy vessel, which it grappled and retained fast by means of a long spike on the underside. The plank had a railing at knee height on each side. It was wide enough to take two men abreast, who rested their shields on top of the railings to provide protection.[1]

There is no record that *corvi* were used after the battle off Ecnomus, although it is thought that they may have been still in use during the battle off Cape Hermaeum in the following year. They were probably abandoned because they made the ships unstable. A gangway thirty feet long normally held in the vertical position could hardly fail to affect the balance and stability of the vessel. They may well have contributed to the heavy losses of ships in an ensuing storm off Camarina.

Battle off Mylae [2]

Apart from the novelty of the *corvus* the battle of Mylae was devoid of tactical ploys, but it is well known for the complacency of the Carthaginians.[3] In the absence of the *corvus* this might have been justified. The Carthaginians were so certain of victory over the Roman landlubbers that their 130 ships sailed out in no sort of order and devoid of any plan. It was a case of each man for himself, selecting a target at will. The Carthaginians were at first dumbfounded at the sight of new contraptions on the Roman vessels and did not know what to make of them. But they got a nasty shock when they found their vessels transfixed by *corvi* and boarded by highly efficient marines. In this way the first thirty ships to be attacked were captured by the Romans with all their crews. Those that followed tried to avoid the *corvi* by veering to one side in the hope of attacking the enemy's broadside. But when the *corvi* swivelled and grappled them all the same, the rest gave up and took to flight with the loss of fifty ships.

After Mylae matters were going well for the Romans on land and so they decided to extend their sphere of activities by invading North Africa. However, before they left Sicilian waters they became involved with the Carthaginians in a second major naval battle, off Ecnomus Promontory in the south coast of the island. This battle was not only much larger in terms of numbers than its predecessor but it is also of considerably greater interest by virtue of the tactics employed. In addition, the *corvus* again came into its own – for the second and last recorded time.

Battle off Ecnomus Promontory [4]

The Romans set out on their expedition to North Africa in the summer of 256 after spending the winter getting a fleet of 330 decked ships in order. First they put in to Messana and then they sailed down the east coast of Sicily. After rounding Cape Pachynum, they proceeded westwards along the south coast to Ecnomus (Poggio di Sant' Angelo). Stationed near here were their land forces, from among whom those required for the expedition were embarked. They were divided into four corps, the first being called the First Legion or First Squadron, and the other three corps were named similarly. The men in the fourth legion, however, were also called the *triarii* in imitation of the rearmost line of troops in the deployment of the army. The total number of men embarked amounted to nearly 140,000. As the normal complement of 270 rowers and thirty crew per ship amounted to 99,000 men, around 41,000 marines must have been embarked. Most of these would have been the normal wartime complement of 120 per ship with a few additions from the Sicilian forces.

When the Carthaginians heard about the Romans' plans, they manned their fleet and sailed to Lilybaeum (Marsala) at the western end of Sicily. From there their fleet of 350 decked ships sailed eastwards along the south coast and anchored off Heraclea Minoa (near Montallegro), about forty miles west of Ecnomus. If it is assumed that each Carthaginian ship carried the same complement as the Roman ships, their total numbers would have been just under 150,000 men. However, the Carthaginians might have carried fewer marines. They were fully aware that Africa could prove to be a soft target for the Romans and their aim was solely to prevent an invasion by a fight at sea. The Romans, on the other hand, were bent on an invasion and were prepared for a sea fight only if it was necessary.

When the two fleets met, the resulting battle was a very different proposition to the encounter off Mylae, quite apart from the much larger

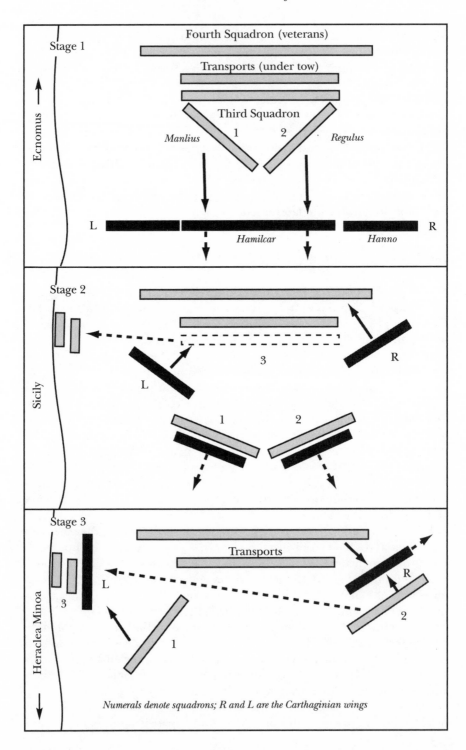

Stage 1

Ecnomus

Fourth Squadron (veterans)

Transports (under tow)

Third Squadron

Manlius 1   2 *Regulus*

L   *Hamilcar*   *Hanno*   R

Stage 2

Sicily

3

L   R

1   2

Stage 3

Heraclea Minoa

Transports

3   L   R

1   2

Numerals denote squadrons; R and L are the Carthaginian wings numbers involved on both sides. The Carthaginians had lost their supreme over-confidence and contempt for the Roman novices. They entered the battle in disciplined order and both sides displayed well-planned (and almost military) tactics, which are of considerable interest. The first two Roman squadrons were in echelon formation, forming a wedge. The two commanders, Marcus Atilius Regulus and Lucius Manlius, sailed side by side at the apex in the two leading ships, Regulus on the left and Manlius on the right. Their ships were larger than the others, being *hexereis* or 'sixes' (believed to be larger than a trireme and having two men to each oar instead of just one). The third squadron was in line abreast across the base of the wedge and converting it into a triangle. These ships towed the transports. The fourth squadron, with the *triarii*, was also in line abreast behind the transports and at the rear of the whole formation. It extended beyond the line of the third squadron, overlapping it at both ends. When the Carthaginian commanders saw the enemy's deployment, they formed their centre and right wing into a single line abreast, extending the line further out to sea than the Romans with a view to outflanking them. Their left wing extended the line shoreward but at an angle to the main body. Polybius does not give a reason for this and, as it is unclear, no angle is shown in the battle plan. The centre was commanded by Hamilcar; Hanno was in charge of the right wing.

The battle was started by the leading Roman squadrons, which launched an attack against the enemy centre. Hamilcar had given orders to the centre to withdraw in the face of such an onslaught with a view to luring the Roman front away from the rear squadrons and disrupting their formation.[5] The Romans fell into the trap by pursuing the enemy. In this way the first and second Roman squadrons became separated from the two rear squadrons and the transports. When Hamilcar judged that they had covered a sufficient distance, the Carthaginians turned to attack their pursuers. While this was going on, Hanno and the Carthaginian right wing sailed across the open sea and fell upon the ships of the *triarii* behind the transports. At the same time, the Carthaginian left wing, on the landward side, deployed into line facing the enemy and attacked the Roman third squadron, which was hitched to the transports. Releasing the tow-lines, this squadron closed with its attackers. In this way the confrontation had developed into three separate fights over a wide area. Out in front, when the 'retreating' Carthaginians turned to the attack, they were relying on their superior speed and flexibility to close and to infiltrate between the Roman vessels in the tactic known as the *diekplous* (p. 118), but they were foiled by the Roman *corvi*, which grappled any ship that came within reach.[6] It was not only the physical damage occasioned by these monstrous contraptions but equally, or even more, the fear of them that broke the attackers. After a while they gave up and fled in earnest. This released the two consuls and their surviving squadrons, allowing them to go to the assistance of their colleagues battling it out in the rear. Lucius Manlius on the right, with the first squadron, got busy taking the captured ships in tow, while Marcus Regulus turned and sailed to attack Hanno in order to relieve the *triarii*. This put heart into those sorely tried men, who promptly regained their fighting spirit. The result was that the Carthaginians, finding themselves attacked on both sides, fled out to sea. Meanwhile, the Roman third squadron had either been driven to the shore by the Carthaginian left wing or had retreated there for shelter. Polybius does not say exactly how this came about. The Carthaginians had then hemmed them in and would undoubtedly have annihilated them if it had not been for their fear of the *corvi*. Lucius Manlius, seeing their plight, sailed to their rescue and was joined by Marcus Regulus, who was able to leave the horse transports and *triarii* in safety. Between them, the Consuls surrounded the enemy and captured fifty of their ships with the crews. In the final tally twenty-four of the Roman ships were sunk against more than thirty of the Carthaginians'. More telling is the statement that sixty-four of the Carthaginian ships were captured with their crews, while not a single Roman ship with its crew suffered this fate.

Thematic Appraisal

At Mylae there were just two outstanding factors at work. The first was the utter complacency of the Carthaginians, born of past experience of the Romans at sea, and it determined their haphazard method of attack.[3] The second factor was the Romans' new weapon – the *corvus*, with its damaging effects on both ships and morale.[1]

At Ecnomus the feint retreat of the Carthaginian centre[5] and the Romans' *corvi* were the two factors which largely determined the course of other events. When the Carthaginian centre stopped withdrawing and turned to attack, its efforts to break the Roman line were foiled by the *corvi* themselves and even more by the fear of them.[6] The Carthaginians fled in earnest, releasing the first two Roman squadrons and allowing them to assist their third and fourth squadrons which were under attack. When the third squadron was bottled up by the enemy close to the shore, it was saved from destruction by its *corvi* until both consuls were free to go to its assistance.

Notes

1   Polybius, 1.22
2   Polybius, 1.23
3   Polybius, 1.23.3.
4   Polybius, 1.25.7–28.
5   Polybius, 1.27.8.
6   J. F. Lazenby, *The First Punic War*, London, UCL Press, 1996, p. 92.

The Trebia (218)

In 218 Hannibal crossed the Rhodanus (Rhône) and headed for the Alps with 38,000 infantry and more than 8,000 horse.[1] His own figures show that when he descended into Italy he had only 20,000 foot and not more than 6,000 horse, indicating that he had lost nearly half his army in the process of crossing the Alps.[2] Advancing across the plains of the Padus (Po), he reached the river and proceeded eastwards along the north bank.

Meanwhile, Publius Cornelius Scipio (father of Africanus) was on his way back to Pisa from the Rhône delta. He and his brother Gnaeus had set sail from Pisa with forces bound for Spain. *En route* Publius had dropped anchor at the eastern end of the Rhône delta and was amazed to learn that Hannibal had already reached the Rhône. There was a clash between reconnaissance cavalry parties from the two sides, but when Scipio followed upstream with his army, he found that Hannibal had already eluded him. He immediately set sail for Pisa, leaving his brother to proceed on his way to Spain. At around this time the Senate recalled the other consul, Ti. Sempronius Longus, and his army from their assignment in Sicily to return to Italy as quickly as possible. Meanwhile, taking command of the legions in the area around Pisa, Publius marched northwards to the Po valley, crossed the river and moved westward to the river Ticinus (Ticino), which he crossed by a bridge constructed by his engineers. Next day he advanced along the north bank of the Po until he heard that Hannibal was close at hand, approaching him from the west on the same bank. Both armies camped where they were and met on the following morning. The resulting clash was little more than a cavalry skirmish in which Hannibal's Numidian cavalry gave him a distinct advantage. On the Roman side, Scipio was severely wounded and owed his life to the timely intervention of his young son, also called Publius and later honoured as Africanus.[3] After this encounter the Romans crossed the Ticinus, destroying their bridge behind them, and then withdrew to the Po, crossed it and marched eastwards. They encamped on the southern bank west of Placentia (Piacenza).

When Hannibal realised that his adversary had departed after the skirmish, he decided to follow him but was unable to cross the Ticinus because the bridge had been demolished. (Livy mistakenly says that it was the bridge over the Po.) He turned and went upstream to find a place where he could cross the Po. After building a bridge of boats, he left Hasdrubal to supervise the crossing of the army while he himself went across first to talk to the envoys who had been negotiating for Gallic recruitments. This was high among his priorities. From the very start of the campaign he had realised that he would be dependent on recruits from the Gallic tribes and had sent out emissaries to put out feelers. Now, after one small success they were hastening to join him. Satisfied on this point, Hannibal marched his army eastwards until he was near the Romans, and he encamped about fifty stades (about six miles) from their position. During the night about 2,000 Gauls who were with the Romans decided to defect to the Carthaginians, who welcomed them. This treachery disturbed Scipio so much that he broke camp during the same night and marched eastwards toward the river Trebia (Trebbia), which runs into the Po from the south and which he crossed. He built a camp and fortified it on the nearest hills, where he felt more secure than in the open plain. Scipio had only just succeeded in crossing the Trebia before Hannibal caught up with him. The Carthaginian camped four to five miles away on the opposite (west) side of the river. In these statements concerning the movements of Scipio in relation to the Trebia, neither of the sources gives a clear account; both are parsimonious with direction indicators. The pointers to the movements as set out above are the statements by Polybius that Hannibal marched 'up the Po' to find a crossing place and then 'marched downstream with the object of encountering the enemy'.[4] This puts Scipio's first camp on the west side of the Trebia.

While Scipio was in his second camp on the east side of the river Sempronius arrived with his forces and immediately took over the command from Scipio, who was still far from recovered from his wound. Sempronius was impatient to engage in a full battle and to show his mettle; so was Hannibal for different reasons, thinking that a decisive victory would encourage the Gauls and aid further recruitment. Furthermore, he had summed up the characteristics of the two consuls and had realised that Sempronius would be impulsive and an easier foe to defeat. Scipio disagreed with his colleague's impatience to fight, but Sempronius decided to adhere to his decision, and the die was cast.[5]

Battle of the River Trebia [6, 7]

By the time of the battle the Carthaginian army which descended into Italy would have been substantially increased by Gallic recruitments. It has been estimated that these might have raised the numbers to as many as 29,000 infantry and 11,000 cavalry.[7] Against them the Romans had 36,000 infantry but only 4,000 cavalry, according to Polybius.[8]

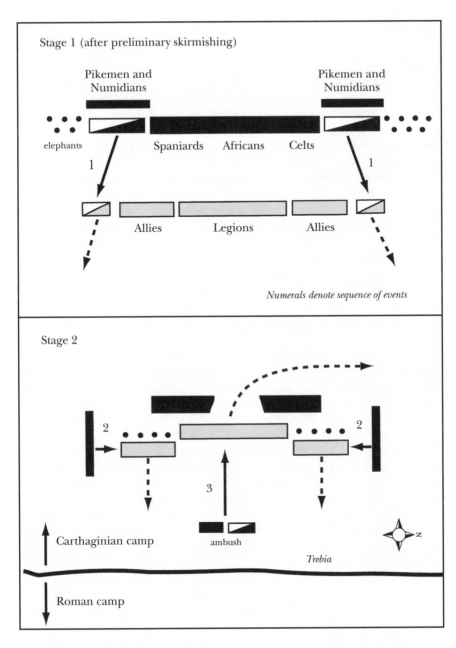

Stage 1 (after preliminary skirmishing)

Pikemen and
Numidians

Pikemen and
Numidians

elephants

Spaniards   Africans   Celts

1

1

Allies   Legions   Allies

Numerals denote sequence of events

Stage 2

2

2

3

Carthaginian camp

ambush

Trebia

Roman camp

When Hannibal reconnoitred the area he achieved two things. He found a suitable site for a battle on his side of the river, which was flat and treeless, and he had also noticed that it was traversed by a water-course with steep banks and heavily overgrown with brambles, which would be ideal for an ambush. He knew that the Romans were suspicious of wooded land with all that it might conceal, but that they were never concerned about traps on sites such as this.[10] During the night he sent Mago out with 1,000 horse and the same number of foot with instructions to conceal themselves in the ditch and to await the timing that he indicated. As soon as the day dawned he ordered the Numidian horsemen to cross the river, ride up to the Roman encampment and start shooting at them to lure them out, giving ground gradually in order to draw the Romans across the river. He then ordered the rest of the army to breakfast well, see to their horses and equipment, and rub themselves down with oil in front of their camp fires.

When Sempronius saw the Numidian horse, he sent out his cavalry to drive them back across the river. Next he ordered his foot javelin men , about 6,000 of them, to follow, after which he began to send out his whole army. It was a freezing snowy day in mid-winter, and the Romans had neither eaten nor taken any precautions to keep out the cold. By the time they had crossed the river, swollen with rains, they were in no fit state to fight. When Hannibal saw that the Romans had crossed, he sent out 8,000 pikemen and slingers followed by his whole army. He drew up his infantry, about 20,000, in a single line and divided his 10,000 horse between the two wings with the elephants in advance. Sempronius withdrew his cavalry, which had been thrown into disorder by the Numidians, and opposed the enemy with his infantry, about 16,000 Romans and 20,000 allies, in the usual three lines (*hastati, principes, triarii*) with light troops in the van. The cavalry he divided between the wings. The light-armed troops began the action and the Romans fared dismally. They had already spent most of their missiles in the preliminary skirmish against the Numidians. The Carthaginian cavalry, superior in numbers, then attacked the Roman cavalry which fell back, exposing the flanks of the infantry. The Numidian cavalry and pikemen then intervened and increased the damage on the flanks, which was completed by the elephants in front. The Roman wings took to flight. In the centre the infantry were putting up a hard fight on both sides when the men in ambush suddenly erupted from concealment and attacked the Roman infantry in the rear.[11] With their avenue of retreat blocked, those in front advanced in desperation and about 10,000 of them managed to break through the enemy line. With nowhere else to go, they continued their advance and retired toward Placentia. Most of the others were killed near the river to which they had been pursued. It is interesting to note that all the elephants except one succumbed to the weather in spite of having traversed the Alps.[12]

Scipio Africanus is known to have said that he learned much from Hannibal. Assuming that he fought at the Trebia, it seems probable that he may have absorbed there the importance of disadvantaging the enemy by subjecting him to such factors as hunger, fatigue and adverse temperatures. He himself employed them with great success at, for instance, the battle of Ilipa (p. 197).

Thematic Summary

1   Planning: Hannibal set the scene for the battle, choosing a place that suited all his purposes including a site for an ambush.
2   Human element: Hannibal had summed up his opponent correctly. Sempronius Longus, the consul in command, was an impatient and impulsive man who was longing for a fight against the advice of his more experienced consular colleague, Scipio, who had been injured and was in no fit state to command.[5]
3   The human element again enters the equation in the form of Hannibal's knowledge of his enemy's thoughts. He knew that the Romans never suspected ambushes in open places and he set one during the night before the engagement.[10]
4   The engagement commenced when the fully prepared enemy cavalry enticed the Romans out before breakfast and then lured them into following them through the icy river. They were in no fit state to fight.
5   Hannibal launched his successful attack on the Roman *wings*, thereby isolating the legions in the centre.
6   A frontal attack on the Roman centre and by the men in ambush in their rear settled the issue.[11]

Notes

1   Polybius, 3.60.5.
2   Polybius, 3.56.4.
3   Livy, 21.46.7.
4   Polybius, 3.66.5, 8.
5   Polybius, 3.70.
6   Polybius, 3.56, 60–70 (background); 71–4 (battle).
7   Livy, 21.38–53 (background); 54–56 (battle).
8   J. F. Lazenby, *Hannibal's War*, Warminster, Aris & Phillips, 1978, p. 56.
9   Polybius, 3.72.11–12.
10   Polybius, 3.71.1–3.
11   Polybius, 3.74.1.
12   Polybius, 3.74.11.

Cannae (216)

Background

Hannibal's invasion of northern Italy in 218 got off to a good start. His victories at the river Trebia in the same year and at Lake Trasimene in 217 shattered the Roman confidence and brought about a change in their tactics as a result of the appointment of Quintus Fabius Maximus as dictator. Realising the necessity of avoiding any further engagement with the enemy for the time being, Fabius instituted a defensive policy of shadowing, dogging and delaying Hannibal which earned him the title of Cunctator (Delayer) and the soubriquet of 'the Shield of Rome'. After Trasimene the road to Rome was open to Hannibal but he refrained from taking it for a number of reasons, notably the facts that he had no base and lacked a siege train. Instead he pillaged his way over to the Adriatic coast, down through Samnium, across to Campania and then back to Samnium. By this time he had amassed an immense quantity of plunder and provisions and was in search of a base. Settling on Gerunium, he seized it and fortified a camp in front of the town for his winter quarters.

At the end of his six-month period in office Fabius relinquished his command. By this time the Romans as a whole had experienced enough of defensive delaying tactics. They had served their purpose of safeguarding the State during a difficult period, but minds were turning toward the thought of an all-out effort to rid them of Hannibal. The next elections were due in March 216, at which the plebeian Gaius Terentius Varro was elected consul for the first time with the more experienced patrician Lucius Aemilius Paulus as his colleague. Neither had any previous experience of Hannibal in action, but the Romans had put everything into raising a new army with an unprecedented eight legions. This, they deemed, would give them a superiority which was more than sufficient for the purpose. The new consuls were unable to assume their commands straight away and so in the interim the retiring consuls retained their commands temporarily as proconsuls. Their camp was not far from Hannibal's base at Gerunium, and they were instructed to skirmish vigorously as training for the new recruits but to avoid major encounters.

In early June of 216 Hannibal left Gerunium, where his supplies were nearly exhausted, and marched southwards. Crossing the river Aufidus (Ofanto) he captured the little town of Cannae with its citadel. As the Romans had been using it as a grain storehouse, he effectively killed two birds with one stone, depriving them while acquiring their provisions for himself. At the end of July the new consuls arrived with their legions and, having joined up with the forces already near Gerunium, they set out for Cannae and encamped about five miles away from Hannibal. At that time the consuls were adopting the usual uniquely Roman system of sharing the command by taking control on alternate days, which led to some altercations. Aemilius thought that the surrounding terrain was too flat and was therefore ideal for the enemy's numerically superior cavalry. He favoured moving away onto hillier ground, but Varro vehemently disagreed. On the following day, on which Varro was in command, he led the army forward toward the enemy. While they were on the march, Hannibal attacked with some cavalry and light-armed troops, but their numbers were small and by nightfall the Roman legions had got the better of them. On the following day Aemilius, now in command, deemed it unsafe to attempt a withdrawal, and he advanced to the Aufidus and encamped two-thirds of the army on the left bank. With the other third he crossed the river and fortified a position on the right bank about two miles from the larger camp, intending to use this to cover his own foragers and harass the enemy's. When Hannibal noted that most of the Romans remained camped on the left bank, he crossed the river and moved his camp from the immediate vicinity of Cannae on the right bank to the southwest of the larger Roman camp on the opposite bank. Two days later Hannibal drew up his army along the river but Aemilius declined the challenge. On the following day (2 August) it was Varro's turn to command. Soon after sunrise he led his men out of the larger camp and crossed the river to join forces with the others on the right bank. Hannibal was eager to accept the challenge and he too led out his men and lined them up. The following description of the battle is based on the account by Polybius.[1] A full account is also given by Livy.[2]

Battle of Cannae

Hannibal's position lay to the southwest of the Roman position. This was to his advantage because the local wind, called the Volturnus, drove over the sandy plain from that direction, whipping up dust which would come from behind him and would blind and choke his opponents. Polybius makes no mention of this, but Livy comments on the advantage,[3] and Plutarch goes so far as to say that Hannibal planned his position accordingly.[4]

Polybius puts the total strength of the Romans at about 80,000, comprising eight legions each of 5,000 men with an equivalent number of

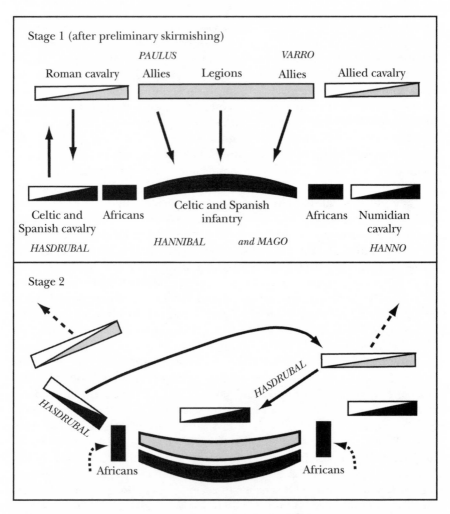

Stage 1 (after preliminary skirmishing)

PAULUS   VARRO

Roman cavalry   Allies   Legions   Allies   Allied cavalry

Celtic and   Africans   Celtic and Spanish   Africans   Numidian
Spanish cavalry   infantry   cavalry

HASDRUBAL   HANNIBAL   and MAGO   HANNO

Stage 2

HASDRUBAL

HASDRUBAL

Africans   Africans

allies, and 6,000 horse. The figure of 80,000 includes the allied skirmishers
and the *velites* as well as the men who were left to guard the camps. Lazenby
deduces that the actual Roman infantry of the line were at most about
55,000, pitted against Hannibal's line of rather more than 40,000.[5]
Hannibal, on the other hand, was markedly superior in cavalry. When Varro
drew up his men in battle line facing southwest, he placed the Roman
cavalry on the right wing close to the river. In the centre were the legions,
the intervals between the maniples being smaller than usual and their depth
unusually large. The allied cavalry were on the left wing, and the light-armed
troops formed a screen in front of the whole line. Aemilius was in command
on the right and Varro on the left. Hannibal, also, led out all his men,
crossed the river, and drew them up opposite the enemy. In the centre he
placed the Spanish and Celtic infantry, who were his weakest members. Next

to them on either side were his veteran African heavy infantry, who were divided between the two sides. On the left wing close to the river were the Spanish and Celtic horse, opposing the Roman cavalry; on the right wing were the Numidian horse. After drawing up this array in a straight line, he took the Spanish and Celtic infantry and advanced their central companies, keeping them in contact with those on either side but tapering the depth and degree of advance. In this way he created a crescent-shaped formation with the convexity facing the enemy. It was deepest in the centre but grew progressively less deep toward the ends.[6] Hannibal commanded the whole centre with his brother Mago; Hasdrubal commanded the left, Hanno the right.

The light infantry of both sides began the action but neither side gained any advantage over the other. The next to engage were the Spanish and Celtic horse on the Carthaginian left, who became embroiled with the opposing Roman cavalry. The ensuing struggle was, as Polybius says, 'truly barbaric'. Instead of indulging in the usual cavalry manoeuvres in the limited space, the riders tried to pull each other off their mounts and eventually both sides dismounted and engaged in man-to-man combat. Although the Romans fought with bravery, the Carthaginians excelled, killing most of the Romans and driving the survivors off the field along by the river. Meanwhile, the battle was shifting to the centre of the stage where the Roman infantry were bearing heavily on the Spaniards and Celts. Although the enemy put up a good fight, they were unable to hold the sheer weight of the Roman legions and were forced back. The Celts bore the brunt of it, being as they were in the very centre of the line where it was most dense. Here the Roman maniples had little difficulty in penetrating the line, but they were unable to effect a breakthrough. Matters were made worse for the enemy when Romans at the ends of the line crowded toward the centre to join in the fracas. With increasing pressure from the Romans, the once convex Carthaginian line began to lose its curve and eventually to bend the other way, becoming concave toward the enemy. By now the Romans had advanced so far that Hannibal's veteran heavy-armed Africans were positioned on the Roman flanks at both ends of the line, as Hannibal had intended. The Africans on both sides then turned inwards to face the centre and proceeded to attack the Romans on the flanks, forcing them to turn and fight while driving them back.[7] The Romans were now becoming crowded together in the centre, some of them facing the Celts in front while others were being forced back onto them from the flanks.

In the meantime, Hannibal's Numidian cavalry on his right wing attacked the opposing cavalry of the Roman allies. In this struggle neither side gained the advantage until Hasdrubal intervened. Having already successfully destroyed the Roman cavalry on the opposite wing earlier in the battle, he now rode across the field to help the Numidian cavalry. This was enough for the Roman allied cavalry, who broke and fled and were driven off the field by the Numidians. Hasdrubal left them to complete the pursuit while he turned toward the struggle in the centre and launched an attack against the rear of the Romans.[8] It was here that the consul Aemilius fell in the thick of the fighting. The Romans were now completely surrounded, and there was nothing that they could do but fight to the end in ever decreasing numbers. Those that could not find an escape route were all killed, including the two proconsuls. While the slaughter was going on, the Numidian cavalry killed most of fugitive horse that they had been pursuing. Few escaped, but they did include the Consul Terentius Varro. Of the original 6,000 cavalry only about 370 escaped, according to Livy.

Polybius puts the Carthaginian losses at about 4,000 Celts and 1,500 Spaniards, hardly surprising figures since these men were sacrificed in the interest of luring the enemy to destruction. He also mentions 200 cavalry killed. On the Roman side, his figure of 70,000 infantry killed is regarded as excessive since, as he himself says, 10,000 had been left to protect the camp while an estimated 3,000 escaped from the field. Moreover, figures given by Livy indicate that over 19,000 were taken prisoner and over 14,000 escaped.[9] Livy puts the total dead at just over 48,000, in close agreement with Appian and Plutarch, both of whom give a round total of 50,000.[10, 11]

Thematic Appraisal

The battle of Cannae was unique. It was the first time that a large army had been totally surrounded by a smaller one. The key to the Roman defeat lay in the brilliance of Hannibal's tactical plan in all its elegant simplicity. Its essence was three-fold:

1 the arrangement of his centre with his weaker troops drawn up in a convex arc pointing toward the Romans to lure them into the depths of what became a concavity wrapped around their front,[6]
2 the attacks on both flanks by Hannibal's veteran heavy African infantry,[7] and
3 the *coup de grâce* dealt by Hasdrubal's cavalry attack on the Roman rear, which completed the encirclement.[8]

Hannibal's convex front was in itself unique. The greater depth in the centre must have been planned to prevent any complete breakthrough by the Romans, an event which would have wrecked the whole plan of encirclement. The purpose of the convexity may also have been to prolong the Romans' advance in order to give Hasdrubal more time to prepare his *coup de grâce*. The successful result of this latter tactic required cooperation between Hannibal who was taking part in the battle and Hasdrubal with his cavalry on the outside. Hasdrubal's decisive finalising blow was timed to a nicety.

A relatively minor item was Hannibal's position with the local Volturnus wind behind him, whipping up dust in the faces of the Romans. This might have been planned by Hannibal, as Plutarch declares,[4] while Livy also seems to concur.[3] As Hannibal was the first to arrive on the scene, it is certainly a possibility. But with Hannibal's known attention to such details, it is more likely to have been the truth.

Notes

1   Polybius, 3.112–117.
2   Livy, 22.45.5–49.
3   Livy, 22.43.10–11, 46.9.
4   Plutarch, *Fabius Maximus*, 16, (1).
5   J. F. Lazenby in his *Hannibal's War*, Warminster, Aris & Phillips, 1978, pp. 79–80.
6   Polybius, 3.113.8–9.
7   Polybius, 3.115.8–12.
8   Polybius, 3.116.7–8.
9   Lazenby, op. cit., p.84 .
10 Appian, *Hannibalic War*, 25.
11 Plutarch, *Fabius Maximus*, 16.8.

Baecula (208)

The Second Punic War was ignited by an affair at Saguntum, the only city south of the river Iberus (Ebro) which was not at that time in Carthaginian hands. The Romans had promised to protect it. When Hannibal, the Punic commander-in-chief, made ominous preparations to attack the place, the Romans protested to Carthage but to no avail. The Carthaginian senate supported Hannibal and upheld his actions as he proceeded to besiege Saguntum and eventually to capture it. The Romans retaliated by demanding the surrender of Hannibal. When the Punic government refused not surprisingly to comply, the Romans issued a declaration of war. The year was 218.

Although the centre of the conflict moved to Italy following Hannibal's crossing of the Alps later in 218, a Roman presence remained in Spain. It pinned down the Carthaginians and prevented them at least from sending reinforcements and supplies to Italy. In 210 the Senate decided to step up its operations in Spain and to make an all-out attempt to force the enemy out altogether, but there was no obviously suitable candidate for the command and nobody came forward to apply. Eventually, the young Publius Cornelius Scipio offered his services and was appointed unanimously. It was an odd appointment. Scipio was only twenty-five or twenty-six years old and had held no previous high office, but the initial misgivings were probably soothed by the fact that his father, who was also his namesake, and his uncle Gnaeus had both been killed in Spain within a month of each other in the previous year. He had good personal reasons for levelling the score.

Scipio was given consular *imperium* (the first person to have received it without having first been a consul) and a force of 10,000 men with which he landed in Spain, bringing the total forces there up to 28,000 infantry and 3,000 cavalry. From the port of Emporiae he moved down the east coast to Tarraco (Tarragona) where he set up his headquarters. He knew that he was opposed by no less than three Carthaginian armies, under Mago, Hasdrubal Gisgo and Hasdrubal Barca (Hannibal's brother) respectively. He also knew that they were a considerable distance away in the interior and that they were separated from each other, but he could not afford to attack any one of them for fear that they would unite against him and outnumber him. Instead he adopted a brilliant strategy, leaving the enemy forces well alone and making his attack against their largest base and most important port and arsenal, New Carthage (Cartagena), around 300 miles (480 kilometres) to the south of Tarraco. He was aware that none of the enemy armies was within ten days' march of his objective, which he besieged by land and sea and captured after one day's fighting. At a stroke this astute move deprived the Carthaginians of their stores, arsenal and workshops. In the aftermath, Scipio assembled all the prisoners and set free those who were citizens of New Carthage after restoring their property to them, while the Spanish hostages were released and sent to their homes without ransom. This was superb diplomacy. It won over many new allies for the Romans, including three of the most powerful Spanish chieftains and many tribes which followed in their wake.

While Scipio was enjoying the sight of Spanish recruits flocking to his flag, Hasdrubal Barca was bitterly aware of the shift away from the Carthaginian cause. About eight years previously he had been ordered by the Carthaginian senate to assemble a force and march to Italy with reinforcements for his brother Hannibal.[1] He was subsequently compelled repeatedly to postpone the journey as a result of the efforts of Publius and Gnaeus Scipio. After both of them were killed in 211, the young Publius Scipio (Africanus to be) was given the command. His capture of New Carthage set Hasdrubal's programme back once again. Hasdrubal became desperate and decided that he must engage the Romans once more – and as soon as possible – in order to prevent the Spanish drift to the Romans from turning into a mass migration. His haste to battle it out suited Scipio well. He, too, wanted a fight before Hasdrubal was joined by the other Carthaginian armies. However, as a precaution against this eventuality Scipio had increased the size of his force before he left Tarraco by laying up his fleet and incorporating the crews into his army. The fleet was no longer required in view of the Roman mastery of the seas.

Hasdrubal had taken up a position near Baecula (?Bailén), which was guarded by cavalry outposts. According to Livy (but not mentioned by Polybius), when Scipio arrived, his vanguard immediately attacked the enemy outposts and drove them back into their camp before even giving a thought to choosing their own camp site.[2] During that night, Hasdrubal withdrew to the top of a nearby hill on which he took up a defensive position. Scipio then set up camp somewhere in the vicinity (not defined in the chronicles).

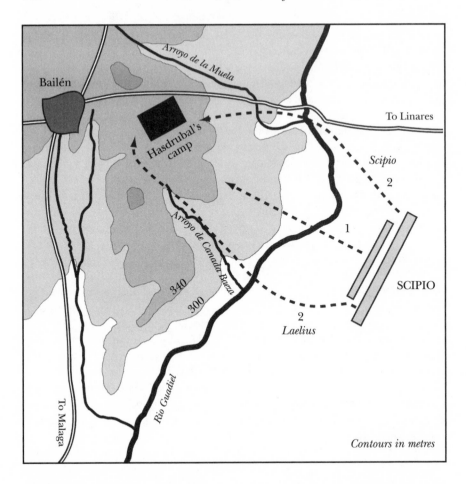

Battle of Baecula

There are two accounts of the battle, by Polybius[3] and Livy,[4] but neither reports the strengths of the opposing armies. An estimate by Scullard puts Hasdrubal's numbers at around 25,000, compared to the Roman strength of between 35,000–45,000.[5] A Roman superiority occasions no surprise in view of the huge Spanish drift in their support from Carthage to Rome. Scullard also gives a reconstruction of the probable battle site, which features in the statements below.

Hasdrubal's chosen position was on the summit of a flat-topped hill. The plateau at the top was large enough to accommodate an army camp and to permit the deployment of a force. At the front and sides the rim of the plateau fell away sharply in a steep and rocky drop. Part way down the slope there was a projecting ledge, like a step, which again terminated in a rocky drop to the bottom. Both Polybius and Livy say that the plateau was protected in the rear by a river.[6] However, this has given rise to some uncertainty. There is no such obvious feature in the site that historians have selected as the likely place of the battle. The nearest river in that direction, the Rio del Rumblar, is at a distance of several kilometres and on the other side of the town.

When Scipio first surveyed the enemy's position, it gave him food for thought. It was undoubtedly a superb defensive site which would present him with difficulties. He waited for two days, pondering the problem, and then felt obliged to act without further delay in case Hasdrubal Gisgo and Mago appeared with their armies, a prime consideration in his mind. Scipio's first act was to send detachments to block up two loopholes. One was a narrow passage though which a river ran; the other was a track which led across the slopes of the hill from the town to the open countryside beyond.[7] The obvious intent was to prevent reinforcements reaching Hasdrubal by these routes. At the same time, however, the blocks would also seal up potential routes for escape by enemy fugitives. Scipio's overall objective at this time was to abort the threat to Rome by eliminating Hasdrubal himself, if possible, or at least destroying the bulk of his forces. After blocking these loopholes, he drew his men up at the bottom of the hill and sent forward his light troops and a picked force of infantry in a frontal assault on the slopes. Hasdrubal's first line of defence was on the lower ledge or platform where he had posted some of his light-armed troops. It was a tough climb for the Romans in the face of all manner of missiles hurled down on them from above. The only missiles available to the Romans were stones in abundance, which were flung at the enemy to good effect. Eventually they dislodged their opponents, who were unaccustomed to close combat and were either slaughtered or driven back up to join their colleagues on the rim of the plateau itself, followed by the Romans. Scipio then sent up the rest of his light troops to consolidate the gain. When Hasdrubal saw that his men were giving way, he led out more troops to reinforce them.

Meanwhile, Scipio divided his infantry into two halves and took charge of one half himself, giving the other half to Laelius. Using a gully, known today as the Arroyo de la Muela, he worked his way to the right around the base of the hill until he found a place suitable for an ascent to the top. Laelius had been instructed to do the same thing around the left side of the hill where the reconstruction shows a similar gully, the Arroyo de Cañada Baeza. When the two groups surmounted the crest, Scipio's was the first to attack on the enemy's left flank followed by Laelius on the other side. At that time Hasdrubal was still in the process of leading his troops out of his camp. With total confidence in the security and defensive strength of his position, he was taken completely off guard. Unable to redeploy his troops in time to meet the threat on both wings, his men were butchered. But they were only a part of his total strength. Those that survived turned to flight together with the others who had never taken part in the battle. When Hasdrubal saw the chaos, he decided not to fight it out but managed to escape, taking his money and elephants with him and collecting as many scattered fugitives as he could find. Scipio's early thoughtfulness in closing two of the escape routes seems to have paid dividends; both Polybius and Livy put the number of captured fugitives at 12,000. But there must also have been many killed, particularly among Hasdrubal's light troops. Polybius gives no figure but Livy quotes the number as 8,000. If this is correct, Hasdrubal would have lost around three-quarters of his men. Scipio deemed it wiser not to pursue the fugitives, ever mindful as he was of the threat from Mago and the other Hasdrubal, son of Gisgo.

Scipio had gained a great tactical victory but his overall strategy was not fulfilled. Hasdrubal escaped and survived to march to Italy, but at least his supporters had been markedly reduced.

Thematic Appraisal

The battle was fought on a strong defensive site of Hasdrubal's own choosing. He lost it primarily through his over-confidence in the security of his position. If he had led out all his men and had deployed them properly, the course of the battle might have been very different, particularly if he had caught the Romans near the end of their climb.

It was Scipio's first major battle as commander, in which he employed unusual tactics. In a preliminary frontal assault he sacrificed his light troops to lure the enemy out to the front of the plateau. His main thrusts were launched against the enemy wings by dividing his force and executing large concealed turning movements to right and left respectively. The enemy was taken completely by surprise. It could have been prevented if Hasdrubal had been less complacent and had provided a modicum of surveillance.

Notes

1   Livy, 23.27.9–11.
2   Livy, 27.18.1–3.
3   Polybius, 10.38.6–40.1.
4   Livy, 27.18–19.2.
5   H. H. Scullard, *Scipio Africanus: Soldier & Politician*, Bristol, Thames & Hudson, 1970, chapter 3.
6   Polybius, 10.38.8; Livy, 27.18.5.
7   Livy, 27.18.10.

The Metaurus (207)

When Hannibal set out in 218 to invade northern Italy, he left his brother Hasdrubal Barca in command of the Carthaginian forces in Spain. In 216, or possibly a year later, Hasdrubal received instructions from Carthage to march to Italy and to reinforce his brother. Once this news became public many of the recalcitrant Spanish tribes openly shifted their allegiance to Rome. According to Livy, Hasdrubal remonstrated with the Carthaginian senate, emphasising the damage that had been caused to their interests by the mere knowledge of his departure and pointing out that there was no adequate commander or force that he could leave in his place.[1] He was proved to be right when the Roman commanders, Publius and Gnaeus Scipio (father and uncle of Africanus), joined forces in an attempt to remove the threat to Rome and defeated Hasdrubal in a battle near Ibera in 215. In the ensuing years Hasdrubal made repeated plans to get away, but one after another they had to be postponed for similar reasons. In 210 the Senate decided to step up its operations in Spain but it was unable to find a suitable and willing candidate for the command. The only man who offered his services was P. Cornelius Scipio (later Africanus) who was only twenty-five or twenty-six years old and had never held a senior appointment. But he was popular with the people and had a suitable family background. Exceptionally he was appointed.

In the spring of 209 Scipio bypassed the three Carthaginian armies in Spain and boldly besieged and captured their vital port, base and arsenal of New Carthage (Cartagena). The material damage inflicted on the Carthaginian cause was immense, but of almost greater moment was Scipio's leniency toward the Spanish. The African prisoners were sold into slavery but the Spanish were sent home without ransom provided they would undertake not to fight him again. It was a masterly piece of diplomacy, which triggered a swing of Spanish support and an increasing volume of desertions to the Romans. No less than three important Spanish chieftains switched their allegiance and a number of other tribes followed suit. This was another set-back for Hasdrubal's planned expedition to Italy because he felt compelled to stay and attempt to stem the ebb tide of desertions. His efforts led to the battle of Baecula (p. 186), in which he was defeated. A few days after the battle Hasdrubal, son of Gisgo, and Mago arrived with their forces, too late to affect the outcome. Between them they decided that if Hasdrubal Barca was ever to go to Italy, he should depart immediately.

Hasdrubal wintered in Gaul and crossed the Alps in the spring of 207. Experiencing none of the difficulties that Hannibal had encountered, his brother arrived in the Po valley earlier than expected. Livy reports that 8,000 Ligures had been recruited for his army and they may have joined him at this point.[2] In Rome, meanwhile, Gaius Claudius Nero and Marcus Livius Salinator had been elected as the two consuls for the year. In the past there had been serious differences between the two men which did not augur well. Eventually they were persuaded to bury the hatchet and to work in harmony for the good of the country. Nero was allotted the south with the task of opposing Hannibal, while Livius was to operate against Hasdrubal in the north. Hasdrubal began his activities with a fruitless siege of Placentia in the hope of impressing the Gauls. From there he proceeded south-eastwards, ultimately reaching Sena Gallica (Senigallia). After abandoning the siege of Placentia he sent off four Gallic and two Numidian horsemen bearing a letter to Hannibal. It never reached its destination. The horsemen rode the length of Italy but finally mistook the route to Metapontum and found themselves near Tarentum, where they fell into the hands of a Roman foraging party. They were taken before the propraetor and confessed to their errand under threat of torture. With the letter still sealed they were then taken under escort to the consul Nero. It transpired that Hasdrubal had told his brother in the letter that he would meet him in Umbria. The point has been raised as to why the letter had not been written in code?[3] Such doubts offer some support for the suggestion that the letter might have been intended to fall into Roman hands and to deceive them with regard to Hasdrubal's intended route.[4] Against this, Livy does mention Hasdrubal's concern that his letter might have been intercepted.[5] The truth will never be known.

Nero decided that the situation warranted urgent and unconventional methods. This was not the time to adhere to the usual practice whereby the consuls would each be confined to his own province. With commendable initiative he formulated a plan, sent the letter to the Senate, and informed them of his intentions.[6] Without waiting for a reply, he left his second-in-command to maintain the surveillance of Hannibal and make the camp appear to be fully manned, while he himself marched out during the night with 6,000 selected infantry and 1,000 cavalry. To maintain the deception he headed southwards until he was well clear of the area before turning toward his intended destination in the north. Only then did he tell his men the true purpose of the march. He had previously sent messengers ahead along his proposed route with instructions to arrange for provisions to be left by the road and horses and mules to be supplied for the transport of those who were in need. They marched day and night, and it is said that they covered the distance of approximately 250 miles to Sena Gallica in seven days. It was here that Nero's colleague Livius was encamped, reinforced by the praetor Porcius Licinus from Gaul, whose army however was below par in numbers. Hasdrubal had already reached the area and was encamped about 500 yards (450 metres) away. When Nero approached, he sent messengers to Livius to inform him of his arrival and discuss the details of their junction. As agreed, he waited until it was dark before silently entering the consul's camp, in which the two forces doubled up together. At a conference next morning Nero strongly resisted any suggestion that his men should rest and insisted that they should take advantage of the hard-gained element of surprise by an immediate attack.

Hasdrubal's army was already drawn up in front of his camp but he had noticed some unusual signs which had made him suspicious that all was not as it had been. His suspicions were confirmed when he heard that the trumpet-call had been sounded twice in the consul's camp. Without any doubt there were two consuls in residence. He hurriedly withdrew his men and marched them off during the night toward the Metaurus with the intention of putting the river between himself and the Romans, but he was dogged by fate. He had with him two local guides, both of whom managed independently to escape.[7] Floundering about in the darkness and following the many twists in the river without the guides, Hasdrubal failed to find a suitable place to cross the river. Even daylight did not solve his problem before Nero appeared with the cavalry, followed shortly by the praetor with the light troops. They harassed him until Livius appeared with the heavy infantry in battle order. Hasdrubal had no alternative but to abandon the camp which he had started to set up and to stand and fight.

Battle of the Metaurus

Livy provides the only full account of the battle and the events leading up to it.[8] Polybius' account exists as a fragment which deals briefly with the battle but contains one or two divergences from Livy,[9] while Appian's version is telegraphic and adds nothing of use.[10] None of these sources gives the strength of the armies. There is a general consensus that Hasdrubal's force may have been in the region of 30,000 (of which the Gauls proved to be useless). The Romans must have topped that figure with Salinator's two legions and the equivalent in auxiliaries, the smaller force of Porcius Licinus, and Nero's picked 7,000 men. Roman superiority is supported in Nero's alleged address to his troops in which he said that the forces in the north were adequate to deal with Hasdrubal and that the purpose of their venture was to turn the probability into a certainty.[11]

The following account of the battle is based on Livy; its actual site near

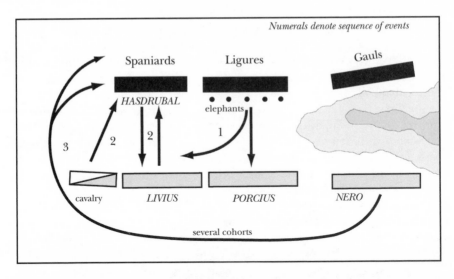

Numerals denote sequence of events

Spaniards   Ligures   Gauls

HASDRUBAL

elephants

cavalry   LIVIUS   PORCIUS   NERO

several cohorts

the Metaurus remains uncertain. Hasdrubal made his line deep but narrow. In the centre he posted the Ligurians (who are not mentioned by Polybius) with the ten elephants in front, and close to them on their right were his veteran Spaniards. The Gallic contingent was posted on the left wing on rough ground with a hill in front of them. A gap almost certainly separated them from the main force. As a result, Hasdrubal's army was virtually divided into two parts: a deep but narrow formation with the Ligurians on the left and the Spaniards close to them on the right, separated from a detached Gallic left wing. Under the circumstances, the term 'centre' is slightly misleading. On the Roman side, Livius stationed himself on the left wing facing the Spaniards, while Porcius opposed the Ligurians. Nero was apart, on the right wing, opposing the Gauls but with a hill or crag between them which prevented either side from catching a glimpse of the other.

The action seems to have been started almost simultaneously along the narrow front occupied by the Ligurians and the Spaniards. In the 'centre' the Ligurians advanced, forcing the elephants to charge forward. They disrupted the opposing Romans and forced the standards back before running amok. Tormented with missiles, they got out of control and did as much damage to both sides, as if they did not know to which they belonged, as Livy puts it. At about the same time the Spaniards became locked in a fierce struggle with Livius and his men. Meanwhile, Nero and the opposing Gauls were idle. Nero had tried to get at the enemy whom he knew to be on the other side of the hill although out of sight, but his attempts were repeatedly foiled by the terrain. Frustrated, he began to wonder why he and his men had come so far to achieve nothing. With commendable initiative he took several cohorts from his force and led them round behind the Roman position to attack the Spaniards in the flank and, after surrounding them, in the rear. They were cut to pieces.[12] Up till then the battle on that wing had been contested ferociously with the upshot hanging in the balance. Nero had arrived in the nick of time. On the Gallic wing, in contrast, there was little fighting. Many of the Gauls had deserted; others were found asleep or in a drunken haze after the battle and were slaughtered.

Livy and Polybius agree that the elephants were stationed initially in front of the Ligurians, but Polybius later says that they were entangled between the Spaniards and the Romans at the time of Nero's attack. This may not be inconsistent. When the elephants were forced into the space between the armies and ran amok, they probably stampeded along the narrow gap in an effort to escape. In the end, six of them were killed with or by their mahouts; the other four were later captured alone.

When Hasdrubal realised that the day was lost, he died a soldier's death by charging straight into the Roman midst. On the next day Nero and his force started their march back to the south, arriving at their camp allegedly on the sixth day, more quickly even than on the outward journey. With them they carried the head of Hasdrubal, which was flung on the ground in front of Hannibal's outposts.[13] It was Hannibal's first intimation of any unusual events and the ultimate realisation that he could achieve nothing more in Italy. It also bears testimony to the effectiveness of Nero's various dissimulations and secrecy and indeed of the whole plan, of which he was the sole architect.

Livy puts the Carthaginian dead at an astonishingly fanciful 57,000, more than Hasdrubal's total force, against Roman losses of 8,000 killed. But then he regards the Roman victory through patriotic eyes when he claims that it avenged the disaster at Cannae. Polybius restores balance to the picture with the reasonable figure of 10,000 enemy killed against 2,000 Roman dead.

The battle on the Metaurus was the turning point in Hannibal's war in Italy. With no further possibility of any reinforcement, he was impotent. Although he hung on in the south for another four years until he was recalled to Africa, he achieved nothing of note.

Thematic Appraisal

The keyword is 'initiative'. The most noteworthy events surround the initiative displayed by the consul Nero both in the run up to the encounter and in the battle itself. In response to Hasdrubal's intercepted letter to Hannibal,[3] Nero's initiative was manifested in his forced march up the length of Italy to reinforce his consular colleague against Hasdrubal in the north. By means of various ruses, it was carried out in complete secrecy and remained unknown to Hannibal throughout and unknown to Hasdrubal until it was too late for him to escape. The Senate was informed of the plan, which involved a breach of accepted practice, but Nero could not afford to wait for official sanction.[6]

When Hasdrubal became suspicious, he withdrew from a confrontation but lost his way as a result of the desertion of his guides and was brought to battle.[7] There is no evidence that the scouts were doing more than acting in their own interests. Their action was probably a chance piece of good fortune for the Romans.

The outcome of the battle was in the balance until Nero took some cohorts from his uninvolved wing and led them behind the Roman centre to attack Hasdrubal's Spaniards on the opposite wing in the flank and rear.[12] This further initiative on Nero's part turned the course of the battle and sealed Hasdrubal's fate.

Dissimulation in Nero's camp opposing Hannibal in the south kept him in ignorance of these events until Hasdrubal's head was delivered to him.[13]

Notes

1   Livy, 23.27.9–11.
2   Livy, 27.39.2.
3   L. Cottrell, *Enemy of Rome*, London, Evans Brothers, 1960, p. 181.
4   J. F. Lazenby, *Hannibal's War*, Warminster, Aris & Phillips, 1978, pp. 183–4.
5   Livy, 27.47.8.
6   Livy, 27.43.5–7.
7   Livy, 27.47.9.
8   Livy, 27.43, 45–7 (background); 27.48–9 (battle).
9   Polybius, 11.1–3.
10   Appian, *Hannibalic War*, 52.
11   Livy, 27.45.1–5.
12   Livy, 27.48.12–15.
13   Livy, 27.51.11.

Ilipa (206)

T he general background to events in Spain down to the battle of
Baecula has already been described under that battle (p. 186).
Following the defeat of Hasdrubal Barca in the fight, he at last
departed on his way to take reinforcements to Hannibal in Italy. The move
had been forcibly postponed so often that it eventually took place eight or
nine years after it was ordered by the Carthaginian senate. Hasdrubal Gisgo
and Mago arrived just after the battle and had a conference with Hasdrubal
Barca. All were agreed that the latter should set out for Italy, then or never.
After that the three of them parted and went their separate ways, Hasdrubal
Gisgo and Mago on recruitment campaigns. Hasdrubal retired into the
remoteness of the Atlantic coastal regions, the only area which had been
unaffected by the swing of allegiance to Rome, and Mago went to the
Balearic Islands to raise auxiliaries. Apart from an illness suffered by Scipio,
the only real threat to the Romans was posed by the arrival of a fresh army
from Carthage under a general Hanno, who joined Mago after his return to
the mainland. Scipio himself was unwilling to move against Mago and
Hanno for fear of exposing his rear to Hasdrubal Gisgo. Instead, he sent his
lieutenant Silanus with 10,000 foot and 500 horse to deal with the emer-
gency. Silanus moved so fast in spite of the rugged nature of the country that
he took the Carthaginians by surprise and utterly defeated them. Mago fled
with the cavalry and a few infantrymen while Hanno was captured and sent
to Rome. In the meantime Scipio confined his activities to besieging various
towns and bringing more tribes over to the Roman side. In the spring of 206
Hasdrubal Gisgo and Mago were emboldened by their numbers and they
decided to risk a last major battle with Scipio. With a large army they moved
to Ilipa (Alcala del Rio, which Livy calls Silpia) near modern Seville. Scipio
marched south from his base at Tarraco to confront them. When he heard
about the size of their army, Scipio deemed that his legions alone were
insufficient to allow him to risk battle with such large enemy numbers and
that he would have to recruit some Spanish auxiliaries, if only to impress the
enemy. On the other hand, he did not want too many in view of his distrust
of them after the part that they played in the disastrous defeat and death of

his father and uncle. Accordingly he sent one of his officers to collect some promised troops, amounting to 3,000 foot and 500 horse, while he himself gathered some more en route. These brought his total numbers up to 45,000.

Battle of Ilipa

There are two accounts of the battle, by Polybius[1] and Livy[2] respectively, but as Polybius was one of Livy's sources, similarities occasion no surprise. As Walsh says in reference to the war-histories of this period, Livy's 'divergences from Polybius are not numerous'.[3] One small one is to be found in the figures for Hasdrubal's strength at Ilipa. Polybius gives it as about 70,000 infantry, 4,000 horse, and 32 elephants. Livy puts a considerably lower figure of 50,000 on the Carthaginian infantry, but he does add that some writers give the number as 70,000. Either way the Romans with their 45,000 men were outnumbered, perhaps to a considerable extent.

Hasdrubal encamped just under some hills near the town of Ilipa with a clear level space in front. When Scipio arrived in the area, he camped on some low hills opposite the enemy. While he was setting up camp, Mago and Masinissa descended on the Romans with most of their cavalry. They were convinced that they would catch their enemy off guard but, with his customary foresight, Scipio had anticipated such an event and had stationed his cavalry under a hill and out of sight. After a brisk encounter the enemy got the worst of it and withdrew.[4] (Livy builds this skirmish up into a proper cavalry battle). After a few days of light skirmishing between the camps, events developed into a pattern. Scipio had decided that when it came to the battle he would employ the same tactics which had been so successful at Baecula by launching his offensive against the enemy wings. Until that moment he contrived to deceive the enemy into expecting a frontal attack. In the pattern which was emerging Hasdrubal was coming out at a leisurely hour with all his forces and was lining them up in front of his rampart with his veteran Africans in the centre and his auxiliaries on the wings with the elephants in front of them. Scipio responded later in the day, perhaps deliberately too late for the enemy to think of starting a battle. In his line up he opposed the Africans with his legions in the centre and placed the Spanish auxiliaries on the wings. Both sides eyed each other for hours but neither side made a move to engage. In the evening Hasdrubal retired, followed later by Scipio. The same procedures were repeated for several days in succession during which they became an established routine.[5] When Scipio considered that it had become ingrained in the enemy's mind, he decided to engage on the following day.

On that day Scipio changed everything to the opposite. The troops were roused early and told to have a good meal and then fall in outside the camp.

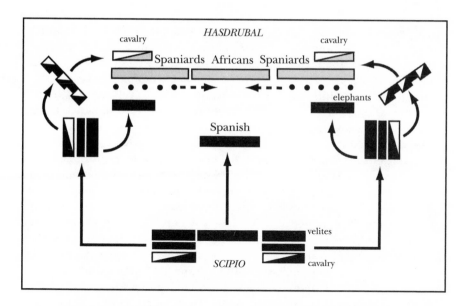

The cavalry and light troops were then sent out to harass the enemy camp and lure them out. At sunrise Scipio himself led the infantry onto the middle of the plain where he drew them up in an order which was the exact converse to that to which Hasdrubal had become accustomed. The Spaniards were placed in the centre and the legions on both wings. Among other considerations, in this ingenious way Scipio ensured that his possibly untrustworthy Spanish troops would have no opportunity to desert and join the enemy's Spaniards. Meanwhile Hasdrubal, taken completely off guard, was forced to line up his hungry men in their usual formation. Whether or not he had noticed Scipio's changed deployment, he himself could not afford to alter his deployment without risking a disaster at the hands of the enemy's cavalry while he was effecting the manoeuvre. Instead he was forced to send out his own light-armed troops and cavalry, which skirmished intermittently with the enemy for some hours. During this period the infantry were just standing, and the Carthaginians who had been forced to line up in a hurry began to suffer from hunger and thirst. When Scipio decided that this ordeal had lasted long enough, his skirmishers were recalled and were withdrawn through the infantry lines, after which they were divided and posted on the wings behind the infantry with the *velites* in front of the horse.[6]

In the next phase, Scipio advanced his whole force to a distance of a little less than half a mile (about 700 metres) in front of the enemy. The Spanish troops were then ordered to continue their advance at a slow pace while the wings were put through a series of complex manoeuvres in which the movements to right or left of one wing were mirrored by movements to left or right of the other wing. The object of these movements was first to extend the distance between the wings until each was opposite the corresponding enemy wing by marching the wings outwards in column, and then to reduce the distance from the enemy by wheeling the right wing to the left and the left to the right and advancing them *rapidly* in column. They were then brought into battle line, the cohorts wheeling successively inwards to face the enemy wing while the cavalry and light troops wheeled outwards to out-flank the enemy line (see the battle plan). During the rapid advance of the infantry, the Spanish auxiliaries continued their slow advance to a position in which they threatened and 'fixed' the enemy centre by refusing contact.[7]

The battle developed entirely on the wings, as Scipio had intended, and from the start the masterly nature and wisdom of his plan was evident. The well trained and disciplined legions were pitted against the Spanish irregulars, mostly raw recruits. The enemy's crack infantry, on the other hand, stood impotently in the centre, inactivated by Scipio's tactics. If they turned to assist their wings, they would have presented their flanks to the Spanish auxiliaries. Alternatively, if they advanced to attack the Spaniards, they would have been open to attacks from the legionaries on both flanks. The first casualties were Hasdrubal's elephants which had been posted in front of the wings. Hit by missiles from the cavalry and *velites*, they became wild and created much damage to friend and foe alike. According to Livy they were forced back to the centre, where there were more friends than foe for them to disrupt. The Carthaginian wings made a brave stand initially but they soon began to tire and retreat. Their resistance was sapped by the effects of the heat, hunger and thirst which they had endured for many hours.[8] It was not long before retreat gave way to rout as they took to their heels and fled back to their camp. They were saved from a further attack by a sudden torrential downpour just as the Romans were approaching their rampart. This put any thoughts of pursuit out of the minds of the Romans, who turned and sought refuge in their own camp.[9]

Polybius account breaks off with the storm but Livy recounts the aftermath. Some of the Carthaginian allies wasted no time in deserting, but the pursuit of Hasdrubal and his remaining followers was resumed swiftly next day. Scipio's cavalry and light troops caught up with them and harassed them continually, holding them up until Scipio arrived with the legions. A bloodbath ensued from which Hasdrubal escaped with only about 6,000 men. Neither Polybius nor Livy gives any casualty figures for the battle itself.

The battle resulted in the withdrawal of all Carthaginians from Spain. Scipio returned to Italy in the following year.

Thematic Content

1. Scipio's anticipation of and preparation against a cavalry attack while the Romans were setting up camp.[4]

2.   The establishment of a routine – a perfect example in which everything was changed on the day of the battle.[5]

3.   The ingenuity of the change in the line-up, resulting in the legions opposing raw recruits while the Spaniards 'fixed' the veterans in the centre.[6]

4.   The additional bonus arising from putting the untrustworthy Spaniards in the centre, from which they would be unable to desert.

5.   The complex manoeuvres for advancing the wings rapidly before the enemy could respond.[7]

6.   The Roman attack directed entirely at the enemy wings. Whereas this was necessitated by the terrain at Baecula, the considerations at Ilipa were more subtle.

7.   The effects of enforced thirst and hunger on the enemy.[8]

8.   The storm which prevented the Romans from seizing the enemy camp and instituting an immediate pursuit.[9]

Notes

1   Polybius, 11.20–24.
2   Livy, 28.12.13–15.
3   P. G. Walsh, *Livy*, New Surveys in the Classics, No. 8, Oxford, Oxford University Press, 1974, p. 19, note 1.
4   Polybius, 11.21; Livy, 28.13.6–10.
5   Polybius, 11.22.1–3; Livy, 28.14.1–7.
6   Polybius, 11.22.7–9.
7   Polybius, 11.22.11–23.
8   Polybius, 11.24.5–6; Livy, 28.15.2–4.
9   Polybius, 11.24.8–9; Livy, 28.15.11.

Zama (202)

A fter completing the subjugation of Spain, Scipio returned to Italy early in 205. Before he left Spain he had been engaged in a meeting with Masinissa which was of outstanding importance and was ultimately a decisive factor in events to come. Masinissa thought highly of Scipio and was grateful to him for the return of his nephew who had been captured at Baecula – another piece of excellent diplomacy.[1] Masinissa had decided to shift his allegiance to the Romans, an invaluable move to which he steadfastly adhered for the rest of his life.

On his return to Rome, Scipio met with rapturous acclaim by the people but only jealousy, criticism and carping on the part of the generals, notably Fabius Maximus. Scipio was intent on carrying the war into Africa and luring Hannibal back to destruction in his own country, but his application for a commission to this effect was turned down, partly on grounds of cost. He was elected consul with Sicily as his province and with a loophole permission to cross to Africa if he deemed it to be beneficial to the State. But he was given no help other than the two legions in Sicily which had been formed from the survivors of Cannae and who were regarded unfairly as being in some disgrace. It took him a year to train this force into shape.

Early in 204 he embarked his legions together with any available volunteers and crossed to Africa where he landed near Utica. He proceeded to besiege the town, intending to use it as a base. In the meantime Hasdrubal and Syphax had combined to raise an army. Syphax, king of the Masaesulii in Numidia, had been an ally of Rome and had repeated his assurances of support to Scipio. Unfortunately for the Romans, he had subsequently married Sophonisba, a Numidian queen who was also the daughter of Hasdrubal, son of Gisgo. Not surprisingly, Syphax had felt obliged to change his allegiance. When he and his brother-in-law appeared in the distance as Scipio was besieging Utica, Scipio withdrew to the tip of the promontory and encamped at what became known as Castra Cornelia. When Hasdrubal and Syphax set up their separate camps close to each other at the base of the promontory, Scipio was virtually cornered and foraging was nigh impossible. His solution to the problem was an incendiary attack on both enemy camps simultaneously. An offer of peace terms enabled him to introduce centurions disguised as servants into his retinue every time he visited the camps for negotiations, when every possible detail was noted. When the talks were suddenly broken off by Scipio on account of some disagreement, he considered himself free to attack. The flames were terrifying and nearly all-consuming. Both Hasdrubal and Syphax escaped, fleeing with all of those who had managed to save themselves – 500 horse and about 2,000 foot.[2]

In spite of their huge losses both Hasdrubal and Syphax set about raising fresh forces. Four thousand Celtiberians who had been expected from Spain arrived at this opportune time. Within a month the two leaders had assembled a joint force of about 30,000 men. They had assembled on the Great Plains of the Bagradas valley when Scipio suddenly appeared with a part of his force, having left the rest to continue the siege of Utica. Anticipating that Hannibal might be recalled from Italy in the very near future, Scipio was anxious to dispose of Hasdrubal and Syphax before they could unite. In an engagement on the Great Plains he routed both their wings with a single cavalry charge on each side, leaving the redoubtable Celtiberians isolated in the centre. They were attacked by the legionaries both frontally and in both flanks and were cut to pieces, but their resistance allowed both Hasdrubal and Syphax time to escape. Syphax was pursued by Masinissa and Laelius to his capital Cirta (Constantine), where he was defeated, taken prisoner, and ultimately sent to Rome. Following these defeats the Carthaginians sued for peace, and while negotiations were in progress Hannibal reluctantly left Italy after his fifteen-year sojourn in the country. It was also around this time and when the peace had just been ratified that a violation of the truce occurred. It was soon to be compounded with a piece of frank treachery when a ship bringing the Roman ambassadors back to their camp from Carthage was attacked by three Carthaginian vessels, ensuring that the war was resumed.

The key to the subsequent movements of the principal participants seems to lie in the activities of Masinissa. Scipio was fully aware that his weakest limb was his cavalry, and he did not dare to contemplate the idea of engaging Hannibal in battle until he had strengthened that arm of his force. Masinissa had repaired to Numidia to re-establish himself in his country, from which he had been evicted by Syphax, but also and at the request of Scipio to collect as large a force of Numidian cavalry as possible. Scipio moved west into Numidia to meet up with him. On the other side, Hannibal, after landing in Africa, moved to Hadrumentum and from there to the vicinity of Zama, where he encamped in the hope that he might be able to prevent the union of Scipio and Masinissa. While he was near Zama, he sent three spies to investigate the Roman camp, probably with the prime object of finding out if Masinissa had arrived.[3] When they were caught in the act, they were treated with courtesy and were given a conducted tour. It was

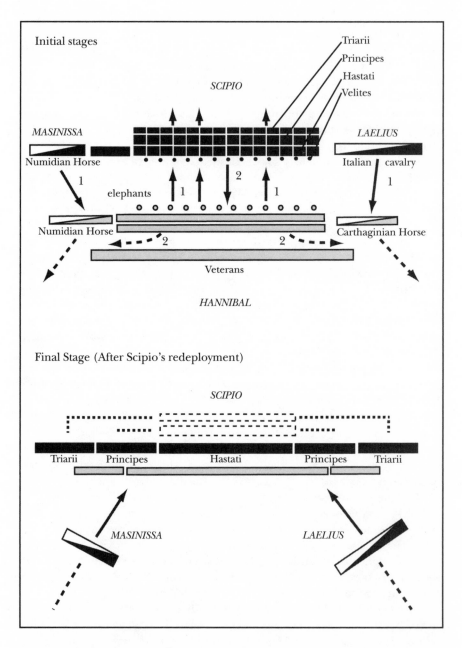

Initial stages

Triarii
Principes
Hastati
Velites

SCIPIO

MASINISSA					*LAELIUS*

Numidian Horse					Italian cavalry

1

elephants	1		2	1			1

2

Numidian Horse				Carthaginian Horse

2					2

Veterans

HANNIBAL

Final Stage (After Scipio's redeployment)

SCIPIO

Triarii	Principes		Hastati		Principes	Triarii

MASINISSA				*LAELIUS*

on the following day, according to Polybius, that Masinissa arrived with 6,000 foot and 4,000 horse.[4] After his spies had reported, Hannibal felt a desire to meet Scipio in person and parley with him, and he sent a messenger to ask for an interview. Soon afterwards Scipio moved to a place called Naragarra [?Sidi Youssef) where he encamped on a hill with a supply of water nearby.

From here he sent a message to Hannibal informing him that he was prepared to grant his request for an interview. Hannibal arrived with his whole army, and the parley took place. As no reconciliation resulted, Hannibal encamped on a neighbouring hill preparatory to a battle on the morrow. Thus, Scipio had neatly chosen the site of the battle. In the process he had also ensured that his opponent had no alternative but to encamp on a hill which was remote from any water.[5]

Battle of Zama

The battle took place on level ground in the space between the two hills. The principal sources for the battle are the accounts by Polybius[6] and Livy[7], but neither of these gives any overall figures. Appian[8] is the only one of the sources who gives a figure for the Carthaginian complement, which he puts at a total of 50,000 men and 80 elephants. His figures for the Romans amount to 29,000 foot and 6,100 horse in total. The few itemised figures given by Polybius suggest that Appian's Carthaginian total of 50,000 is probably too high but that they nevertheless outnumbered the Romans.

Hannibal placed his 80 elephants in front of his whole force in the hope that they would impair the Roman morale. Behind them he lined up his mercenaries, a mixture of infantry and light troops such as archers and slingers from many nations, numbering about 12,000. Behind these, in his second line, he placed the Libyans and Carthaginians. The third line consisted of his experienced veterans who had fought with him in Italy, and these he stationed well behind the rest at a distance of more than a stade (around 200 metres). The cavalry were placed on the wings with the Numidian allies on the left and the Carthaginian horse covering the right flank. Scipio drew up his men in the usual three lines but with an unusual difference. The *hastati* in the first rank were deployed in the normal way with gaps between the maniples. In the second rank, however, the gaps between the *principes* were aligned behind the gaps in the first rank instead of being offset in the usual chequerboard (*quincunx*) arrangement. As the gaps between the *triarii* in the third row were placed as usual in line with the gaps in the first row, the configuration left corridors between the maniples as escape routes for elephants.[9] The intervals in the first row were then filled with *velites*, who were ordered to retire to the rear through the corridors or to move aside through the spaces between the lines. Scipio posted Laelius with the Italian horse on the left wing; on the right were the Numidian infantry and then Masinissa with his Numidian cavalry on the extreme right.

The action had begun with some skirmishing between the Numidian cavalry of the two sides when Hannibal ordered a charge by the elephants. Scipio countered this by telling his trumpeters and buglers to make as much noise as they could. The resulting cacophony had the desired effect. Some of the elephants on the left wing turned back against their own Numidian cavalry and either killed or disrupted them as they were preparing to advance. Masinissa seized the opportunity and charged the enemy cavalry, driving them off the field and exposing the left wing of the infantry. The rest of the beasts fell on the unfortunate *velites* out in front and inflicted much damage on them. Some of the elephants in their terror found their way or were driven into the lanes between the maniples and managed to escape by one route or another. At this point Laelius availed himself of the disruption to charge the Carthaginian cavalry who took to flight. Both he and Masinissa pursued their respective quarries off the field, leaving the infantry lines of both sides facing each other in unprotected isolation.

The next phase of the battle was ushered in when the infantry lines of both sides slowly closed, with the exception of Hannibal's third line which remained stationary and kept its distance. In this engagement Roman superiority in arms and discipline readily showed itself, and the enemy's first line was pushed steadily back into their second line. Hannibal had ordered his men not to allow their lines to be disrupted by admitting the defeated into their ranks. In consequence, the Carthaginians and Libyans in the second line refused to offer any support to the mercenaries and pushed them off. The mercenaries were aggrieved by this lack of cooperation on the part of their own side and, feeling abandoned, began attacking and butchering the Carthaginians. Set on by the Romans as well as their own men, the Carthaginians developed a courage born of desperation with which they managed to throw the *hastati* into disorder and kill quite a number of them. This brought the *principes* to their assistance and the Carthaginians were butchered in large numbers. Any who escaped and sought refuge in the third line were again denied admittance and were repelled by levelled spears. Their only course was to retreat to open ground.

The final phase of the battle began with pools of blood and piles of corpses littering the ground and making any orderly progress almost impossible. The *hastati* gave up the attempt and, after abandoning their formation, contented themselves with pursuing any fugitives toward the wings. Scipio ordered that the wounded should be taken to the rear. He then recalled the *hastati* from their pursuit and ordered them to cross over the carnage and position themselves in close formation opposite the centre of Hannibal's veteran third line, which was still at some distance. The *principes* and *triarii* were then ordered to 'close up on both wings' and to 'advance over the dead' after which they 'found themselves in a line with the *hastati*'.[10] This is taken to mean that the whole force was reorganised into one line with the *hastati* in the centre, the *principes* divided on each side of the *hastati*, and the *triarii* divided between the two wings. In this way Scipio lengthened his line to equal or even overlap the enemy line.[11] The whole process was effected in the face of the enemy and yet without undue haste, presumably because Scipio was biding his time hopefully awaiting the return of Masinissa and Laelius with the cavalry.

When the opposing lines closed for the final count, they were approximately equal in numbers and determination.[12] The Carthaginians had the advantage of being fresh whereas the *hastati* and *principes* had already seen much action. Nevertheless, the outcome was in the balance until Masinissa and Laelius returned with the cavalry from the pursuit. Arriving at just the right moment, they fell upon the rear of the Carthaginian line. Many were slaughtered; few escaped. Hannibal himself rode away with a few others and did not draw rein until he reached Hadrumentum. According to Polybius, more than 1,500 Romans fell while the Carthaginian slain amounted to 20,000. Livy gives the same figures.

Thematic Summary

1   Background: Scipio's diplomatic return of Masinissa's captured nephew to his uncle. A factor which encouraged Masinisa in his shift of allegiance.[1]
2   Hannibal's spies in the Roman camp, probably to find out if Masinissa had rejoined Scipio.[3]
3   Scipio's 'choice' of a waterless camp site for Hannibal and of the battle site.[5]
4   Scipio's unusual deployment to deal with Hannibal's elephants.[9]
5   The refusal of the Carthaginian second line to help and accommodate their beleaguered first line, resulting in active hostilities between the two lines.
6   In the final phase, Scipio's redeployment into a single closed-up line to cover the enemy's line.[10, 11]
7   The timely return of the Roman cavalry from their pursuit to attack the enemy line in the rear.

Notes

1   Livy, 27.19.8–12.
2   Polybius, 14.3.7–5; Livy, 30.3.8–6.
3   Polybius, 15.5.4–7.
4   Polybius, 15.5.12–13.
5   Polybius, 15.6.2.
6   Polybius, 15.9–15.15.3.
7   Livy, 30.33–35.
8   Appian, *Punic Wars*, 40–41.45.
9   Polybius, 15.9.6–10.
10   Polybius, 15.14.4–6.
11   B. H. Liddell Hart, *Scipio Africanus: Greater than Napoleon*, London, Greenhill, 1992, p.184
12   Polybius, 15.14.6.

Cynoscephalae (197)

For more than two centuries after its foundation, traditionally in 509, the Roman Republic was not involved in any conflicts outside Italy. It was not until the onset of the First Punic War in 264 that the Romans had to transport an army across the waters and then only as far as Sicily. Her first expedition across the Adriatic did not take place until 229, when she became involved in a policing operation to curb the activities of Illyrian pirates against foreign shipping, including her own. This led to two brisk Illyrian Wars in the following ten years.

From 218 onwards Rome was totally involved with the crisis of the Second Punic War. She had uneasy suspicions about Philip V of Macedon and some of his dealings, but the crisis at home ensured that events across the Adriatic went largely unnoticed. It was not until after the catastrophic defeat of the Romans by Hannibal at Cannae in 216 that they were forced to take note when Philip offered to ally himself with Hannibal. He proposed that he should raid the Italian Adriatic seaboard in exchange for a stake on the eastern Adriatic seaboard after the war. At that time the Carthaginians needed no help, and nothing came of the plans. But at the same time nothing could have been more conducive to confirming Roman suspicions and laying the groundwork for future hostilities. The First Macedonian War (215–205) consisted of little more than actions on the part of Philip to enhance his control over the Greek states. The Romans were scarcely involved. The events which triggered their involvement – and ultimately the Second Macedonian War – arose from Philip's behaviour in the Aegean. Immediately after the Peace of Phoenice, which terminated the First War, Philip built a sizeable fleet and launched it in piratical expeditions against the Greek islands, seaboard and shipping. This enraged the Rhodians and others whose prosperity depended upon trade. But what really incensed the Greeks was the barbarous nature of Philip's actions, which included the enslavement of the entire populations of towns which he captured. In 202 the Rhodians declared war on Philip, and they were joined the following year by king Attalus of Pergamum, a friend of Rome. Although not involved at the start, Attalus began to wonder whether he would be the next victim.

He decided to make a preemptive strike, and in 201 the combined fleets of Rhodes and Pergamum brought Philip to battle off Chios. They defeated him in terms of losses but failed to curb his activities, and so they appealed to Rome where the memory of Philip's alliance with Hannibal still rankled. The thought of another embroilment so soon after the Second Punic War was distasteful to the Romans, who were unwilling to make a formal declaration of war. But they did send a stiff ultimatum to Philip. When this was predictably rejected, a preemptive attack on Philip was reluctantly sanctioned and in 200 a force crossed the Adriatic and established a base at Apollonia in Illyria late in the year. The following year saw only a couple of minor confrontations with Philip near the Macedonian border, and nothing significant was achieved.

The year 198 saw the arrival of the consul Flamininus. When he tried to gain access to Macedonia by the Aous (Vijose) valley, Philip blocked his passage in the fortified defile and held him up for several weeks before the Romans were enabled to turn it. The terrain was so unsuitable for pursuit that the enemy suffered minimal losses and withdrew to fight another day. It was not until the start of the following campaigning season that both Flamininus and Philip decided that it was time to end the struggle decisively. Both armies were somewhere in Thessaly but neither side knew the position of the other. Flamininus moved from his base at Elatia to Thebes and then northwards to camp about six miles from Pherae. While he was there, he heard that the king was at Larissa about twenty-five miles to the northwest. The king, hearing of the Roman position, marched down and camped about four miles from Pherae in a different direction. While they were in these positions both sides realised that the surrounding terrain was totally unsuitable for battle because of numerous trees, walls and gardens. Independently, both commanders decided to move to a more suitable area in the direction of Scotussa, and they marched for a couple of days without setting eyes on each other. Eventually the Romans pitched their camp at Thetidion (near Pharsalus) while Philip set up his on the banks of the river Onchestos, a few miles further to the north. Even at this point the two parties were uncertain of the position of the other. Unknown to them they were separated by a ridge of high ground known as Cynoscephalae (Dog's Heads, now Chalkodónion) and it was for the control of these heights that the battle was fought.

Battle of Cynoscephalae [1]

Livy says that the Macedonian army consisted of 16,000 heavy infantry, 6,000 peltasts, around 1,500 mixed mercenaries and 2,000 cavalry.[2] The Roman complement is unstated but it is said to have approximately equalled the enemy's number. Plutarch is in general agreement, putting the Roman total at a minimum of 26,000, which included their only allies in the form of 6,000 Aetolians. He adds that the Macedonian total was about the same.[3] The two armies were therefore well matched in numbers. Polybius gives no figures.

On the day after they had pitched their respective camps the weather was damp, dark and foggy. In spite of this Philip seized the initiative. He advanced with his whole army to the foot of the hills and sent out a force which managed to reach the summit of a pass between the peaks. There they left a strong outpost of infantry and cavalry, after which they set up camp at the base. The Romans, on the other hand, contented themselves with sending out a reconnaissance party of 1,000 light-armed troops and ten squadrons of cavalry. On ascending to the pass from the opposite side to the Macedonians, they were startled when they confronted the enemy at the top.[4] In the ensuing hostilities the Romans were getting the worst of it. They sent a messenger to their camp to ask for reinforcements, whereupon Flamininus sent out 2,000 foot and 500 horse. These turned the tide. The Macedonians fled to the summits and sent for help to the king, who sent out all the Thessalian and Macedonian cavalry and all those mercenaries who were not out foraging. Once again the tide was reversed and the Romans retreated down the slope. Flamininus then mobilised his whole army and, after drawing it up at the foot of the hills, he advanced with the left half while leaving his right half below. Philip had not expected a full encounter on that day and he was unhappy about the suitability of the terrain for his phalanx, but he decided reluctantly that he would have to see it through. Accordingly he too drew up his whole force at the bottom and ascended the slope with his light-armed peltasts and the right wing of his phalanx. Suddenly his mercenaries reappeared at the top of the pass with the Romans in hot pursuit. The left wing of Philip's phalanx had not as yet reached the top but he ordered the right wing to double in depth. (This manoeuvre would probably have been effected by withdrawing alternate files from the right, lining them up behind the files that had been on their right in order to double the depth, and then closing the files up to the file on the extreme right).[5] They were then ordered to lower their pikes and charge. The Romans had no chance of standing up to the weight of this charge, bristling with pikes to the fore and descending on them from higher ground. They were driven back and were being slaughtered.[6]

Flamininus decided that his only hope of rescuing the battle lay in creating a diversion by attacking the enemy's left wing which had so far not been engaged. With his elephants in the lead he took his whole right wing up against them. It was an easy victory. The left wing of Philip's phalanx had only just surmounted the ridge and the men were still in column formation and were idly watching the battle. The approach of the elephants and the legions threw them into confusion and they were routed and pursued.[7] At this point the battle might have ended indecisively but for the initiative of an unnamed tribune, who saw no point in staying with the pursuit of a defeated enemy. Taking twenty maniples from among the pursuers, he wheeled them to the left and charged across to attack the enemy's victorious right wing in the rear. At one fell swoop this turned the battle into a Roman victory.[8] A phalanx with its *sarissae* (pikes) protruding about four-and-a-half metres (over fourteen feet)[3] was a cumbersome instrument which was incapable of any abrupt change in direction. Unable to turn to fend off the attack, the Macedonians were slaughtered where they stood. At the same time the Romans in front of the phalanx, who had been the victims, turned to join in the attack. Some of the Macedonians held up their pikes vertically in token of surrender. The Romans, however, had never met this signal before and, unaware of its significance, continued the slaughter. The few Macedonians that escaped only did so by dropping their pikes and fleeing. Polybius and Livy agree that the Romans lost about 700 in the battle in contrast to the enemy losses of around 8,000 killed and 5,000 captured.

In the following year Philip requested an armistice, which was granted. It confirmed that all Greek cities should be free. Philip was left in possession of Macedon to which he was confined, but his fleet was confiscated and a modest indemnity was imposed upon him. The execution of these conditions was entrusted to Quinctius Flamininus as the victorious general, but he ran into difficulties over the disposal of the Greek cities which had been evacuated by Philip. The Aetolians provided the problem. As the only Greeks who had given material assistance to the Romans during the war, they expected to be awarded the whole of Thessaly for inclusion in the Aetolian League. When they were given only a part of it they became disgruntled and, acting on impulse and pique, they invited Antiochus III to liberate Greece. In doing so, they provided the trigger for the next war, the War against Antiochus. Philip, on the other hand, abided by the terms imposed on him. When the war against Antiochus materialised, he sided with the Romans and gave them good assistance.

Thematic Summary

1   A chance encounter between the advance parties of the two armies at the summit of a pass. They had approached it from opposite sides.[4]
2   The right half of the Macedonian phalanx formed in double depth and charged downhill against the Roman left wing.[6] Their relentless advance foretold doom.
3   The consul saw that his only hope lay in creating a diversion. He directed his elephants followed by his right wing uphill against the enemy left wing.[7]
4   The enemy left had just arrived on the summit. Still in column formation, they were thrown into disorder and were easily routed and

pursued. If matters had ended there, the result would have been indecisive with the loss of a wing on each side.

5   A Roman victory was gained through the initiative of an unknown tribune. He abandoned his part in the pursuit of the left wing, took 20 cohorts and launched an attack on the rear of the victorious enemy phalanx.[8]

6   This was the first time that Romans had encountered a Macedonian phalanx and defeated it, establishing the superiority of the more flexible legionary system The second and last time was at Pydna (p. 220).

Notes

1   Polybius, 18.19–26; Livy, 33.4, 6–10; Plutarch, *Flamininus*, 7.2–8.
2   Livy, 33.4.4–6.
3   Plutarch, *Flamininus*, 7.2.
4   Polybius, 18.21.1–2; Livy, 33.7.5.
5   P. Connolly, *Greece and Rome at War*, London, Greenhill, 1998, p. 83.
6   Polybius, 18.24.8–9, 25.2.
7   Polybius, 18.25.4–7; Livy, 33.9.6–7.
8   Polybius, 18.26.1–5; Livy, 33.9.8–11.

Magnesia (190)

The battle of Magnesia was the final confrontation which brought to an end the two-year Roman war against Antiochus III the Great. Antiochus had succeeded to the Seleucid throne as a young man in 223 after the assassination of his elder brother. At the time of his accession the empire had been crumbling fast and was in a state of almost total disintegration. In the next eight years Antiochus dealt with various internal dissensions, after which he launched into a series of campaigns in the east which included a grand anabasis through Persia and Bactria. This resulted in the restoration of much of the former empire, for which he was acclaimed 'the Great'. He was also involved in two Syrian wars against the Ptolemies for possession of southern Syria. However, none of these matters encroached on Roman interests or gave cause for alarm.

The War against Antiochus was triggered directly by the terms of the armistice after the Second Macedonian War in which the Aetolians felt that they had had a raw deal. As they were the only Greeks who had given material assistance to the Romans during the war, they expected to be awarded the whole of Thessaly for inclusion in the Aetolian League. When they were given only a part of it, they became disgruntled. Acting on impulse and pique, they invited Antiochus to liberate Greece. Whatever his motives may have been, Antiochus made the fatal mistake of accepting the invitation. It is probable that he was only prodding the Romans on the diplomatic front, but they had good reason for viewing it in a different light. Only two years previously they had learned that Hannibal had escaped from Carthage and had joined Antiochus at Ephesus. In their eyes he could now be putting into effect his plan for a joint re-invasion of their country. They responded by declaring war.

Antiochus landed in Greece at the port of Demetrias in 192. To assist him the Aetolians had wrested the place from Roman control. Antiochus had with him only a small force of 10,000 men, 500 cavalry and six elephants, hardly sufficient to 'liberate' Greece let alone sustain a war against the Romans. He spent the whole of the rest of the year touring the towns and cities endeavouring to drum up support but to little effect. Some of them promised support but did not give it; others sided with the Romans. Yet others asked from whom Greece was supposed to be liberated. Even the Aetolians were divided among themselves as to their best course, but they did produce 4,000 men, the only allies that joined Antiochus. Eventually he chose to confront the Romans in the pass of Thermopylae, where he was soundly defeated and was forced to return to Asia. In short, the whole invasion was a fiasco. The war was then extended into Asia where the king's preparations for defence rested on his fleet. Until the final battle on land at Magnesia there was only a succession of naval battles – off Corycus, Side, and Myonnesus – all in a single campaign in 191/190 and in all of which the king's fleet was defeated. (The battle off Side was of particular interest in that the king's fleet was commanded by Hannibal in his one and only naval venture.)

The consequences of these battles were disastrous for Antiochus. He had lost any control of the sea, withdrew from the Thracian Chersonese, and was unable to defend the Hellespont or indeed any of his seaboard against invasion. He retired to Sardis where he made frantic efforts to collect reinforcements from every possible source, while making peace overtures to the Romans which were not accepted. He then moved to Thyatira where he set up his camp. In the meantime Lucius Cornelius Scipio had been appointed consul for the year with his famous brother, Scipio Africanus, as his subordinate at his own request. In view of his great experience and background, Africanus was the one who in reality did the leading and shaped the events. They marched with their army to Macedon and were escorted to the Hellespont by Philip, who had made all the preparations including repairing the roads. They then crossed the Hellespont without any opposition and marched down to the mouth of the river Caicus about 50 miles from Thyatira as the crow flies. Here he was joined by Eumenes II of Pergamum with about 3,000 of his men. While they were there, Scipio Africanus was taken ill. When Antiochus heard about this, he made a magnanimous gesture in reuniting him with his son, who had been captured at some uncertain point in the campaign.

Although Antiochus had a much larger force than the Romans, he was very hesitant about facing them. He crossed the river Phrygius and established his base near Magnesia-ad-Sipylum, situated on the slope of Mount Sipylus in Lydia (to be distinguished from Magnesia on the Maeander in Ionia). Here he dug a ditch, eighteen feet wide by nine feet deep, and surrounded his camp with a double palisade outside the ditch. To cap it all, inside the ditch he built a wall with numerous towers. The consul, believing the king to be still at Thyatira, advanced to that place and then followed the king's track westward, eventually camping about four miles from his enemy. For the next two days all was quiet. On the third day the Romans crossed the river and advanced their camp to a site two-and-a-half miles from the enemy. For four days after that the battle lines of both armies were drawn up but no engagement followed. The Romans then moved forward yet again into the middle of the intervening space, but again Antiochus did not respond. To the utter contempt of the Romans, he was funking the challenge. On the next day the Romans again advanced and drew up their lines with the left wing resting on the river Phrygius. This time Antiochus could delay no longer without incurring further shame and aggravating the demoralisation of his men. He led out his force and drew it up.[1]

Battle of Magnesia

The best account of the battle is given by Livy.[2] Appian's account is more disjointed, and his deployment of the Roman forces is at times ludicrous.[3] However, the two sources agree that the king's force totalled around 70,000 men, in contrast to the Romans who sported less than half that number.[4]

The battle took place on a murky morning in December of 190 (or January 189). The Romans had a total strength of about 30,000 men at most, of whom around 3,000 were cavalry. The two legions each of 5,000 men were deployed in the centre of their line with a contingent of Latin allies 5,400 strong on either side. (Appian places the legions on the left wing resting on the river and the allied contingents behind the legions with yet other contingents behind them. This is patently wrong. The Romans with their gross numerical inferiority must have needed to extend their line as far as possible). On the right wing there were the troops of Eumenes II with a mix of targeteers to a total of 3,000, after which there were 3,000 cavalry, largely Roman, and finally 500 each of Trallians and Cretans. As the left flank rested on the river it was deemed unnecessary to station any auxiliaries there, but the consul placed four squadrons of cavalry in support.[5] There were also 2,000 Macedonian and Thracian volunteers who were left to guard the camp. Finally there were sixteen elephants of the small African 'forest' type, which were no match for the enemy's large Indian beasts and were therefore stationed behind the legions. The principal uncertainty surrounds the question of the Roman leadership, about which there is a divergence of opinion. As Scipio Africanus was still unwell, his place as lieutenant and adviser to the consul Lucius Scipio was taken by the experienced Gnaeus Domitius Ahenobarbus. According to Appian, Domitius was in effective command of the Romans. Livy, on the other hand, gives the ultimate command to the consul Lucius Scipio, who took his place in the centre, and Livy only mentions Domitius once when he was 'sent out' to reconnoitre.

The strength of the king's force is said to have been 60,000 infantry and at least 12,000 horse. The centrepiece was the phalanx of Macedonian type. Livy puts this at 10,000 men and Appian at 16,000, but both agree that it was divided into ten sections. Apart from the fact that a phalanx of 16,000 would have been quite exceptional, both sources agree that the files were 32 men

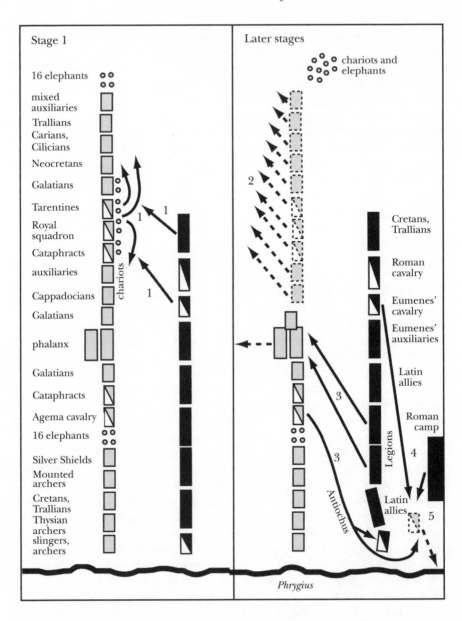

deep which indicates that it must have been a double phalanx, one behind
the other. This may explain Appian's statement that 'the appearance of the
formation was like that of two armies, one to begin the fight, the other held
in reserve', also that 'the phalanx... was crowded together unskilfully in a
narrow space'. Both chroniclers agree that elephants with towers containing
four men were stationed in each gap between the sections (Livy says two per
gap; Appian considerably more). Livy then gives an itemised account which

adds up virtually to the stated totals of 60,000 men and 12,000 horse.[6] To detail all the contingents here would be both superfluous and largely irrelevant as none of them played a specific role in the battle. (They are shown in the Plan). An impression of the assorted horde confronting the Romans is best conveyed in terms of the number of contingents involved. On the right of the phalanx there were eight contingents totalling around 19,000 men. They included Galatians, the Silver Shields, *cataphracti* (heavy-armed cavalry with hooded cuirasses), Dahae and several bodies from other nations, with sixteen elephants in the middle and eighteen on the extreme wing. The left wing was composed of a further twelve assorted contingents amounting to 26,000 men, which must have extended far beyond the Roman line. Next to the phalanx were two contingents of infantry, then a multinational mix of auxiliaries followed by *cataphracti* and other cavalry. In front of the cavalry were stationed scythed chariots and dromedaries carrying Arab archers. Beyond all these was another host ranging from Tarentines, Galatian cavalry, and Neocretans to targeteers and contingents from various other nations. On the extreme wing were a further sixteen elephants.[6] The king commanded from the right flank; his son, Seleucus, was in command on the left.

On the day of the battle the morning was initially so misty that the Macedonian wings could scarcely see their centre let alone each other, so extended was their line. This was less of an inconvenience to the Romans with their much shorter deployment; in fact, it was to their advantage in that Antiochus on his right wing cannot conceivably have been aware of the damage inflicted to his left half.[7] The action began when Antiochus' chariots on his left wing were unleashed, but from previous experience Eumenes knew how to deal with them. He directed his slingers, archers and some cavalry against them, instructing his men to act individually and to attack from all directions while aiming at the horses and not the men. The missiles and the noise so terrified the horses that they dashed about wildly in all directions and were eventually driven from the field.[8] The panic and confusion created by the chariots had infected the auxiliaries nearby, who turned and fled, exposing the adjoining contingent. With the Romans maintaining the pressure on them, they in their turn rushed away in flight. It was like a fuse, igniting the next in line until it reached the infantry next to the phalanx. When these sought shelter in the phalanx, the ranks, according to Appian, opened to admit them resulting in overcrowding and disorder. The Roman legions then advanced and hurled their spears into the maelstrom. The disruption was completed by a stampede of the elephants in the intervals between the sections.[9]

At this point the Romans heard shouting from their extreme left. Antiochus had noted that the Romans had put so much reliance on the protection afforded by the river that they had not posted any auxiliaries there. Staking everything on his manoeuvre, Antiochus had charged along the bank with his auxiliaries and heavy cavalry and attacked the Roman left wing in a frontal assault. In addition, he outflanked them by the river and drove them back toward their camp in the rear.[10] The camp commandant and his guard had considerable difficulty stemming the flight of their own side; he was even forced to order the guard to cut down the first of the fugitives and make the rest turn and face their pursuers. Help was at hand when Attalus, brother of Eumenes, on the victorious right wing noticed what was happening on the extreme left. Collecting 200 horse, he charged across the field and counter-attacked at just the right moment.[11] When Antiochus saw that the troops whom he had driven to the camp were returning to fight and were being joined by others from the field, he turned and fled. In his extended pursuit he had thrown away any chance of victory by failing to support the phalanx in its hour of need. It had been driven back behind the rampart, which it struggled fiercely to hold. For the Romans, this provided the hardest fighting of the whole battle. When they did eventually manage to force their way through the defences, the slaughter was bitter.

Both of the sources state that about 50,000 of the enemy were slain, although Appian includes 1,400 prisoners in this figure. The overall figure is probably an exaggeration as it represents most of the force, but the losses were clearly enormous. According to both sources, the Romans lost 300 infantry and 24 cavalry but there were also many wounded.

Why did Antiochus with his large numerical superiority suffer such a major defeat? His main tactical blunder was his prolonged pursuit of the Roman right wing and failure to return to support his phalanx in its hour of need. This was a carbon copy of his actions at Raphia (p. 127) and he had not learned the lesson. But there was another reason too. His forces, though numerous, were a disparate lot from many nations, each with its own ways and with no training as a unit. The Romans, by contrast, had trained as a disciplined, cohesive and interactive force.

The peace terms stipulated that Antiochus must keep out of Europe and abandon all his possessions in the near East, west of Mount Taurus. He was ordered to surrender most of his fleet and all his elephants, and to pay a huge indemnity. The territories in Asia Minor which he had to vacate were divided between the Rhodians and Eumenes. The Romans pocketed the indemnity, but they did not have their sights on territory and took no land for themselves. In 188 they evacuated all their troops from Greece and the Eastern Mediterranean.

Thematic Content

1   The human element: Antiochus' shameful hesitation to fight in spite of his huge numerical superiority was reflected in the demoralisation of his men.[1]

2   Poor visibility. Antiochus' line was so extended that the wings could not see each other.[7]

3   The defeat of the scythed chariots by Eumenes' methods. The chariots caused damage almost entirely to their own side.[8]

4   The disruption of the phalanx when adjacent contingents sought shelter in it.[9]

5   Antiochus' charge along the river bank and extended pursuit of the enemy, leaving his phalanx leaderless.[10]

6   The principal cause of Antiochus' defeat was the assorted composition of his army. The twenty or more contingents of different nationalities practised varying forms of warfare and had never operated together as a whole. Compare the disciplined unity of the Romans.

Notes

1   Livy, 37.39.1–6.
2   Livy, 37.37.6–44.2.
3   Appian, *Syrian Wars*, 30–36.
4   Livy, 37.37.8; Appian, *Syrian Wars*, 32.
5   Livy, 37.39.11.
6   Livy, 37.40.
7   Livy, 37.41.2–4.
8   Livy, 37.41.5–12.
9   Livy, 37.42.1–5; Appian, *Syrian Wars*, 35.
10 Livy, 37.42.7–8.
11 Livy, 37.43.5–6.

Pydna (168)

Background

Philip V of Macedon abided by the terms of the treaty after the Second Macedonian War and until his death. During the war against Antiochus he was firmly on the Roman side. His younger son Demetrius visited Rome, where he was widely acclaimed and developed excellent relationships which boded well for the future. But trouble did come – in the person of Philip's elder son, Perseus. His brother's diplomatic success made Perseus suspicious and aroused in him fears for his own prospects of succession. By means of a forged letter he managed to engineer the execution of his brother on a trumped up charge of treason. After the fraud was revealed, Philip was on the point of disinheriting Perseus when his own death intervened in 179 and Perseus gained the throne.

Although the new king extended his father's programme of internal development, some of his actions raised doubts about his intentions. These included the enlargement of his military forces and, worse, his alliances with Illyrian and Thracian chieftains. He had an enemy in Eumenes II of Pergamum, who had inherited a tradition of alliance with Rome and who sedulously kept the Romans informed on the matter of Perseus' actions and behaviour. Oddly unlike his father, he was a retiring, timid creature who would almost certainly have towed the line if Rome had appealed to him with sufficient force. But Rome's responses to complaints were half-measures, neither conciliatory nor openly demanding.

Rome drifted into war on a pretext, of which alternative versions are cited in the literature. The version described by Livy concerns a visit to Rome by Eumenes with a list of complaints against Perseus. On his return journey by way of Delphi he was struck on the head by a boulder, which might have tumbled down from Mount Parnassus, nearly killing him. This could have been an accident of nature, although Livy dresses it up in great detail as a deliberate attempt at murder.[1] Whatever the truth, Eumenes chose to regard the incident as an attempt on his life and made accusations against the king of attempted assassination. With this as a pretext, the Romans sent Perseus

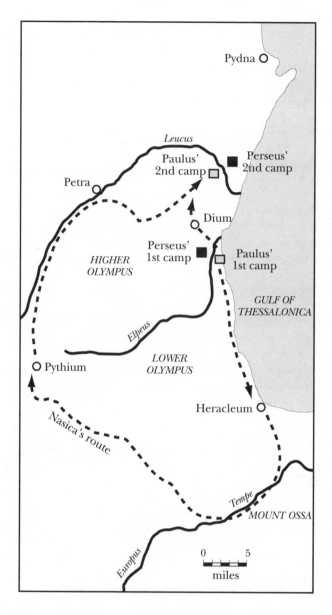

an ultimatum demanding his disarmament. When this was declined, the
senate voted for war. On at least two subsequent occasions Perseus made
peace overtures to Rome, but the senate retorted that war had been
declared and so war it must be. It was almost certainly an unnecessary one
which might have been avoided by more astute diplomacy. When it came, it
was a straight trial of strength between Rome and Macedon; neither side
had acquired any significant support from other sources.

In 171 a Roman army crossed the Adriatic, disembarked at Apollonia in
Illyria and marched across Epirus into Thessaly. After two engagements with
Perseus, which caused him some dismay even though he was the undisputed
victor in a cavalry battle near Larissa, he withdrew into Macedonia. In the
next couple of years there was no significant progress on that front.
Attempts to penetrate into the country failed until eventually a determined
consul, Marcius Philippus, breached the border after a perilous march
across the shoulder of Mount Olympus. When he got there he was unable to
achieve anything except to cause Perseus to panic. At the end of the
campaigning season for that year (169) Perseus moved from his base to the
river Elpeus, on the north bank of which he set up a strongly fortified
position. Here he spent the winter months.

In the following year the new consul with responsibility for Macedonia
was Aemilius Paulus. At the beginning of spring he crossed the Adriatic with
his forces and marched to Macedonia. Having already been told the
whereabouts of Perseus' camp, he advanced to the Elpeus and took up a
position on the south bank of the river opposite his enemy. The Elpeus (unidentified) was a river which arose in Mount Olympus and flowed down past
Dium to the sea. In summer it was reduced to a trickle and its bed became
dried up, rough and uneven. The consul's first action was to deal with the
shortage of water which had been annoying the troops. Looking around, he
noted the greenness of the trees on the hills and surmised that there must
be water underground. Setting some men to dig down, they had no sooner
removed the surface than water began to bubble up. The solution to the
problem greatly enhanced the prestige of the consul in the eyes of his
troops.

It seemed to Aemilius that the enemy's fortified bank presented an
insuperable obstacle. The river bed was approximately a mile wide and a
frontal assault across it was out of the question. For two days engagements
took place in the middle of the river bed between light-armed troops of the
two sides. There were heavy casualties on both sides, particularly among the
Romans, who were also attacked by missiles from the enemy fortifications.
However, these were no ordinary skirmishes for supremacy and control.
They were engineered by the consul to divert the prying eyes of Perseus
away from events elsewhere while he strove to find a way of circumventing
the enemy's position.[2] He learnt that all the mountain passes were guarded
with the sole exception of the Petra Pass, probably because the terrain was
so inhospitable that no one in their senses would want to use it. The consul
resorted to a feint by sending Cornelius Scipio Nasica Corculum (son-in-law
of Africanus) with 8,000 men, 200 Thracians and Cretans, and 120 horse to
Heracleum on the coast to give the impression that they were leaving by sea.
After dark the force moved off in the opposite direction, skirting to the
south of Mount Olympus and halting below Pythium, the sanctuary of
Apollo on the west side of the mountain.[3] In the meantime Perseus, noting

that Aemilius was still in position on the opposite bank of the Elpeus, was unaware of Nasica's departure until a Cretan deserter from Nasica's force alerted him to the facts. Perseus immediately sent out 2,000 Macedonians and 10,000 mercenaries under a man called Milo to seize the passes. By this time Nasica had taken Pytheum by surprise. When he advanced from there, he encountered Milo and his force sleeping off their fatigue. After a brisk fight Milo and his men took to their heels in a shameful flight, leaving Nasica with a free ticket through the Petra Pass. He proceeded to the area north of Dium.

Meanwhile Perseus hastily broke camp and departed northwards from the Elpeus to take up a position near the coast between Dium and Pydna. The place which he selected was a level plain, suitable for a phalanx, with the sea to the east. At the west end of the plain it gave way to the foothills of Mount Olocrus. Across the plain ran two small rivers, the Aeson and the Leucus, which were shallow at that time of year. When news of his enemy's position reached Paulus, he marched northwards and joined up with Nasica north of Dium. Together they descended to confront Perseus and, presumably from what follows, they camped on the slopes of Mount Olocrus with the plain and the river Leucus between them and the enemy. To the disgust of his impatient men Paulus refused to give battle until they had completed their camp and were thoroughly rested. Moreover, he did not want to fight until well into the afternoon when the sun would be behind them and facing the enemy.[4] On the night of June 21–22 there was an eclipse of the moon, which dates the battle to a nicety. It is said that on the following afternoon a Roman horse broke loose and galloped down to the river. Both sides drew their water from it and each side maintained a protective guard near the bank. Three Romans set out catch the horse while two Thracians did likewise from the Macedonian side. In the ensuing scuffle one Thracian was killed, which so enraged the 800 Thracians on guard that some of them crossed the river and attacked the Roman guards. More came out on both sides and the fight escalated until it developed into a general confrontation. It has been said that Aemilius himself might have engineered the whole incident by releasing the offending horse in order to 'make the enemy begin the attack'. But it is perhaps more plausible that he merely accepted it as a trigger, occurring as it did at his planned time of day.

Battle of Pydna

Polybius' account of the battle has unfortunately been lost and so has a report by Scipio Nasica, while Livy's version is confused and incomplete.[5] There remains Plutarch's *Aemilius Paulus*, which does incorporate parts of Nasica's report.[6] Where Plutarch's account is deficient, for example in the deployments, the conjectures of General Fuller have been adopted here.[7]

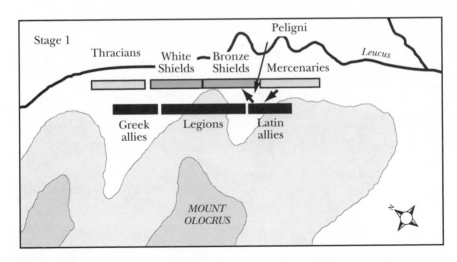

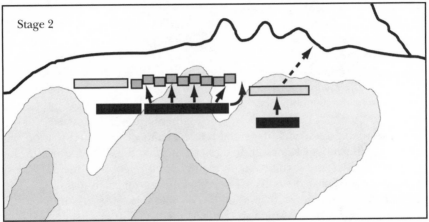

Plutarch gives the Macedonian strength as 'not much fewer' than 40,000 heavy infantry and 4,000 horse, but Livy puts the infantry at only about 30,000. This figure is consistent with his later statements that few survivors escaped altogether, and that the casualties amounted to 20,000 slain and 11,000 captured. (Plutarch gives only a total of over 25,000 slain). These figures exclude the cavalry which played no significant part in the battle and escaped unscathed, headed by Perseus. The Romans are reported as being numerically inferior but neither Livy nor Plutarch give any figures for actual numbers in the battle. When the forces were allocated in Rome shortly before the departure of Aemilius, two legions each of 5,200 men and 300 cavalry were allocated to Licinius, Aemilius' consular colleague, for the Macedonian campaign, and Licinius was instructed to add 10,000 allied infantry and 800 cavalry.[8] If this was the total of their forces, they were distinctly inferior in numbers.

Plutarch gives the order of advance but this provides no indication of the deployments. However, there are one or two pointers. It will be seen later that the mercenaries were on the left of the Macedonian phalanx. If it is assumed that the phalanx was as usual in the centre of the line, the Thracians were presumably placed on the right. The phalanx was composed of the 'White Shields' (*Leucaspides*) on the right and the 'Bronze Shields' (*Chalcaspides*) on the left. These probably formed the two halves of one phalanx, which may have had a total strength of 16,000 (a phalanx of this magnitude has been attested only in the battle of Pydna).[9] On the Roman side the legions may again be presumed to have been central with the Latin allies on the right (as seen later) and the Greek allies on the left. On both sides the cavalry were probably on one or both wings, but as they played little or no part they are not shown in the present battle plan. Some elephants were also held back on the Roman right flank.

It is probable that the Macedonians started the action by crossing the river with their whole line. Hostilities began with an advance by their Thracians, men of terrifying appearance equipped with heavy iron-headed battleaxes, but there is no mention of any ensuing action. The next to advance were the mercenaries on the left wing, after which the phalanx also began to advance. By the time Aemilius arrived on the scene the phalangites had already planted the tips of their *sarissae* in the Roman shields, which rendered their victims effectively useless. The Romans were totally unable to get at or stand up to this weight of men with their shields locked in close formation and levelling an array of up to ten pikes at every legionary. They were being forced back inexorably. The Pelignians among the Latin allies on the Roman right attempted a counter-attack but they were unable even to dent the enemy formation. Their commander, Salvius, then resorted to the ancient trick of picking up his company standard and hurling it into the enemy midst and telling his men to recover it (p. 112). Nothing was more calculated to drive Roman troops into frenzied effort, but in this instance it was to no avail and the Pelignians suffered terrible losses.[10] The survivors were repulsed by the Macedonian mercenaries. The very sight of the phalanx instilled such terror into Aemilius that he never forgot it and frequently used to reminisce about it later. His men appeared to be facing total destruction as they retired step by step until suddenly the consul noticed that the phalanx was running into difficulties. As it reached the end of the level ground of the plain, it was moving onto rougher terrain at the base of the foothills. Under these conditions a phalanx could no longer maintain an unbroken line and gaps would begin to appear between the files.[11] This is precisely what was happening at Pydna. Aemilius immediately reacted by dividing his legions into small groups and ordering them to infiltrate the gaps in the phalanx. On account of his enormous pike, up to about 6.3 m (twenty feet) long, the phalangite was unable to turn aside. His only recourse was to abandon his pike and resort to his sword, which was shorter than the Roman weapon and no match for it. By infiltrating into gaps in the phalanx, the Romans could attack the Macedonians in the flank and rear as the opportunity presented. As a result, the Macedonians were overcome in droves and the conflict underwent a complete reversal of fortune, as narrated by Plutarch.

The beginning of Livy's description of the battle is missing. His account begins cryptically with another aspect of the battle by telling us that *the legion filled the space between the Macedonian targeteers and the phalanx.*[12] After the Pelignian attack early in the battle had been repulsed, the Macedonian mercenaries ('targeteers') who repelled them continued their advance presumably in pursuit of the fleeing Pelignians. This put them well out in front of the line and created a large gap between their right wing and the left wing of the Macedonian phalanx. Livy proceeds to tell us that Aemilius himself then led one of the legions into the gap, and that he directed the other legion against the White Shields. This is contradicted by Plutarch, according to whom the legions were already opposing both halves of the phalanx without success at the time that the Macedonian mercenaries drove the Pelignians off the field. If the accounts of Plutarch and Livy are viewed together, it seems obvious that Aemilius' first move would have been to oppose the phalanx with both of his legions, as reported by Plutarch, with himself in command of the legion opposed to the Bronze Shields. It is equally credible that a large gap would appear between the mercenaries and the Bronze Shields, as told by Livy. It is feasible then that as soon as Aemilius noticed this gap, he would have either led or directed a part of his legion to the right to fill it, as expressed in Livy's opening statement. The legion would still be in contact with the Bronze Shields in front but, in addition, it would also be in a position to attack them in the flank from the gap. If this is what happened, it was probably around this time that the Macedonian phalanx started to run into difficulties on account of the uneven terrain, with the results that have already been described by both sources.

Livy alone further tells us that the mercenaries, who were separated from the rest of the Macedonian army, were attacked from the front by some cohorts of allied cavalry and by the elephants which had finally been pressed into service. When the beasts proved useless, their place was taken by the Latin allies who routed the enemy.[13]

The whole battle took place within one hour from start to finish. When Perseus saw that he had lost, he fled with his cavalry which had seen little action. Later he surrendered, leaving Macedonia without a king. According to Plutarch, the Macedonians lost 25,000 men killed; Livy says 20,000 were killed and a total of 11,000 captured. Roman losses are variously put at between 80 and more than 100, but they did suffer many wounded. This battle was only the second and last occasion on which the Romans encountered a Macedonian phalanx in full cry. It demonstrated again the superiority of the more flexible Roman legion under varying conditions.

The phalanx had had its day.

The political upshot of the battle was the abolition of Macedonia as such. It was divided at first into four federated republics. Twenty years later, In 146, it became a Roman province.

Thematic Content

1   The feint engagements on the river bed initiated by Aemilius to divert the prying eyes of Perseus away from a turning movement.[2]

2   The large turning movement executed by Nasica to circumvent the enemy's position.[3]

3   Aemilius aim to fight in the afternoon when the sun would be behind the Romans and facing the enemy.[4]

4   The ancient ploy, executed by Salvius, of hurling the standard into the enemy midst to arouse ferocity in his men.[10] In this instance, it was to no avail.

5   The development of gaps in the phalanx when it moved onto uneven terrain, and the consul's initiative and response.[11]

6   The development of a large gap in the line between the Macedonian phalanx and the mercenaries.[12] The Romans penetrated the gap and attacked the flank of the phalanx.

7   The ineffectiveness of the elephants against the mercenaries.[13]

Notes

1   Livy, 42.15.3–15.5.
2   Livy, 44.35.16–24.
3   Plutarch, *Aemilius Paulus*, 15.
4   Plutarch, *Aemilius Paulus*, 17.13.
5   Livy, 44.40–42.
6   Plutarch, *Aemilius Paulus*, 16.4–22.
7   J. F. C. Fuller, *Decisive Battles of the Western World*, London, Eyre & Spottiswoode, 1954.
8   Livy, 44.21.9–11.
9   P. Connolly, *Greece and Rome at War*, London, Greenhill, 1998, p. 75.
10   Plutarch, *Aemilius Paulus*, 20.1–4.
11   Plutarch, *Aemilius Paulus*, 20.7–10.
12   Livy, 44.41.1.
13   Livy, 44.41.3–5.

Carrhae (53)

Background

In the era in question the term 'long-range fighting' or 'fighting at a distance' implied any method of attacking an enemy which avoided direct contact with him. The battle of Carrhae is included here expressly to highlight this topic because the Parthians were renowned as the most formidable adversaries and advocates of long range warfare. There are two accounts of the Parthian campaign, by Plutarch and Dio Cassius respectively. Dio gives a short but clear description of Parthian arms and methods;[1] for everything else, including the battle, Plutarch's excellent version is more complete and readable.[2]

The battle of Carrhae (Haran) was one of the greatest disasters in Roman history, but the senators were nevertheless entitled to divorce themselves from any responsibility. They had never decreed a Parthian war and the blame for it lay entirely on the head of a newly appointed consul.[3] Marcus Licinius Crassus Dives, the consul in question, was a vain and ambitious man of sixty years or more and looking old for his years. In league with Pompey, the pair of them got themselves voted as consuls by somewhat devious means, and when lots were drawn for the provinces, the Spains fell to Pompey and Syria to Crassus. This sent Crassus into ecstasy. The appointment would give him the opportunity to do great things and satisfy his ambitions. Above all, he intended by majestic achievements to gain renown and recognition in excess of anything that Pompey or even Caesar had achieved. As the decree defining the mission made no mention of a Parthian war, he decided to take it on himself as his claim to fame. It would be his own private war, intended to bring him great renown.[4]

In the course of his martial preparations Crassus fell into the clutches of a certain wily Arab chieftain by the name of Ariamnes. (Dio calls the traitor Abgarus of Osroëne in Mesopotamia. If not the same man, both seem to have got up to similar tricks). This man had enjoyed a good relationship with Pompey and had pledged himself to peace with the Romans. He used this as a reference to ingratiate himself and worm his way into the consul's confidence. Unknown to Crassus, Ariamnes was acting as a double agent and was informing the Parthians of all his plans. There was no doubt that the safest route into Parthia lay along the banks of the Euphrates, which would provide both protection from encirclement and a supply route. Ariamnes, however, managed to persuade the impatient Crassus that he was wasting valuable time and would do better to head off inland. The Parthians, he said, were not far away and their general Surena had only a small force with him. Crassus' quaestor Cassius was sceptical and not so easily taken in. He distrusted Ariamnes and repeatedly tried to dissuade the consul from accepting the traitor's advice but to no avail.[5]

Battle of Carrhae

Crassus had no knowledge of the country or its people; worse he was totally ignorant about their military forces and methods of making war. The Parthians practised the art of riding from childhood and were expert horsemen on their short stocky Nisaean mounts. In addition they were accomplished archers. They did not use shields. Surena had 10,000 of them in his force. He also had some heavy cavalry who wore metal armour and carried long spears, and their horses were usually mail-clad (*cataphracti*). Of infantry there were only a few from among the poorer brethren but even these were all archers.[6]

Crassus had under his command a force of at least seven legions and 4,000 cavalry with as many light-armed troops. His cavalry force, which by Parthian standards was small, consisted of Gallic horses and was under the direction of his son. Crassus himself had been negotiating with Artavasdes of Armenia for reinforcements, but he was too impatient to wait for the promised squadrons to materialise. Even before the start of the expedition ominous portents had abounded, such as legionary standards which seemed to have become embedded in the earth and could only be raised with difficulty. Undeterred, Crassus set out with his army to penetrate the hinterland in accordance with Ariamnes' advice. At first the going was easy but the track soon degenerated and led into a treeless and waterless desert as far as the eye could see. There was no sign of human activity apart from some tracks made by horses which appeared ominously to have turned and withdrawn into the distance.[7] Eventually they caught sight of the enemy who, to their surprise, seemed neither numerous nor formidable. When the consul formed his men into an open square and advanced closer, the truth was revealed. Surena had placed his main force behind the advance forces and had ordered the former to cover themselves with skins to conceal the gleam of their armour. On a signal they suddenly filled the whole plain with a deep and terrifying roar accompanied by a 'low and dismal tone' from their drums which were covered with bronze bells. The skins were then suddenly cast aside, revealing numerous warriors 'blazing in helmets and breastplates and their horses clad in plates of bronze and steel'. After this demonstration they proceeded to surround the Roman square while keeping at a distance.[8]

The term 'battle' is hardly justified because it was entirely one-sided. The Romans were not given a chance of hitting back. The Parthians maintained a safe distance and proceeded to circle round the Roman square discharging a perpetual shower of arrows at it. Shot into the densely crowded square no arrow could miss hitting a mark. The Parthians' bows were large and imparted a high velocity to the barbed arrows, which could penetrate Roman armour. If the Romans did charge out and attempt to make close contact, the Parthians temporarily withdrew while shooting arrows in the process, a tactic at which they were highly proficient. Crassus' only hope was that the enemy would run out of arrows, but when a camel train arrived with fresh supplies, he lost heart.[9]

When Crassus had formed an open square formation he had placed his son Publius in charge of one wing and Cassius on the other, but the meaning of this is unclear. It appears that a 'wing' might have been a separate formation, largely of cavalry, because at this point Crassus sent messages to Publius ordering him to attempt a break-out before he was entirely surrounded. Accordingly, Publius took 1,300 horsemen, 500 archers and eight cohorts with whom he charged the nearest Parthians. He was exhilarated when they wheeled about and 'fled'. When he had been lured away from the main body for a considerable distance, the Parthians turned to the attack and were joined by many of their fellows. Publius and his men were then subjected to the same long range treatment with arrows as the others had received. When Publius urged his cavalry forward in a vigorous charge and made contact with the enemy, his attack was countered by the *cataphracti* in a hopelessly unequal match. It was a matter of small Roman spears against breastplates of hide and steel, and of long pikes against the unprotected Gauls, who formed much of the Roman force. Five hundred of the Romans survived to be captured; most of the others were killed but a few chose to kill themselves. Publius chose the latter course, but he was unable to use his injured hand and ordered his shield-bearer to do the job for him. The Parthians subsequently chopped his head off and paraded it on a spear before his father and his men. After demoralising the Romans even further by this act, the Parthians continued to attack them until dusk. The *cataphracti* first crowded them back into an ever decreasing space before countless arrows caused devastation in their midst.[10]

When dusk came the Parthians took themselves off and bivouacked for the night. Crassus and other ambulant Romans managed to walk away and were not molested by the enemy although the latter were aware of their departure. On the following morning the Parthians returned to the battle site and slaughtered all those who had been left behind, 4,000 of them, as well as others found wandering in the countryside. In all a total of 10,000 escaped. Crassus was subsequently murdered treacherously when he obeyed a call to a peace conference, and it was said that some unknown man in the party then cut off his head.

Plutarch adds a macabre note. When the messengers bringing tidings of the Parthian victory reached the King's court, the *Bacchae* of Euripides was being performed. In place of the dummy head of Pentheus, the actor substituted the real head of Crassus.

The battle of Carrhae was notably similar in just one respect to the events at Cannae (p. 180). In both cases a large Roman army was totally surrounded by a smaller force. There the similarity ends. The composition of the encircling armies of Hannibal and Surena and their respective methods of warfare bore no resemblance to each other. The Parthian numbers at Carrhae are not mentioned directly in connection with the battle, but in a previous dissertation on Surena and his army Plutarch reports that altogether, as horsemen, vassals, and slaves, he had no fewer than 10,000 men.[11] This is a minute force by comparison with the seven legions of Crassus which, with the cavalry, must have totalled around 40,000. It was the mobile equestrian composition of the Parthian army and its long range method of warfare that enabled it to defeat an overwhelming opposition with a great economy of forces and with ease. By means of his distinctive methods Surena outdid Hannibal on the basis of the ratio of the number of men surrounded to the number who encircled them.

Thematic Summary

1   The vain and ambitious personality of Crassus.[4]
2   Crassus' ignorance of the Parthian army and its methods of warfare.
3   The disinformation, espionage and treachery of Ariamnes.[5]
4   The dissimulation by disguised Parthian warriors with the object of making the force seem smaller than it was, and terrifying the Romans.[8]
5   The nature of the long range warfare of the Parthians.[9, 10]
6   The effortless encirclement of an army about four times its size.

Notes

1 Dio Cassius, 40.15–21.1 (background); 40.21.2–25 (battle).
2 Plutarch, 20–2 (background); 23–28.2 (battle).
3 Plutarch, *Crassus,* 16.3.
4 Plutarch, *Crassus,* 16.1–2.
5 Plutarch, *Crassus,* 21.1–4.
6 Dio Cassius, 40.15.
7 Plutarch, *Crassus,* 22.1–2.
8 Plutarch, *Crassus,* 23.6–24.4.
9 Plutarch, *Crassus,* 24.5–25.1.
10 Plutarch, *Crassus,* 25–27.2.
11 Plutarch, *Crassus,* 21.6.

Pharsalus (48)

Background

In January 49 Caesar knowingly ignited the Second Civil War. He had refused to give up his command at the end of the Gallic War and had crossed the Rubicon and invaded Italy in contravention of the Senate's orders. His great rival Pompey was in no position to confront him militarily. Although he had large resources available to him throughout the Roman empire, in Italy he had only a few trained troops and a lot of recruits. Caesar's army, on the other hand, was a seasoned force which had become battle-hardened during the Gallic War. Pompey decided that he had no alternative but to leave Italy, and he marched his army southwards to Brundisium (Brindisi), where he embarked for Illyria. Caesar followed him to the port but was prevented from pursuing him for lack of ships. He decided to adjourn to Spain to deal with Pompey's lieutenants Afranius and Petreius, who with five legions between them were operating unopposed. After two indecisive encounters in 49, the war became a war of attrition. Caesar hounded and harassed his opponents wherever they went, depriving them of water and preventing them from foraging until eventually they sued for peace and their armies were disbanded. After the end of hostilities in Spain Caesar again turned his thoughts to his principal opponent, Pompey.

Meanwhile Pompey had been building up his strength on the eastern side of the Adriatic, where he made his base at Dyrrhachium (Durrës). By withdrawing the equivalent of four legions from the Roman garrisons on the eastern frontiers he brought his infantry up to eleven legions. At the same time he acquired a considerable body of cavalry and built up a large fleet which controlled the seas. Caesar, on the other hand, had still managed to amass only sufficient ships to transport half of his army by packing the men in tight. Banking on his enemy's assumption that he would refrain from a winter crossing, he succeeded in landing seven legions on the Epirote shore south of Apollonia. The inhabitants of the town willingly surrendered it to him. The transports were sent back to collect the rest of the army, but they fell foul of Pompey's ships. This led to a frustrating delay in uniting the two halves of the force. It was not until the approach of spring that Mark Antony crossed with his four legions and just managed to shake off pursuit and land them safely, north of Dyrrhachium. In this, an element of Chance saved the day in the form of a fortuitous change in direction of the wind.[1] Caesar set off to meet up with Antony – and so did Pompey; but when the latter realised that he would be between two armies, he abandoned his plan and retreated to his camp at Asparagium. Caesar and Antony followed him there and lined up for battle, but the challenge was refused. There had been repeated opportunities for a showdown but Pompey was ever unwilling, probably wisely, to take on even a smaller force. He was always conscious of the inferior quality of his own. Caesar's objective was Dyrrhachium; Pompey's fear was that Caesar would get there first. However, the next morning saw Caesar marching off in an opposite direction before, pre-dictably, making a detour. Outwitting his rival in this way, he did get there first, just as Pompey appeared in the distance.[2] In the end it did not help Caesar. What followed was a double siege in which Pompey built a line of defences around the centre while Caesar built another ring outside the first. But there was a flaw in the defences which allowed Pompey to penetrate the outer ring. Caesar was defeated and he withdrew from the area. If at this point Pompey had crossed to Italy to seize power, there would have been nothing to stop him. But he decided that Caesar must remain his principal target.

Caesar moved first to Apollonia where he could give his men a rest and boost their shattered morale. He then moved into Thessaly in search of a place providing good foraging and a suitable battle ground. On the way he joined up with Gnaeus Domitius, who had been sent – but failed – to confront Q. Caecilius Scipio. The latter was returning from Asia to join Pompey. Together Caesar and Domitius found a suitable place near Pharsalus (Farsala) or, more precisely, Palaepharsalus a few miles away.[3] They camped on the right bank of the river Enipeus. Pompey followed him to Thessaly, where he joined up with Scipio, and they set up camp on the foothills of a mount facing Caesar's camp. Every day Caesar lined up his men in battle array, but the challenge was invariably refused. Eventually the pleadings and taunts of Pompey's officers overrode his caution and, on the very day that Caesar was arranging to decamp in disgust, Pompey's line was seen to be advancing a little further forward. The battle was about to take place.

Battle of Pharsalus

There are accounts of the battle by Caesar,[4] and Appian,[5] and two by Plutarch in his *Caesar* and *Pompey* respectively.[6, 7] In another version Dio Cassius is verbose but adds virtually nothing of note.[8] The following description is based largely on Caesar, who had with him eight legions (eighty cohorts), totalling 22,000 men, and 1,000 horse. Against him were Pompey's eleven legions which, with the addition of numerous other contingents, amounted to 45,000 men, but he also had a vastly superior cavalry force amounting to nearly 7,000 horse. Both Appian and Plutarch agree with these figures. Pompey drew up his force in three lines, with Scipio holding the centre, and Lentulus in charge of the right wing, which rested on the Enipeus. As no additional protection was needed for this wing, all the cavalry were mustered together beyond the left wing with numerous archers and slingers. They were commanded by Labienus, and it was on them that Pompey pinned his hopes. Caesar, also, drew up his force in three lines with his cavalry beyond the right wing. Antony held the left, which rested on the river, Domitius was in the centre, and Sulla was on the right. When Caesar surveyed the enemy dispositions, he noted the heavy concentration of cavalry and light troops opposite his right wing and foresaw the risk that it could be outflanked. To counteract this threat he withdrew one cohort from the rear line of each legion and formed them into a fourth line.[9] With eight legions this suggests that there were eight cohorts but Plutarch in his *Pompey* says the number was six.[10] Caesar, however, had left two cohorts to guard his camp, and this may perhaps explain the discrepancy. He stationed this body obliquely beyond the wing and behind the cavalry so that they were screened from the enemy's view and were in effect in ambush.

The action began when Caesar's line began to advance and charge toward the Pompey's lines. They had covered half the intervening space when they realised that the enemy were not responding. Pompey had told his men not to move but to keep their breath and await the charge. As there was no movement from the other side, Caesar halted his men and allowed them to regain their breath. The charge was then resumed, and as they approached the enemy Caesar's men threw their javelins and then drew their swords. The charge was met steadfastly by Pompey's men, who in turn threw their javelins and resorted to their swords. It was at this point that the Pompey's cavalry left their place beyond the left wing and charged the Roman cavalry, followed by the archers and slingers. The Roman cavalry, with their inferior numbers, did not have a chance of standing up to this onslaught. In Caesar's words they were 'dislodged and gave ground a little' before, in reality, turning to flight. This revealed Caesar's fourth line. The legionaries in this line had been previously told not to point their javelins at the bodies of their opponents but at their faces. According to Caesar, the enemy cavalry, who had started to surround his wing, were so unnerved by this experience that they shied away and fled in turn.[11] This left the archers and slingers unprotected, and all were killed. The fourth line then carried on to attack Pompey's left wing in the flank and rear. Caesar's final move was to order his third line, which had seen no action, to move forward and

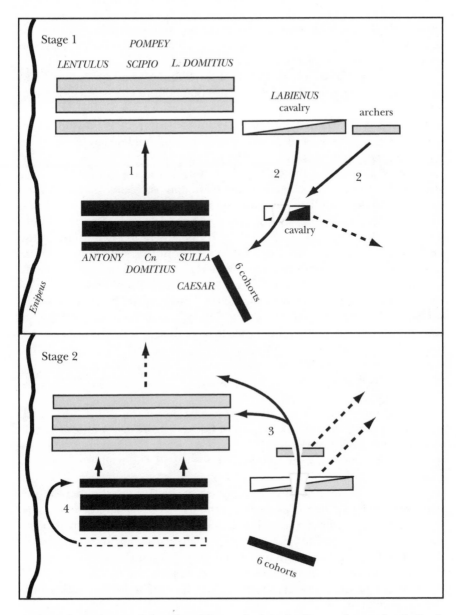

replace the exhausted first line. The arrival at the front of completely fresh men put an end to Pompey's resistance.[12]

When Pompey saw that his case was hopeless, he fled to his camp where he removed his insignia. He then rode on horseback to Larissa and thence to the coast where he boarded a fishing boat. Later in the year he was murdered as he was about to step ashore at Alexandria. After the battle many of his men retreated to a hilltop, around which Caesar built an earthwork. But as there was no water there the men retreated over the hills behind. Eventually they gave up and surrendered to Caesar, who spared them all and ordered that none should be hurt.

According to Caesar, about 15,000 of the Pompey's army were killed and more than 24,000 surrendered. He relates that he himself lost no more than 200 troops and 30 centurions.

Caesar was right when he said that the outcome of the battle would depend on the actions of his fourth line. For, as he himself says, it was these men who first repulsed the cavalry, then massacred the archers and slingers, and finally surrounded the enemy left wing. This seems to be an amazing string of feats when one considers that eight cohorts could have amounted to only 2,200 foot soldiers (the total force of 80 cohorts contained 22,000 men). If there were only six cohorts they would have numbered a mere 1,650, and they were pitted against 7,000 horsemen, to say nothing of the archers and slingers. Fuller has a lot to say about this.[13] He recounts what Labienus ought to have done to secure victory, and castigates him for being a rotten leader who had no plan and led his men from behind. It would seem that Caesar was probably aware of these deficiencies in a man who had served under him throughout the Gallic War. If it had been otherwise, Caesar must have exceeded the pinnacle of foolhardy optimism.

Thematic Summary

1   The element of chance: a fortuitous change in wind direction which allowed Antony to disembark the rest of Caesar's army.[1] Without this Caesar would have been in sore straits.

2   Caesar's feint by means of which he reached Dyrrhachium ahead of Pompey.[2]

3   The two-to-one disparity in numbers in favour of Pompey. It was counteracted by a disparity in quality of the troops in Caesar's favour.

4   Caesar's confidence versus Pompey's reluctance to fight, an issue of morale.

5   Caesar's concealed fourth line and its achievements.[9]

6   The tactic of pointing javelins at the faces of the enemy.[11]

7   Caesar's action in moving his fresh third line to the front to replace the exhausted first line.[12]

8   The poor leadership of Labienus.[13]

Notes

1   Caesar, *Civil War*, 3.26.
2   Caesar, *Civil War*, 3.41.
3   J. F. C. Fuller, *Julius Caesar, Man, Soldier & Tyrant*, Ware, Wordsworth, 1998, pp. 231–2.

4   Caesar, *Civil War*, 3.85–99.
5   Appian, *Civil Wars*, 2.70–82.
6   Plutarch, *Caesar*, 42–45.
7   Plutarch, *Pompey*, 68.3–72.
8   Dio Cassius, 41.52.3–61.1.
9   Caesar, *Civil War*, 3.89.
10   Plutarch, *Pompey* 69.2.
11   Appian, *Civil Wars*, 2.78; Plutarch, *Pompey*, 71.4; *Caesar*, 45.2.
12   Caesar, *Civil Wars*, 3.94.1.
13   Fuller, op. cit., p. 237.

Conclusions

Who won or who lost the battle? And why? Is it possible to draw any valid conclusions from such a disparate wealth of observations and events as those that have been presented in these pages? This brief overview provides good reasons for replying in the affirmative. Several chapters in this work begin with a statement that the subject, be it surprise, deception, or secrecy, is a most important – even fundamental – element. That may be true, but we are looking for the dominant element. These factors may determine the outcome of a battle, but there is always a human element behind them, initiating and controlling them. Also to be considered are factors such as weapons, weight of numbers, and methods of warfare. These will be taken into account but they too provide no evidence of being of supreme and far reaching importance. The human element in one form or another is the nearest approach to a universal controlling factor. It will be argued here that the dominant factor in classical warfare, overriding all others, was the human element and, in particular, the character of the man at the top – the commander. His universal nature is patent since every military force, big or small, has a leader and the object here is to establish that his character, abilities and actions were the most fundamental determinant of the ultimate outcome, whether it be victory or defeat. To do this it is pertinent to see what lessons can be learnt from the great leaders, about whose characters we are best informed, and to make the reasonable assumption that the lessons can also be applied to lesser mortals and smaller confrontations.

Alexander the Great has often been regarded as the greatest military figure in ancient warfare. He never lost a battle, except finally against his own men when he had to give in to their demand to go no further. However, it has been pointed out that his opponents were always ' barbarians' or tribesmen, people with less 'sophisticated' machines and methods of warfare. In the larger encounters, their armies usually consisted of contingents from many tribes, each with its own methods of fighting. They may never have fought side by side in the past, and therefore they could not act as a cohesive whole that was bonded together. Contrast that with the Macedonian army of Philip II, the best trained and most efficient military machine of the day. Alexander may have been assisted by the inferior quality of his opponents, notably the pusillanimous Darius III of Persia. At Gaugamela in 331, for instance, he won a decisive victory over Darius who had an overwhelming majority of around five to one. Alexander' s narrowest victory was in Pakistan at the river Hydaspes (p. 149) where he was up against Porus, his greatest opponent and a very different figure of speech from Darius. Alexander's victory was dependent upon his proverbial foresight, which told him that Porus would need to withdraw his cavalry from his right wing and amalgamate it with the rest on his hard-pressed left. Alexander had previously concealed some cavalry with orders to break cover and follow the enemy cavalry to the left, where they forced the enemy to divide his forces and face both ways. Alexander' s subsequent tactic of crowding the cavalry and elephants back onto their own line was another winning move. The Macedonians suffered heavy losses but the Indians had no space to manoeuvre and were trampled to death.

Hannibal was another genius who never lost a battle until he was defeated at Zama in 202 (p. 202) His nemesis was Scipio Africanus called 'the Great' by Plutarch, who added superb diplomacy to his military credit. Both of these generals were excellent planners who gave attention to detail down to the last minutiae. Although Scipio fought fewer battles than Hannibal, he was responsible for the total ejection of the Carthaginians from Spain, where he won every time. Further examples of great com- manders and their greatest victories are to be found in Epaminondas, outnumbered by nearly two to one but nevertheless the victor at Leuctra (p. 136), Philip II, the winner at Chaeronea (p. 142), and Caesar, triumphant against a force of more than twice his numbers at Pharsalus (p. 232). It may be argued that all these commanders were thought to be great because they won, but this is putting the cart before the horse. All of them have been acknowledged as men with that inherent trait called military genius. This includes what is perhaps the greatest of all military characteristics, namely an ability to put oneself in the enemy' s position and divine his thoughts and reactions to situations. It is also apparent so far that sheer numbers were not a major determining factor, an observation which is amply confirmed below.

These generals were great leaders, but what about their tactics and the part which they played in ensuing victory? To list a few examples:

1 the ambush during the battle on the Trebia in 218 (p. 175) where Hannibal personally surveyed the site and set the trap in motion before the battle;
2 his sheer good planning and tactics at Cannae in 216 (p. 180) achieved the almost unthinkable by surrounding a large Roman army with a smaller force;

3 at Leuctra in 371 (p. 136) Epaminondas adopted a novel procedure, amassing a phalanx fifty deep and concentrating the whole of his attack against one point, the enemy command post;

4 at Chaeronea in 338 (p. 142) Philip II made a feint withdrawal of his right wing. It determined all the subsequent events, exactly as he had planned;

5 at Pharsalus in 48 (p. 232) Julius Caesar took a cohort from each legion to form a fourth line for the purpose of countering a threat to his wing; and

6 the routine established by Scipio before the battle of Ilipa in 206 (p. 197). When he decided on a day for battle, he changed everything around to the utter dismay and disadvantage of the enemy. Hasdrubal's veteran troops, for instance, found themselves ' fixed' and unable to attack.

These examples are but a few of the many that could be cited, but they make it abundantly clear that well-planned tactics could and often did determine the outcome of a battle. However, it is equally clear that each of the above examples was the brain child of the respective commander, who devised it, organised it and directed it often from start to finish. In themselves tactics are mere tools, but to think of them solely in such simplistic terms does not make good sense. It ignores the vital human element and all that goes with it. Every tactic depended at the least upon a prime mover who, in the larger confrontations, was almost invariably the commander himself.

What has been said above has been derived largely from a study of winners. What about the other side of the coin, the losers? Antiochus III may have been called 'the Great', but he was accorded the title in respect of his anabasis of the eastern provinces and the recovery of parts of the empire which had been lost. In other respects he was not a great general. At Raphia in 217 (p. 107), he threw away any chance of victory by indulging in an extended pursuit, which left his phalanx leaderless and demoralised. Failing to learn the lesson, he repeated the blunder at Magnesia in 190 (p. 213). Demetrius Poliorcetes made the same mistake at Ipsus in 301 (p. 165) and lost the battle for his father. The only difference at Ipsus is that Demetrius' return to his phalanx was blocked by elephants, a winning point to the enemy leader. It is worth noting here that at Magnesia Antiochus' army contained no less than twenty assorted contingents from various countries. Were they able even to understand their neighbour's language? It is not surprising that a cohesive Roman legionary army of less than half the size was able to defeat them, confirming what has already been said about heterogeneous forces as a recipe for defeat. Nevertheless, the complement of a mixed army like that of Antiochus was decided by the man himself and was his responsibility. Turning again to Hannibal, he was a leader who was adept at finding out the character of his opponents and using the knowledge to good effect. He knew that his opponents at the Trebia (p. 175), Trasimene (p. 74) and Cannae (p. 180) were all tainted with ambition, over-enthusiasm and a tendency to make hasty decisions. They were not up to his standard, and they failed to assess his abilities and paid the price accordingly. The disaster at Trasimene could have been avoided by a little forethought and judicious scouting, an omission on the part of the consul. The same applies to the equally catastrophic ambush at the Caudine Forks in 321 (pp. 73–4), where a Roman army and two consuls surrendered to the Samnites without lifting a finger or, at any rate, a sword. The ambush was the decisive tactical element but the dominant element was undoubtedly the human one, seen in the good planning of the Samnite command, on the one hand; on the other was the Romans' naive acceptance of disinformation about the whereabouts of the enemy and their failure to take elementary precautions. This was particularly poignant because the consuls were aware that their chosen route was a potential trap. Neither Hannibal nor Scipio would have been guilty of such an omission. At Carrhae in 53 (p. 228) the consul Crassus had openly admitted his aim to gain renown exceeding that of both Pompey and Caesar, but he knew nothing whatever about the Parthian army and its method of fighting. Against advice, he allowed himself to be tricked into exchanging the security afforded by the Euphrates for a desert which was ideal for Parthian warfare. The defeat of the Roman army numbering about five times the enemy complement was primarily the result of human failure, on the one hand, and a brilliant enemy general, Surena, on the other. Once again, we return to the view that the character of the leader is paramount in either winning or losing the fight. Other considerations, such as the Parthian method of warfare, played a major role in the outcome, but the dominant factor was surely the relative quality of the opponents at the top. There is one point which emerges repeatedly from these observations: the numbers involved in armies do not provide a reliable indicator of the outcome. The great generals seem to have had an aptitude for winning against apparently overwhelming odds.

If the commander was the dominant factor in these examples of great generals and major combats, what about the lesser generals and the less well-known battles? In these instances it is much more difficult to argue a case, because less is known in detail about the personalities involved. Nevertheless, it seems unlikely that what has been said for the one would not apply in general to the other. It is hard to conceive of one principle for the best and another for the 'lower orders' . In these cases it is also easier to argue that a commander was thought to be a good one because he won, and vice versa. But this is shifting the terms of reference or, in modern parlance, moving the goal posts.

To return to the basic question, it is argued here that the dominant factor in the warfare of the age was the human element as exemplified in the character of the leader, no matter who he was and whether he was a winner or a loser. There were of course exceptions and dubious cases. The outcome at Cynoscephalae in 197 (p. 208) was turned from an utter Roman defeat into what would have been an indecisive draw by a diversion initiated by the consul. But indecisive it would have been had it not been transformed into a resounding Roman victory by the initiative of an unknown tribune. Although he was not the leader, save of a few cohorts in his moment of glory, the final outcome nevertheless rested decisively on his quick thinking. By and large, the present conclusions remain intact. It is normally the human element that counts, and it is usually the character of the leader that is the dominant factor whether he is a winner or a loser. If his name was Eumenes or Julius Caesar, there would have been a plot against him, but he could almost certainly be held responsible even for that!

Glossary of Tactical Definitions

Ambush: A sudden and unexpected attack from a place of concealment.

Countermarch: A complex 'internal' manoeuvre by a phalanx or part of a phalanx by means of which it was inverted from back to front so that the original front rank became the new front rank facing in the direction from which it had come, i.e. the file leaders remained at the front, etc. In the process the right became the left and vice versa, but this did not entail any great disadvantage. A subsequent countermarch would restore the status quo.

Decoy: An action designed to lure an enemy into danger or a trap, e.g. a prepared ambush (q.v.).

Diekplous: A Greek naval tactic, also known as 'breaking the line'. It occurred when a ship penetrated between two enemy ships in a line abreast and then relied on its superior turning speed to swing round and attack one of the enemy vessels in the rear or preferably its broadside. The Rhodians perfected the man-oeuvre by approaching the enemy prow to prow, then veering abruptly to one side. With its own oars shipped, the attacker then passed alongside the enemy vessel with the aim of shearing its oars before executing the diekplous around its stern.

Disinformation: False information given with the aim of deceiving.

Dissimulation: A concealment or disguising of an intention, action or identity. See also Impersonation.

Diversion: An action which was designed to draw the attention of the enemy away from other events. The distracting action may have been either feigned or genuine.

Double bluff: A statement or action which is intended to appear to be a deception but which is in fact genuine and true.

Feint: A mock (dissimulated) emotion or action to deceive an enemy, e.g. a mock retreat in feigned fear or apparent defeat preparatory to a surprise attack. A feint was also used to draw the attention of the enemy away from other events in preparation for a diversion (q.v.).

Hit-and-run: A form of individual warfare which was common notably among tribespeople. It consisted of closing with the enemy and discharging one's missile before retreating to a safe distance. The procedure was usually repeated, the attackers taking it in turn so as to maintain a steady stream of missiles.

Impersonation: A specific case of dissimulation. A pretence by an impersonator that he is someone other than the individual that he is thought to be.

Kyklos: Greek term for a defensive naval circle in which a fleet forms up radially with the prows facing outward. Non-combatant craft were usually placed in the centre of the circle.

Misinformation: Incorrect information which is given without any intention to mislead.

Periplous: A nautical manoeuvre in which a ship or ships at the end of an extended line abreast outflank the opposing enemy line and turn to attack the enemy amidships. The nautical equivalent of a small turning movement (q.v.).

Repetition tactic: The term used in this work to denote the deliberate establishment of a regular routine in the period before battle. If the enemy conformed to the routine, it was abruptly changed to his disadvantage.

Secrecy: The withholding of information by means of silence or deception. In military matters secrecy is the most widespread form of deception, involving a pretence that relevant intentions or actions do not exist or are other than the true ones.

Surprise: Emotion evoked by unexpected events. In warfare the events are usually deliberate and aimed at catching a foe when he is off guard and unprepared.

Turning movements (large): A movement to circumvent an obstacle such as a river, defile, or mountain, with the object of taking the enemy by surprise, usually in the flank or rear. Total secrecy is essential for success.

Turning movements (small): In battle, an outflanking movement to turn an enemy's wing with a view to attacking him in the flank or rear.

Index

Key headings for the battles in Part Two are indexed in bold type

Chares, Athenian general: disagreement at Embata, 49; natural elements, 115

Chios island, off Ionia: naval tactics, 119

Claudius Cento, Ap: legate at Uscana, lured by disinformation, 68

Claudius Nero, C.: expedition before battle of the Metaurus river and tactic during battle (q.v.); strategy, 32; secrecy, 99; chance, 105–6

Claudius Marcellus: attacked in mid-manoeuvre at Canusium, 62

Claudius Pulcher, C.: sacrificial portents disregarded 40; his incompetence, 50–1

Cleombrotus, king of Sparta: at battle of Leuctra (q.v); attacked in mid manoeuvre, 62

Cleomenes I, king of Sparta: at Sepeia, deception leading to attack while enemy eating, 58

Cleomenes III, king of Sparta: victim of a diversion at Sellasia, 76

Cleonae (Kleonai), Argolis, S Greece: ambush & sortie, 55, 72, 86

Cleonymus, Spartan pretender: disagreement with Pyrrhus, 48

Cnemus, Spartan commander: impatience of his vanguard at Stratus, 45

Conon, Athenian admiral at Aegospotami: victim of Lysander's 'repetition tactic', 80

Cornelius Scipio, P., father of Scipio Africanus: chance effects of wound, 105

Cornelius Scipio Aemilianus, P.: initiative at Nepheris, 44; personalised combat at Intercatia, 110

Cornelius Scipio Africanus, P.: at Baecula (q.v.), at Ilipa (q.v.), at Zama (q.v.); planning, 32–3; elephant lanes at Zama, 28; diplomacy, 32–3; military genius, 36; incendiary attacks at Utica, 58, 113; siege of New Carthage, 91; turning movement, 79; established routine ('repetition tactic') at Ilipa (q.v.)

Cornelius Scipio Calvus, Cn. (uncle of Africanus): made surprise naval attack at the mouth of the Iberus river, 55–6

Cornelius Scipio Nasica Corculum, P. (son-in-law of Africanus): turned enemy position in the Pydna

campaign (*see* battle of Pydna)

Cornelius Sulla Felix, L.: attacks enemy while in mid-manoeuvre, 62–3

Corupedium (Plain of Cyrus), unidentified, Lydia, W Anatolia: battle of, 31

corvus: gangway for boarding, 47, 120; at Mylae (q.v.)

Crimisus river (Fredolo), NW Sicily: storm, chance, 104; enemy baggage abandoned, 108–9; natural elements, 115–16

Croton (Crotone), Bruttii, Calabria: unfitness of Sybarites in battle, 39

Cuballum (unknown), Galatia: surprise attack on Romans, 54

Cunaxa, Babylonia, Iraq: personalised attack of Cyrus against his brother, 45; extended Greek pursuit, 108

Cynoscephalae (Chalkodónion), Thessaly, N Greece
battle of (197): 209–12; thematic summary, 211; chance encounter, 103; diversion in battle, 75–6; initiative of unknown tribune, 43

Cynoscephalae, Mt: personalised attack by Pelopidas in battle (364), 45–6, 110

Cyrus the Great, founder of Persian Empire: military genius, 36

Cyzicus, on Arctonnesus Peninsula in Propontis: decoy by Alcibiades, 75

Darius I, king of Persia: invasion of Greece, 113

Darius III, king of Persia: personalised assaults by Alexander the Great, 109

Dascylium, Phrygia Minor, NW Anatolia: Agesilaus repeatedly deceived Tissaphernes, 85

Decius Mus, P., father: 'devotion' at Veseris, 112

Decius Mus, P., son: 'devotion' at Sentinum, 112

Delium (Dilessi), Boeotia, S Greece: battle (424), depth of Theban phalanx 29; turning movement, 79

Demaratus, exiled Persian: cryptography, 94

Demetrius I Poliorcetes of Macedon: rejected advice before battle of Gaza, 46; at battle of Ipsus (q.v.), extended pursuit, 38

at Complega: counters guile by feigning fear before returning to attack, 69

Sempronius Longus, Ti., consul at the Trebia river: his character at the Trebia (q.v.), 105

Sentinum, Umbria, N Italy: 'devotion' in battle, 112

Sepeia, Argolis, S Greece: Spartan ruse followed by attack at meal time 58

Sertorius, Q., leader of anti-Sullan group in Spain: decoyed Pompey into ambush at Lauro, 73

Servilius Caepio, Q., proconsul at Arausio: disagreements among the leaders, 49

Shipka Pass, in Haemus range, Bulgaria: dissimulation by Thracians, 96

Silver Shields, elite veterans of Alexander's army: at Paraetacene (q.v.) and Gabiene (q.v.); mutinied at Gabiene, 109

Sogdian Rock, Sogdiana: captured by Alexander the Great, 90–1

Sphacteria, bay of Pylos, Messenia, S Greece: turning of Spartan position by Athenians, 77–8

Stratus, Acarnania, W Greece: impatience of Spartan vanguard under Cnemus, 45

Sulla *see* Cornelius

Surena, Parthian general: unusual 'ambush' at Carrhae, 92

Susian Gates (unidentified), SW Iran: turned by Alexander 79, 97–8

Sybarites, inhabitants of Sybaris in Bruttii: a byword for luxurious and unhealthy living, 39

Sybota islands, Straits of Corfu, off Epirus: tactics in old style naval battle, 118

Syme island (Simi), Sporades, Aegean: natural elements affect naval battle, 116

Syphax, king of Masaesulii (Numidians): incendiary attack on his camp at Utica, 58, 113

Syracusan expedition, E Sicily: morale, 38; feint withdrawal by Syracusans, 70; superstition delays Athenian withdrawal, 40–1

Tamynae, Euboea, Aegean: Phocion

prolonged sacrifices before giving battle, 40

'Tearless battle', near Malea, Arcadia: chance encounter led to battle, 102

Tegea, Arcadia, S Greece: Philopoemen's chain-letter ruse, 98; Agis II's aquatic ruse before Mantinea I (q.v.), 103

Tegyra, Boeotia, S Greece: chance encounter between Thebans and Spartans, 102; gap in the Spartan line, 64

Tellias, Phocian soothsayer and leader: planning of night attack, 26–7; the attack, 57

Terentius Varro, C: consul at battle of Cannae (q.v.), his personality, 48–9

Thapsus (Ras Dimas), Tunisia: Caesar's illness, a chance event, 101

Themistocles, Athenian politician and leader: strategy, 28; his disinform-ation at Salamis, 84–5; backing water at Salamis, 117

Theodotus, admiral of Antigonus: ambushed by land and sea at Aphrodisias, 73

Thermopylae Pass, E Locris, S Greece: turning of pass by Persians, 77; Spartan hit-and-run tactics, 69

Tifernum (unidentified), Samnium, S Italy: failed ambush, 72

Tigranes II the Great of Armenia: at Tigranocerta scorned advice of Mithradates and lost to the Romans, 46–7; his baggage captured, 109

Timoleon, liberator of Sicily: attack on enemy camp at Hadranum, 59; natural elements at Crimisus river, 104, 115–16; enemy baggage train abandoned, 109

Timotheus, Athenian general: disagreement between leaders at Embata, 49

Tissaphernes, Persian satrap: victim of disinformation and double bluff by Agesilaus, 85

Trasimene, Lake, Umbria, N Italy: Hannibal's ambush of whole army, 74; complacency of consul, 47; natural elements, 116

Trebia river (Trebbia river), Gallia Cispadana, N Italy
    battle of (218): 175–9; thematic